BIGLAW

BIGLAW

LINDSAY CAMERON

ANKERWYCKE

Cover design by Kaitlyn Bitner/ABA Publishing.

Printed in the United States of America.

19 18 17 16 15   5 4 3 2

Library of Congress Cataloging-in-Publication Data

Library of Congress Cataloging-in-Publication Data

Cameron, Lindsay.
  Biglaw : a novel / Lindsay Cameron.
     pages cm
  ISBN 978-1-63425-027-6 (alk. paper)
  1. Women lawyers—Fiction.   2. Lawyers—New York (State)—New York—Fiction.
3. Law firms—Fiction.   I. Title.
  PS3603.A4526B54 2015
  813'.6—dc23
                          2015022972

Discounts are available for books ordered in bulk. Special consideration is given to state bars, CLE programs, and other bar-related organizations. Inquire at Book Publishing, ABA Publishing, American Bar Association, 321 N. Clark Street, Chicago, Illinois 60654-7598.

www.ShopABA.org

To my husband, for encouraging me to take a risk.

PROLOGUE

As the revolving doors twirled, spilling grey suits into and out of the Death Star, I pressed my fingertips against my eyes and repeated these words: *Don't panic.*

"Oof." A portly man in an ill-fitting pinstriped suit jarred past me, swinging his brown paper bag spotted with grease. The Midtown lunch crowd was especially ravenous today, reminding me that the salad I'd bought over thirty minutes ago was sitting uneaten in the plastic bag digging red marks into my wrist. I gazed up at the fifty-two story, cavernous black steel building that housed F&D and gave myself one final mental pep talk before tossing the bag into the garbage can on the curb and pushing through the doors, about to hear my fate.

"Happy Tuesday!" Eugene called out from behind the security desk as I swiped my ID and cleared the turnstile. "Monday's in the rearview mirror and we're racing towards Friday!" I grinned tightly, willing my expression to be friendly, while my stomach plunged into a pit of nerves. I'd been counting down the minutes until Friday. Wonderful, magical, I-get-to-see-my-guy-again Friday. I'd even snuck out of work this morning to buy new lingerie from La Perla in anticipation of the evening. "What's the occasion?" the lipsticked sales lady had asked, hanging two lace bras on the hook in the dressing room. "Just a date," I'd sing-songed, trying to suppress my smile.

I filed into the elevator with six other suits. A middle-aged woman in a red power suit squeezed in just as the doors slammed shut. She nodded a greeting in the direction of a grey-haired man in the corner wearing a flashy purple tie undoubtedly picked out by someone under thirty. Probably his third wife.

"Case settle?" Purple Tie asked.

"Yup, an hour ago."

"Client happy?"

"Very." Red Suit beamed.

Happy. That was exactly the feeling that should be coursing through my veins. I was twenty-eight years old. I'd graduated from Georgetown Law School, passed the most difficult bar exam in the country, and after two years at a top New York law firm, I was on the cusp of obtaining the prestigious secondment I'd been busting my butt for. Even better, there was a text on my cell phone that said, "I can't wait to see you Friday," from a man whose kiss sent waves of ecstasy through my body. I should be skipping through a field of sunflowers somewhere, reveling in pure delight. But it wasn't over-whelming joy requiring me to force my body to perform a function that (I remember quite clearly from biology class) was supposed to be automatic. No, it was sudden, all-consuming, bone-crushing stress.

Breathe in. Breathe out.

I stepped off the elevator, pausing to check my BlackBerry in hopes I'd simply imagined the summons that had arrived during my lunch break—my body so uneasy with the newfound feeling of romantic bliss that it had sought a way to return itself to the anxious state it had become accustomed to, sort of like how a newborn baby, unfamiliar with freedom of movement, is more at ease being swad-dled. But there was the email, just as it had been an hour ago when it had first popped in to my inbox. From: Saul Siever, CC: Sarah Clarke—who, in a twisted stroke of bad luck, was actually my men-tor. Or at least she was the mentor Human Resources had assigned to me back when I was a first year associate.

Breathe in. Breathe out. One foot in front of the other. One foot in front of the other.

My secretary leapt from her desk and scurried to intercept me before I entered my office.

"Where have you been?" she whispered anxiously, studying my face. "And why do you look so . . . sweaty?"

I swiped my forehead. "I was just at lunch. It's hot outside." It was a lie, but Rita already looked flustered enough for both of us.

"Mackenzie," she hissed, her eyes darting around the hallway to ensure she wasn't being watched. "Saul's called three times. And he sounded really pissed-awf. I mean, REALLY pissed awwwf," she emphasized in her thick Long Island accent. "He wants you in conference room 27C—ASAP. He asked for your *personnel* file." Her kind eyes filled with concern.

My stomach dropped. If my gut hadn't already warned me this meeting would be bad news, the request for my personnel file solidified it.

"He wouldn't tell me what the meeting was about, but I don't think it's good, Mac." She wrung her hands. "If they're lettin' you go, I don't want you goin' down without a fight, so I printed out a spreadsheet of your billable hours to take with ya' to the meeting." Rita dashed back to her desk, knocking over the Starbucks cup perched precariously on the counter of her cubicle, sending pools of coffee over a pile of papers.

"Oh, crap! Crap! Crap! Crap!" She frantically wiped the coffee with a balled-up napkin. "Good enough." She pushed the coffee-stained document into my hands. "Let them see what you've given this firm." Her eyes burrowed into mine, the way a trainer stares into the eyes of a boxer during a pre-fight pep talk.

"Thanks," I mumbled, heading into my office to grab a legal pad. I squinted at the clock on my computer, silently willing time to stop so I could catch my breath.

"Is there anything else I can do?" Rita peered into my office, tugging nervously at her short leather skirt.

"No, that's fine, Rita." My tone was clipped as I breezed past her on my way to the elevator.

Get it together, Mackenzie, I repeated, punching the button for the twenty-seventh floor. *Don't panic.*

Yesterday I'd been practicing my best surprised face so I would be prepared when they inevitably knighted me with an honor bestowed on only a select few associates. Things couldn't have changed drastically in the past twenty-four hours. Unless . . .

A tight band of stress constricted around my lungs. Unless they'd found out about my one teeny, tiny transgression.

When the elevator doors opened, the large group standing there startled me. Sixty eager-to-please law students dressed in shiny new suits and smelling like the leather from their recently gifted briefcases were reporting for their first day as summer associates. I remembered my first day at Freedman & Downs ("F&D" as they had branded themselves) when I too had that same confident glint in my eye. How could I not? We were the chosen ones—the Type A personalities who'd graduated top of our class from the most prestigious law schools and now had the good fortune of nabbing a coveted summer associate position. The standards had been stringent. F&D was part of an elite group of New York mega-firms, the ones that housed 500+ lawyers, with offices that were run like small cities. Lawyers referred to this collection of firms simply as "Biglaw," and landing at one of them meant earning close to $200,000 right out of law school. The students who secured a position at one of these firms during the summer between second and third year of law school were virtually guaranteed a job offer following graduation. Thousands applied to F&D, only sixty were chosen. It was a dream job.

Is this how I used to look? I wondered, studying their fresh faces with annoyance and fascination. No glassy eyes from long, obedient hours staring at a computer screen. No physical signs of prolonged sleep deprivation. A few of them even had a summer tan. A tan is practically forbidden in Biglaw. It shows you're spending too much time outside the office. Maybe even have a hobby. They had no idea what was in store for them, just as I hadn't. Like war, Biglaw is something that has to be experienced firsthand to truly be understood.

I pushed through the crowd and down the hall as another associate scurried past me. Nobody walked at F&D. They scurried. Walking was for people with time on their hands. I recognized him—he was the associate with the peculiar habit of carrying around a briefcase with a huge block of cheese inside and nothing else (and could often be seen munching on his cheese like some oversized mouse). Cheese Boy might stand out as strange outside of Biglaw, but at F&D he fit right in. F&D was a repository of distorted personalities: the associate with the pornography addiction, the one who spontaneously fell asleep during conversations, the partner that had the nervous nose pick, visibly picking his nose whenever he was talking to a female colleague, the guy who swears he invented the internet. In Biglaw, some form of eccentricity is practically a job requirement.

"Mackenzie!" A familiar shrill voice spat out my name venomously from the end of corridor.

Cheese Boy whipped around to locate the target of Sarah's wrath. A mix of sympathy and fear filled his eyes as they met mine for a second. He quickened his pace. Clearly he didn't want to be in the middle of what was about to go down.

"Get your ass in here," Sarah hissed, gesturing towards the door. Her neck was covered in red blotches and her stick straight hair looked so frizzy you'd think she'd just run a marathon. I'd never seen her look so unnerved. "Everyone is waiting!" She disappeared back inside the conference room.

I could feel my underarms growing wet. Taking a long breath, I stepped into the conference room, prepared to hear my fate.

But there had been no need to practice my surprised face, because my face contorted into a genuine expression of shock quite naturally when I saw the man in front of me extending his hand.

5

"Miss Corbett, I'm Tucker Sullivan with the Securities and Exchange Enforcement division. I have a few questions for you regarding some unusual trading activity we've uncovered. Why don't we all take a seat?" He strode briskly behind me and pushed the conference room door shut.

1

SEVEN MONTHS EARLIER

"WE'VE GOT A NEW TIMELINE, people! This deal has gotta sign before the markets open in the morning!" A tall man with a physique that had earned him the nickname "Stay Puft Marshmallow Man" thudded down the corridor. "Somebody bring me the goddamn disclosure schedules!"

Russ Tornelli poked his head into my office, mopping his brow with a handkerchief. "Mackenzie, Maxwell needs the disclosure schedules. Print them out and bring it to the war room."

"I've got them right here, Russ." I thumbed through a pile of papers before remembering I'd stuck them in my drawer as part of my nightly clean-up. Being privy to confidential information that could mean the difference in millions of dollars in stock value required strict adherence to the firm's clear desk policy, but clearing my desk at 9 P.M. had clearly been a tad optimistic. I passed the stapled document over to Russ's eager hands.

"I finished the material contracts portion, so they're good to go. And I've just started drafting the press release."

"Good, we'll need that ready to go so it can hit the wires right after signing. It's going to be a long night. Hunker down."

I nodded like an obedient foot soldier before Russ took off down the hallway at breakneck speed. I let out a long, weary sigh. The adrenaline that comes with working on a high-profile acquisition has a time limit and it usually expires right about the time you hear the words "hunker down." I gulped back the last of the can of Red Bull and shut my eyes, waiting for the caffeine to work its magic. Where I wanted to be hunkering down right now was right beside Jason, my boyfriend and fellow F&D associate, in a cozy bed. Maybe somewhere with a couple of glasses of champagne on the nightstand and the sound of the ocean outside our door.

"Mackenzie! What are you doing?" An irate voice cut through my fantasy.

My eyes flew open. Looming over me was a balding, paunchy Indian man of indeterminate age. When I first walked into my new office at F&D, I'd remembered a good friend telling me how she and her officemate were so close they'd been each other's bridesmaids. I'd pictured crouching in the Biglaw trenches with someone glamorous and fun. We'd make each other laugh doing choreographed dances in the unisex bathroom (à la Ally McBeal) before heading out to happy hour with our well-dressed colleagues. Or, if it was a guy, we'd be like *When Harry Met Sally*, but without the eventual hookup. Instead, what I'd gotten was Sadir.

"That was my last Red Bull!" He pointed to the can still clutched in my hand.

"Sorry," I sputtered. "I thought you'd gone home for the night and I was going to replace it."

He eyed me warily. "You know I'm usually willing to share my stash with you, Mackenzie. You're not one of the hypercompetitive freaks around here so I don't mind. But drinking my last Red Bull is crossing the line." He snorted. "And P.S., I don't think I've ever left for the night before you."

This was probably true. Sadir was always in the office—day or night—whether or not work actually required him to be there. "Face time," he'd say when questioned. And if you're looking to cast someone to play the part of a guy who spent that much time in the office, Sadir would be your man. His age was hard to pinpoint—he could pass for anywhere from twenty-eight to forty. His thinning hair and furrowed brow aged him, but his chubby chipmunk cheeks made him look young. He had the beginnings of a double chin and a flabby chest that made his man boobs visible through his ill-fitting dress shirt. His eyes were slightly squinty behind Coke-bottle glasses, but you could still see they were bloodshot and tired. Not exactly a specimen of health or vitality.

"Won't happen again. Promise." I gave him a Girl Scout salute.

Sadir may not have been the officemate I'd pictured, but he'd grown on me. He wasn't exactly warm and fuzzy, but he gave me advice—cynical but usually spot on—when I needed it. The first time a senior associate dumped a pile of documents on me and asked me to tell him if there was anything "relevant" in them, it was Sadir who had walked me through the ins and outs of due diligence. I'd spent three years at law school memorizing the rules of evidence, countless Supreme Court decisions, and the details of negligence law, but had been left woefully unprepared for the work of a Corporate first year associate. When I was still in college, Georgetown law students, recognizing their lack of real-world skills in a lackluster economy, had pushed for classes that were more practical. The faculty response had been, "We're teaching the Law, not training lawyers." The Ivory Tower prevailed, and at the time I understood their position—law school isn't a trade school. But at F&D, I often found myself wishing the classes I'd taken in school had been just a little more useful.

I pulled my chair close to the computer, rested my fingers on the keyboard, and felt my eyelids grow heavier. If I was going to draft a press release that, when it hit the wires, would result in the company stock doubling in price, I was going to need some bottled energy. I pecked out a quick IM to Alex, Jason's best friend, who I knew would be working on the other side of the floor. *Need more caffeine. You around?*

We were now into our second year as associates, and day-to-day life at one of New York's top law firms was a far cry from the wining and dining we'd experienced as wide-eyed, euphoric summer associates. Back then, the schedule for our eleven week summer job was more like a social calendar—Yankees games, cooking classes, Broadway shows, guided tours of the Bronx Zoo. There were free lunches at the finest restaurants in the city and evenings filled with firm-sponsored cocktails. For this we received checks for $4,500 every two weeks. It would have been an amazing summer under any circumstances, but it was also the summer I fell in love. I wasn't looking for a boyfriend—I'd worked my ass off to get this job and didn't need the distraction—but one glance at Jason's easy smile and I was smitten.

"There's a reason this place is called the Death Star," was his opening line to me. It was our first day and we were standing in the polished marble lobby of F&D waiting for the elevator. My nose had been buried in my leather portfolio folder, reviewing the schedule for the hundredth time since I'd received it in the mail. It took me a moment to realize he was talking to me. When I looked up, the most gorgeous deep brown eyes were staring back at me. "Oh," I replied, feeling my face flush. He was tall, with close cropped dark curls, and dressed in a navy blue Brooks Brothers suit, but with his tanned skin and square jaw he looked like he would be more at home in a button down shirt and shorts on Martha's Vineyard, radiating the classic New England prep school look. He smiled sheepishly, like he knew he was handsome and was somewhat embarrassed about it.

I silently thanked the expensive makeup I'd purchased from Saks that the saleswoman swore would accentuate my best features. Hey, nobody said I had to use the *entire* three thousand dollar travel stipend on relocation expenses. My brand new heather-gray Theory suit and Prada slingbacks with a practical one inch heel completed the transformation from frumpy law student to polished, sleek lawyer.

"Is that what they call it?" I grinned.

"Yeah, this building I mean." He gestured around the lobby. "I think it has something to do with the ominous big, black steel *looming* over the Empire of New York." I noticed the most adorable glint in his eye when he emphasized the word "looming."

"I'm Jason." He extended his hand.

When he asked me out for dinner a week later, I couldn't believe my luck. I was certain he was going to go for Fiona, easily the prettiest summer associate, with her long blond hair, sparkling blue eyes, and yoga instructor's body. I won't be modest, I'm pretty, but I haven't always been that way. Mom used to tell me that one day I'd be a beautiful swan, but she failed to mention the whole ugly duckling stage I'd have to suffer through first. I hit every awkward stage possible: braces, pimples, unfortunate haircuts, tragic fashion choices. But when I went away to college the braces came off, the pimples cleared up, and I left my scrunchies behind. Boys finally started to notice me, but none of them in any way, shape, or form had been on the same level as Jason.

We left right from work (separately, of course, not wanting to arouse any rumors) and headed to an oyster bar in the West Village. With no awning, it was the kind of place that you would never know was there unless you were an insider. Jason had confidently, but not cockily, taken my hand and navigated me to our table. As he pulled out my chair, he leaned down and whispered—no, more like growled—in my ear, *You look fantastic*. It sent a scrumptious, involuntary shiver down to my toes. More importantly, though, I *believed* him.

It was one of those perfect New York City dinners, where everything from the butter served with the bread to the whipped cream on top of the dessert makes you feel like your taste buds have been amplified tenfold. We chatted easily and I found myself amazed that, despite his good looks and exclusive boarding school background, he was down to earth and fun and even a tiny bit goofy. "Why do you want to work in the corporate department?" he'd inquired, forking out a mussel and popping it into his mouth. "You do realize it's the most intense department in the firm, don't you?" After briefly debating which version to share, I gave him the same answer I'd given the on-campus interviewer from F&D—I like to look at a corporate contract the same way I do a crossword puzzle, figuring out the words that fit, and I love the challenge of a puzzle. Not only did he not laugh at my nerdy answer, he'd beamed and said, "I love how ambitious you are." I'd rolled my eyes playfully, but could think of nothing other than how the word "love" sounded coming out of his mouth.

The rest of the summer flew by in budding-relationship bliss. Jason and I were inseparable, taking turns sleeping at each other's apartments, sneaking kisses at summer associate events, and making out furiously on cab rides home. The goal of the firm that summer was to introduce us to law firm life while preventing us from getting a significant glimpse into the inner workings of Biglaw. F&D spared no expense to shield us from the reality so we would return to the firm after graduation to work as first year associates. "Fattening you up for the slaughter," one associate termed it.

Our relationship survived long distance during our final year of law school and even our first year as associates, which seemed like a hazy blur to me now. We learned to adapt to the unpredictable Biglaw timetable, spending time together whenever work allowed—sometimes a quick lunch at a deli close to the office, other times a lingering Saturday night dinner at the latest hot restaurant, putting our large paychecks to work. Jason's schedule in the Trusts department wasn't as demanding as mine.

Being in the corporate department meant being on call twenty-four hours a day, seven days a week, and never leaving the office until the partner you're working for has left the building for the night. It could be eight in the evening or two in the morning, but most days it was impossible to tell. Some days I would bite the bullet and sneak out before eight. Sneaking out was a finely honed survival technique that involved a fair amount of planning and forethought. Above all, it must appear to other lawyers that you are returning to your office, not actually leaving to go home for the night. When you leave, you have to pretend you are just going to the word processing center to drop off a document for revision or to the cafeteria to grab a Red Bull (*Gonna need some help staying up all night!*). Always be carrying a file. Your office has to look like you are coming back shortly—a coat left on the back of the chair, your computer logged on, a half empty cup of coffee beside a document left open on your desk. You only take the elevator down to the lobby when there isn't anyone senior to you in it. If there's a partner in the elevator when you enter, you get off on the next floor, take a lap, and try again. If you happen to be really unlucky and there's a partner in the lobby when you exit, have your back-up plan ("*Just picking up my Seamless delivery!*"). These were details I had mastered. They may sound ridiculous, but they were necessary to Biglaw survival. Otherwise, you risked getting caught leaving early, meaning you'd suddenly find yourself staffed on a deal no one wanted to work on because, clearly, you had too much time on your hands. Some associates resorted to taking the stairs down twenty-seven floors to avoid being caught in the elevator, but I never did that. Too desperate.

"Who's the partner on the deal?" Sadir called from the other side of the partition, knowing full well who it was.

"Maxwell Gold."

"Stay Puft?" Sadir whistled through pursed lips. "Wow—a deal with a four corner partner and you're just a second year associate. You're moving up in the world."

I rolled my eyes. The only thing that excited Sadir more than gathering information on his fellow associates was the rigid law firm hierarchy. He'd actually ranked all ninety-five attorneys in the corporate department in order of alleged importance, on a list he referred to as "The Power Players." Of course, if anyone wanted to discern the pecking order, all they had to do was look at the offices. Partners had the biggest offices with the best views and the partners that brought in the most business were rewarded with a corner office. In the corporate department, associates called them the "four corner" partners. They were the top rainmakers, the partners who enjoyed the bulk of the profits, while the other partners, the "service partners," sweated it out in the trenches. After the "service partners" came the senior associates, who had their own offices. Next were the junior associates, who shared an office with another junior associate. Enter yours truly. Share a 150-square-foot space with another person for fifteen to twenty hours a day, and even the most unobtrusive, agreeable officemate will eventually get on your nerves. It reminded me of an experiment I'd studied in tenth grade science—a cage of rats are supplied with food and water, replenished to support an increasing population, but the size of the cage remained fixed. The result was hyper-aggression and increased mortality. Some rats even ate their own offspring in an effort to prevent the overcrowding. After more than a year sharing a small space with Sadir, I could relate. At least I hadn't killed him . . . yet.

13

My computer pinged with Alex's response. *Still here and you're going to need a boatload of caffeine. I just heard Russ tell his secretary to have breakfast delivered to the war room at 5 A.M.*

I groaned, suddenly reminded of why I never liked working with Russ Tornelli. He lived at the office. "Literally," Sadir had emphasized when he'd passed on this tidbit of gossip. When his lease ran out a year ago, Russ had apparently slept in his office for two months because he was too cheap to rent another apartment. He was currently sleeping on his parents' couch when he wasn't at the office and still had no intention of getting his own apartment.

As part of my preparation for hunkering down I reluctantly sent an email to Jason, who I knew was waiting patiently for me at my apartment, as he was most nights when he left the office before me.

To: Jason Kermode
From: Mackenzie Corbett

It's going to be another late night here—you can go ahead and order the pizza and watch Mad Men without me. Sorry!! If you're awake when I get home I promise to greet you like Megan greets Don ;)

To: Mackenzie Corbett
From: Jason Kermode

Now there's no way I'll be asleep! 1-4-3

A wide smile broke across my face. 1: *I.* 4: *Love.* 3: *You.* It was a special code we had developed early in our relationship, a way to secretly connect at work. Sometimes Jason would tap out the code on the table when we were in the same meeting, other times I'd arrive at work to find a yellow sticky note on my monitor with the code. It still felt unreal that I was the girlfriend of such an irresistible guy. Not that I was inclined to ever resist him.

1-4-3, I wrote back, wishing I was snuggling up with him on the couch instead of holed up in my office.

"I'm going to grab some caffeine," I announced to Sadir. "Need anything other than Red Bull?"

"Just get me the Red Bull," he mumbled without looking up.

I pecked out a quick IM to Alex. *Wanna join me on a coffee run?*

See you at the elevator, he wrote back.

I grabbed a random file, ensuring I looked busy, tucked it under my arm and made my way down the corridor. Despite the late hour, lights were still gleaming in offices, phones were still ringing, photocopiers still whirring. F&D, like all Biglaw firms, ensured its lawyers could work twenty-four hours a day, seven days a week. There were night time secretaries that could be reserved when your own secretary went home and a round-the-clock photocopy and document support center to ensure that the marked-up drafts lawyers dropped off before leaving for the evening were retyped and waiting for them in their inboxes first thing in the morning. The full-service cafeteria, complete with a salad bar, sushi bar, grill station, and sundae bar, was available for all three meals. If you didn't have time to leave your desk a cafeteria worker could bring it right to your office, piping hot. Prefer food from the outside world? No problem—simply place an order (or have your secretary place an order) with Seamless, an online food delivery service offering any type of food available in the city. A uniformed deliveryman would bring it right to the lobby. Dinners were always billed to the client automatically, so no need to bother with cash. If you were one of the lucky ones leaving for the night, you simply emailed the firm's operation center and they ordered you a Town Car home. Pantries were stocked with snack food and toiletries for those spending the night at the office. There was even a fully stocked medicine cabinet should you require . . . oh, I don't know . . . three Advil and a swig of Pepto-Bismol at 3 A.M.? All of it set up so that associates never had to stop working. There might as well have been a large neon sign erected outside that blinked "Open 24 Hours."

I pushed through the glass doors to the elevator bank, expecting to see Alex. Instead, there stood Sarah, looking hostile and unpleasant with her arms folded and her brow furrowed. Shit.

The earliest sign that Sarah and I weren't exactly going to be Oprah and Gail was when she'd stood me up for the mentor/mentee introductory lunch. Giving her the benefit of the doubt, I'd gone to her office to introduce myself and discovered, behind a meticulously clean desk, a woman so full of tension that even the air around her seemed to emit stress. One look at her and I knew I wouldn't be picking her brain for advice on surviving in the male-dominated Corporate group or "leaning in," as they say. The crease in her pin-striped pants was so flawlessly pressed it could have been used as a paring knife, and her pointy-toed Jimmy Choos could've doubled as weapons. All in all, she'd expertly cultivated a look that screamed, *I can crush you.*

I grinned tightly at Sarah now, nodding what I hoped was a friendly hello. She glared in my direction before facing the elevators, not even acknowledging my presence.

Taking her cue, I stood stiffly in silence, keeping my distance, gripping my hands around my file. I couldn't help stealing a surreptitious peek at Sarah out of the corner of my eye. Everything about her was rigid and taut—from her long blond hair pulled back into a severe pony tail, to her pointy hip bones that looked like they might poke out from beneath her skin at any moment. Even the sides of her squared manicure looked razor-sharp. Every part of her was precisely in place, but precariously so. I imagined that if you pulled out one bobby pin from her perfectly slicked back hair, she would completely unravel.

What little I knew about Sarah I'd learned from Sadir. He'd given me the run-though of all the senior associates in my first week. Derek Boyle, he explained, was an eighth year associate who was "riding his ponies to partnership," which meant he staffed deals heavily with junior associates, had them do all of the work, and then took all of the credit. Brian Gambrill, on the other hand, was a seventh year associate famous for emailing associates while they were on vacation and demanding an immediate response. According to Brian, vacation was no excuse for not continually checking your BlackBerry. "I was responding to emails while on the Matterhorn ride at Disney World with my nine-year old daughter during our *only* family vacation all year," Brian would brag. His daughter will be telling *that* story to a therapist one day, I'm sure. Although something tells me she won't be hunting for material.

"What about Sarah?" I'd asked, figuring that while Sadir was dishing I might as well get some information on my mysteriously bitchy mentor.

"Never worked with her. I try to avoid working with women. No offense," was his response. "But I know she's a fifth year associate who graduated top of her class from Columbia, is supposedly brilliant in a diabolical kind of way, and is gunning for partnership. Which means she'll throw anyone under the bus to save her own ass. You definitely gotta watch your back with that one." He made a stabbing motion with his hand to emphasize the point.

I was shivering at the memory when, to my surprise, Sarah broke the chilly silence.

"So what's keeping my mentee here so late?" she asked icily, her eyes still fixed forward.

My body jolted, startled not only that she'd spoken, but also that she'd remembered she was *supposed* to be my mentor.

"I'm just working on a merger that's signing tonight," I answered, a little too manically. "For uhh . . . a client of Maxwell's."

She turned her head slowly to face me, giving me a frigid once-over.

I was suddenly aware that after being at the office nineteen straight hours, I was looking as disheveled as I felt.

"Well, I hope it's *work* keeping you here and not something else, Mackenzie." Her overly glossed lips curled into a smirk. "Rumor has it you're hooking up with another associate."

Hooking up with? That sounded so tawdry. "I'm in a relationship with another associate." I struggled to keep my tone as pleasant as I could. Suddenly realizing neither of us had pushed the button for the elevator, I pressed the down button three times, hoping the high speed elevator lived up to its name.

"I guess you didn't get the memo on how unprofessional it is to engage in a romantic relationship with a work colleague." She raised one overly plucked eyebrow, and with her thin nose and slight sneer,

I swear she was a dead ringer for the evil witch in *Wicked*. "I hope you don't end up like my last mentee. She got married after ten months at the firm, pregnant immediately thereafter, and was never heard from again. It's women like *her* that put the women's movement back decades. Why would any firm promote us if they think we're just here to meet men and make babies? I choose to counteract that stereotype by putting my *career* first. I suggest you do too."

As if on cue, the elevator doors opened and she stepped inside and turned around, facing me.

"Oh, go . . . go ahead, I'm just waiting for someone." I pointed at the glass doors to the elevator bank.

"Of course you are," she said frostily as the elevator door slammed shut.

2

TRUTH BE TOLD, MY fondness for crossword puzzles wasn't the reason I chose the corporate department. In Biglaw, the corporate department was a mark of success and I'd been fixated with success ever since I saw my sister, Margaret, draped in four first place medals at the regional swim competition when I was ten years old. Mom had signed Margaret and me up for the swim team at the community center that summer after reading an article on the importance of sports in building girls' self-esteem. Margaret had groaned, but I was excited—I loved swimming. When the season started, it didn't take a stopwatch to tell me that Margaret was easily the fastest swimmer on the team, often finishing races a full length ahead of everyone else. And I would know, being that I was usually the one bringing up the rear. "I think you just need to practice more," Mom would gently instruct when I complained to her about being last. "You can achieve anything with hard work." So I spent the summer in the pool, with Dad dropping me off early on his way to work while Margaret was still in bed, and stayed long past when Margaret skipped out to head to the beach with her friends. I didn't mind, though, because I couldn't wait to show my parents how good I'd become in the final match of the summer—the All East swim competition. But things didn't go exactly as my optimistic ten-year old mind had planned. Margaret won four first place medals, and all I walked away with was a cruddy participation ribbon. Watching my sister standing on the makeshift podium, the medals draped around her neck, nodding humbly at the rousing applause, somewhere deep inside I was filled with a burning, pulsing *need* to be up there. But so long as I embodied the athletic ability of Charlie Brown, it wasn't going to happen.

I didn't want to just be a hard worker. I wanted to be a winner. And in that moment, I knew what I would be plagued with for the rest of my life if I embraced the same things Margaret, a year older than me, did—new coaches looking at my last name on the roster, certain they had a gem with "another Corbett girl." Until they saw me play. Unless I wanted to grow up in Margaret's superior gene pool shadow, I had to find another way to get noticed. Soon, I learned that if I studied hard enough and had a 4.0 GPA, I'd earn awards, scholarships, and feel the thrill of victory when called up on stage to give the class valedictorian speech while my parents cheered proudly in the audience. I discovered that if I steered clear of sports or sororities in college and filled my time with lawyer-friendly extracurricular activities like the debate club and civil liberties club instead, Georgetown Law School would offer me a spot.

In law school our career resources counselor told us that a corporate associate position at a Biglaw firm was the most difficult spot to obtain. Of those lucky enough to land a summer associate position, only a handful would be asked to join the corporate department. It was the epitome of success for the eternal striver in me. When F&D offered me a spot, it felt like a huge achievement, assurance that I'd chosen a career path that I was good at. But most important, it quelled the worries in my head that Margaret was the only winner in the family. Which was why it really got under my skin when Sarah implied that I was at the office late at night for any reason other than work.

"Seriously? Unprofessional? That's what she called you?" Kim's voice cut through my brief fantasy about yanking on Sarah's pony tail until she cried "uncle."

"Yup." I nodded, stifling a yawn. The mandate from Maxwell last night that the merger sign before the markets opened meant that I'd pulled an all-nighter, but it was worth it because as of seven thirty this morning two companies were joined in holy matrimony. The best thing about signing up a deal early in the day was that it meant you could actually leave the office at the same time as the majority of the population. It was a rare occurrence to be out of the office while it was still light outside, one that had to be seized. So, despite my sleep-deprived state, here I was having dinner on a sidewalk patio with my best friend, Kim, filling her in on my run-in with my Ice Queen mentor.

"Oh, and apparently I'm in grave danger of putting the women's movement back decades."

"Wow, I didn't realize you had that kind of power, Mac. Impressive." Kim ripped off a piece of bread and swirled it around in the plate of olive oil. "Remind me to blame you when they take away my right to vote."

I laughed. Other than my unpleasant run-in with Sarah last night, I had a lot to celebrate. The deal had signed on time, meaning my press release hit the wires just before the markets opened. News of the merger resulted in the stock nearly doubling in value, leaving our client overjoyed. Even Stay Puft had been jovial during the congratulatory handshakes around the conference room. "Good work, Mackenzie," he'd boomed while clapping me on the shoulder. "You're a real up-and-comer around here." As he shook my hand I felt a swell of pride. It was definitely a booster shot to my ego to get a compliment from Maxwell. Biglaw partners had a knack for giving just enough praise to make your all-nighters feel worthwhile. Yes, being an up-and-comer in the eyes of a four corner partner was definitely cause for a toast.

I raised my glass. "To the women's movement—may it be solid enough to survive my intra-office dating."

"Hear, hear." Kim smiled, clinking my glass.

I took a swig of Chianti, recommended by our waiter as the perfect accompaniment to our dinner selections. It was a far cry from the suburban Olive Garden back home. "Mmm . . . this is good. What's it called again?"

"Wine," Kim answered, smiling wickedly. Despite Kim's well-off upbringing, or maybe because of it, she always rebuffed anything that sounded even slightly haughty.

"Ha, ha." I deadpanned. "Whatever it's called, I may crawl into that bottle."

"Well, I think your maniac mentor story trumps any maniac four-year old encounter I've had lately, so I'll forgive you if you drink the bulk of it."

Kim loved to mock her job as a teacher at an Upper East Side preschool, sarcastically announcing she was "shaping our future," but I knew her job was probably the one thing she took seriously. When Kim was four her parents went through a messy divorce, each using Kim as a pawn in their dysfunctional relationship. With a complicated custody schedule in place, she'd often been left at school long past the 2 P.M. dismissal time, as her parents fought about whose turn it was to pick her up. Thankfully, a kind teacher took Kim under her wing, reading or doing special art projects long past the final bell, and always explaining away her parents' absence. "Stuck in traffic. That's what she would always say," Kim scoffed when she would recount the memory. "I thought Greenwich was the most congested town on earth until I was about ten." Although she would never admit it, I knew Kim's career choice was formed in her preschool classroom.

I peered at my BlackBerry, placed visibly on the table, as it was at every meal. Seeing it blinking, I picked it up and did a quick check.

To: Mackenzie Corbett

From: Mom

Hi Honey!

I heard you had dinner with Uncle Nigel last week. He mentioned anytime you're out there you're always welcome to spend the night so you don't have to take the train back to the city late at night. Take him up on it next time—you know how your old mom worries!!

xo Mom

P.S. Make sure you and Kim get your flu shots!! Tis the season . . .

Kim raised a questioning eyebrow.

"Just my mom checking in." I tossed my BlackBerry back on the table.

"I'm still amazed your mom even lets you live in this city all by yourself," Kim teased.

"Please," I scoffed. "The only reason she's not consumed with worry on a daily basis is that Uncle Nigel lives close enough to put out any emergencies."

Kim snickered.

My parents were the complete opposite of Kim's—they'd been married thirty years, worked jobs that meant something to them, but didn't provide a windfall (Dad was a principal and Mom was an ER nurse), and while they bickered over small things, they rarely fought. They centered their lives around their children, proudly drinking their morning coffee out of their "World's Best Mom/Dad" mugs, and would love nothing more than to have me living closer to their safe suburb just outside of Boston.

As my best friend, Kim was under Mom's worry umbrella too. And although Kim never mentioned it, she loved having a parent actually be concerned about her wellbeing.

I first met Kim orientation day of freshman year at Princeton. She was sitting on an unmade bed in our dorm room painting her toenails when I arrived, Mom and Dad in tow, schlepping labeled Tupperware storage containers I'd spent weeks organizing. "Macken-zie!" she'd sung, hopping off the bed, duck walking to avoid smudging her freshly painted toes, and embracing me the same way you would an old friend. "I've been waiting for you to get here. Welcome to Chez KimMac." She'd gestured grandly around the tiny dorm room. "Or MacKim, whatever." Something about the way she confidently assumed we'd be friends charmed me, melting away my usual new person shyness. Mom and Dad had set to work unpacking my clothes into contact paper-lined drawers, putting up shelves, and making both beds. "My mom dropped me off, but she had to go," Kim explained as Mom spread Kim's flowered comforter over her bed. "Something about staying in Jersey not being good for your skin." She'd rolled her eyes, but I noticed the tiniest blush when she said it. When Mom finished her long, tearful goodbye, and Dad, the emotional opposite of Mom, had simply reminded me of the dangers of overloading the outlet with too many electronics, they finally closed the door behind them. Kim turned to me, eyes glinting with freedom and possibility, and said, "So what should we do tonight?" We'd been inseparable through the rest of college, talked daily when I was in law school, and blessedly ended up in the same city together, which wasn't really an accident. We'd spent countless nights lying on our beds talking about our plans to live in New York City. We complemented each other well. She'd been my anchor when academic pressures threatened to push me off the deep end and I'd kept her safely moored through her multiple tumultuous relationships.

"So where's Jason tonight?" Kim inquired, changing the subject.

"At the Rangers game with Alex. I doubt Alex will get to stay for the whole game, though. He's still working with Saul, so he'll probably get the usual 'get your ass back to the office' email." I shrugged.

"Is Saul the really crazy one?" Kim asked, drawing out the word "really."

"Yup, Saul's the really crazy one," I affirmed, nodding. The partners in the corporate department all used intimidation and public humiliation as teaching tools. Frankly, each of them was really crazy in his own way. But Saul Siever had something extra—he was a sadist. He actually derived real pleasure from the torture he inflicted. Rumor had it that the only time Saul could be seen with a smile on his face was after he yelled at someone. Particularly if he brought them to tears. It was well-established firm lore that he once threw a stapler at the cleaning lady for moving his beloved ficus plant while vacuuming. It hit her in the back of the head and drew blood. Apparently after the settlement the partnership requested that he be put on medication. Whatever medication he was taking didn't seem to stifle his ongoing atrocities against associates, though. "They can't make a medication strong enough to give that monster an empathy gene," I remembered an associate slurring after one too many margaritas at a Cinco-de-Mayo party. He had a client list that rivaled those of the top partners in the city, and because of it, the firm ignored all the ways in which he was a severe liability.

"How does Alex manage to survive working for that nut?" Kim shook her head in disbelief.

I shrugged. "You know Alex, everything rolls off his back." Which unfortunately was not a trait I possessed. Lucky for me, I'd so far managed to avoid being staffed on one of Saul's deals. In my mind, Saul had chosen his favorite associates to abuse and, thankfully, I wasn't one of them.

Kim sighed dramatically. "I wish I was the one rolling around with Alex's back."

"Kim!" I laughed.

She clinked her wineglass against mine. "Don't claim you aren't aware of how incredibly sexy he is."

Alex possessed a distinct "just rolled out of bed" sexiness that clearly appealed to Kim, but he and I had always been close friends—platonic work spouses. I'd thought about setting Kim up with Alex at one point, but quickly came to my senses—Alex went through girlfriends the way a bad golfer goes through balls. If he made my best friend his next mulligan, I would have to kill him.

"Nothing wrong with looking," she added, holding her hands up in surrender. "With my record I need to have a back-up."

I squinted one eye in a mock reproachful look. It was true that Kim didn't have the best track record. Her fondness for relationship-phobic men meant her boyfriends typically stuck around about a month, just short enough to not actually be categorized as a "relationship." But her current boyfriend, Quinn, was different. For starters he actually had a source of income, something none of her previous boyfriends had. I'd initially been suspicious of the dubious occupation of "bar owner," so I'd run a title search confirming that (a) the bar "Cordova" did in fact exist and (b) Quinn did in fact own it. Yes, I did due diligence on my friend's boyfriend. I may have inherited Mom's tendency to worry.

"You don't need to have a back-up when you've found the perfect guy for you."

"Mac, don't jinx it!"

It was true, though. If I had to design a guy specifically for Kim, Quinn would be it. He was attractive, but not intimidatingly so. His

25

nose was just a tad too big, but his endearingly wide smile compensated for that. He was effortlessly cool in the "hipster without even trying" way. He was funny, but never made jokes at her expense. On their second date he cooked her lasagna because it was her favorite, and later confided to me that he'd watched a YouTube instructional video eleven times to learn how to make it. Most importantly, unlike her other beaux, he hadn't run in the opposite direction when she referred to him as her boyfriend.

"How are things going with Quinn anyway?" I asked.

Just hearing his name, Kim's face brightened. "Welllll . . . He wants me to meet his *family*." She drummed the table in delight.

"What?" I squealed.

Kim nodded enthusiastically.

"That's huge!"

"I know, right?" She picked up her wineglass and took a long, wistful gulp. "Remember that guy I dated in college who I thought wanted me to meet his family and it turned out he just wanted me to babysit his kids?"

"Yeah, you've come a long way from dating that gem."

"Who'da thunk it?"

Our waiter suddenly materialized, balancing the plates on his arms. "Just put them all in the middle," Kim instructed. He set down the caprese salad, brown butter gnocchi, and beef ravioli in the center of the table and an empty plate in front of each of us.

I speared a piece of gnocchi with my fork, grateful for Kim's indiscriminate ordering. It melted in my mouth in a ball of yummy, buttery goodness. Nights like tonight made me feel beyond lucky that the paths Kim and I had taken had led us both to New York.

"So, if you and Quinn get married and have babies, do you realize how cute they'd be?" I pointed my fork at her. "You two owe it the world to procreate."

She snorted. Never one to look too far into the future, she quickly changed gears. "Hey, do you think you'll be free tomorrow night? Every Friday is 90's movies trivia night at Quinn's bar—winner gets a $100 tab."

"Oh, we could so win that!" I raced through my mental checklist of work to-dos. With Stay Puft's deal now done, I planned on laying low for a while and enjoying a social life again. Lately it felt like I was taking up residence at F&D, but now I could finally see the light at the end of the tunnel.

"I'm in." I grinned.

Kim clapped excitedly.

But I must have had one too many glasses of wine because I had momentarily forgotten the one truth, the biggest truth I'd learned: In Biglaw, the light at the end of the tunnel is always—always—an oncoming train.

3

"Mackenzie," Rita's voice burst out of my speaker phone. "Ben Girardi needs to see you in his aw-fice."

"Did he say what it was relating to?" I asked, silently praying it wasn't a new deal. I didn't want to be smoked out of my hole a mere twenty-four hours after the merger was announced.

"No, but it bett-ah be about givin' you a raise for all the haw-d work you've been puttin' in lately."

Sadir let out a laugh from the other side of the partition. "Not likely," he scoffed.

It used to bother me that Sadir was privy to nearly everything that happened in my life on a daily basis. He could hear one side of every personal conversation, knew that I sometimes snored in my sleep, and could rattle off my schedule better than I could. But after he witnessed my attempt to discretely shave my legs at my desk one morning, I came to grips with the fact that there were never going to be any secrets between us.

"Have you heard anything about a deal Ben would be staffing?" If anyone would be in the know, it would be Sadir.

He shrugged his shoulders. "Maybe you've been picked for the associates committee."

The newest thing in Biglaw propaganda was to have an "associates committee" that supposedly dealt with associate satisfaction issues. In reality, the committee would meet with the partners once a month and suck up to them by telling them they were all doing a bang-up job and the associates were blissfully happy. What associate would risk saying anything to the contrary? No one. Then the committee would institute something like "Jamba Juice Fridays," and somehow this was supposed to miraculously increase morale. Like a free Jamba Juice made up for our indentured servitude.

"Wouldn't that be nice?" I responded sarcastically, grabbing my notepad and heading out the door. But inside I was secretly hoping that Sadir was right. Ben was a partner who had many roles in the department. I could see him being the one responsible for staffing the associates committee. Or it could be any number of things—he wants to know how the CLEs are going? Suggestions for the next department lunch? My opinion about the success of Jamba Juice Fridays?

I reached Ben's office and noticed two first year associates were already sitting on the couch off to the side of Ben's desk, legal pads perched on their laps. Ben was in a large leather chair behind his desk, his greying temples framing what anywhere else would be considered an average looking face, but in a law firm was considered handsome. I felt as if I was walking the plank as I took a few slow steps from the door to the seat across from Ben's desk. Patrick O'Shea, another first year associate, entered the office last and took the last spot on the nubby maroon couch. Ben continued to scan his email, ignoring us, while we waited to hear our fate.

I'd never worked for Ben before, but had attended a dinner at his house when I was summer associate. Every summer the partners with the nicest houses hosted a dinner for the summer associates. A sort of "this could be yours" party. Personally, I think the plan backfires because you end up getting a rather unfortunate glimpse into their lives. Of course, Ben's house was amazing—a huge old brick colonial home on a large piece of land in Scarsdale with a pool, tennis court, and a circular driveway that took visitors to the private parking lot behind the house. Inside, there was a grand staircase descending down into the foyer—wide enough that a car could probably drive down it. From the foyer, double French doors led to a large room where the furniture had been cleared out to accommodate the party. It was clear from the food and drink that

30

the dinner had a Mexican theme—waiters holding silver trays with sangria and pomegranate margaritas greeted everyone at the door and tiny empanadas and spicy shrimp were being offered by waitresses circulating through the crowd. Ben had done his best to portray the "laid back fun partner" look, wearing a cream colored linen shirt rolled up to the elbows and matching linen pants. To me it ended up looking more like a pair of oversized pajamas Hugh Hefner might wear.

Ben's wife, Katrina, was easy to spot. She was the petite, blue-eyed blonde floating through the crowd with a blinding amount of diamonds around her wrist and neck, talking a little louder than everyone else. Her tanned skin was flawless and perfectly set off by her white, flowing linen dress. She'd be the first to tell you she was from a prominent Russian family and clearly embraced her roots in her home decorating. Large, gilded arm chairs and ornate tables were proudly displayed in the foyer, but didn't really mesh with the exterior of the house. Clearly their decorating plan was simply "anything expensive and showy" rather than one particular style. The party was meant to impress us, but, even though I couldn't put my finger on it, there just seemed something a little tacky about the whole thing. Did we really need to be taken on a tour of Ben's luxury goods? And be forced to listen to the silly reasons for each purchase? I mean, he actually told us he bought a piece of art for three hundred thousand dollars just so he could out-bid George Soros at the Sotheby's auction.

Of course, just when I thought the party couldn't get any more over the top, our attention was directed towards the foyer where a five-piece mariachi band descended down the grand staircase, singing and playing their large stringed instruments, making the whole setting unquestionably one of the most bizarre firm events I'd witnessed. A mariachi band. For a dinner party. As if a further element of absurdity needed to be added to the whole situation.

The mariachi band continued to play throughout dinner as we feasted on lobster ceviche and braised short ribs. I sat two seats away from Katrina, who downed red sangria like it was water and regaled the table with stories of their extravagant vacations.

31

"'Scuse me please, but it's time to kick this up a notch," she slurred to the table midway through dinner and stumbled towards the band. We all turned to see what would happen next as she grabbed a microphone and started to sing. And by sing, I mean rolling her tongue and shrieking, "Ya ka ka ka ka" while clapping to the rhythm and swinging her hips. The members of the band looked puzzled, but kept playing. She dropped the microphone and stumbled back and forth attempting to dance with one of the band members. Finally, the train wreck ended and she returned to the table and fell into her chair.

"Ben just hates it when I sing," she announced to no one in particular. "But Ben hates just about everything I do, don't you, Benny?" She patted his face a little too hard. Ben just sat there stiffly, clenching his teeth together like his jaw was wired shut. "Awww . . . now I'm being ignored." Her lower lip dropped into a pout.

"Nothing a little Xanax can't fix though, right, sweetie?" She laughed and swilled back more of her drink.

I can personally attest to the fact that nothing kills a dinner party faster than the hostess talking about her happy pills. We were ushered to our coats just as she was breaking out in song again. After that night I couldn't look at Ben without thinking of his medicated wife and his pajama outfit. Now here I was, in Hugh Hefner's office.

"Okay," Ben started, looking down at his clasped hands. "I just got off the phone with a new client and we've been given the go ahead to start work on their latest acquisition. And it's a big one. Big." He looked around the room significantly. "We've been retained by Pegasus Partners, the private equity firm that made headlines last year for their unfortunate foray into the arms manufacturing business. The bad publicity cost them two major investors."

I looked up from my notepad as though this wasn't news to me.

"Pegasus has decided to target Highlander Hotels and Resorts, hoping that a move into the more PR friendly hotel industry will scrub their image," Ben went on. "They reached a handshake deal last night. We're looking at a purchase price well north of seven billion." He raised his eyebrows. "Now we've got to do the diligence and paper the deal. They want a fully signed purchase agreement by the end of February and the deal closed by the end of May."

I felt a bubble of dismay growing inside. Taking a multibillion dollar acquisition from a handshake to a fully signed purchase agreement typically took over six months. We had four. Couldn't I just give him my thoughts on Jamba Juice Fridays and call it a day?

"Mackenzie, set a kick-off meeting for today at two."

I nodded, scribbling orders on my notepad.

"Any questions?" Ben asked, clearly expecting none.

The room fell silent.

"Great." Ben smiled. "Pegasus usually uses Skadden for their M&A work, so if we bring this one home it could mean a lot more work for us from these guys." Ben pushed back his chair and stood. The rest of us followed suit.

"Oh, Mackenzie, hang back for a second. The rest of you can go." He dismissed the first years with a curt nod of his head.

I stood awkwardly, not knowing if I should sit back down. I noticed Patrick turn and give me a look on his way out that said, *Better you than me.*

Ben waited for them to scurry out of the office before fixing his eyes on me, "Mackenzie, I'm sure you realize what a privilege it is for a second year associate to be entrusted with this deal. Your efforts on Maxwell's deal didn't go unnoticed and Maxwell is a hard guy to please. It's not easy for an associate to stand out at F&D. There's a lot of driven and smart associates here. That's a given." He hesitated. "Those who distinguish themselves in my eyes go *above* and *beyond*. Do you understand what I'm saying here?"

I nodded, not entirely sure I did.

"Good." He folded his arms over his chest and rocked back on his heels. "Then I'm sure you know that I'm the partner responsible for picking the associate that lands the StarCorp secondment."

My pulse quickened. Every year the firm selected one mid-level associate to work for the firm's largest client, StarCorp Investments, for six months. Not only does the lucky associate get an opportunity to work on the business side, gaining valuable experience, but the hours were far less demanding, essentially amounting to a six month break from the grind of Biglaw. It was the most sought after reward for a corporate associate at F&D and landing it was essentially a declaration that you were on partnership track. Every associate that has been selected for the plum position has gone on to make partner. Every single one. And the last three associates that had been graced with the opportunity made partner a year earlier than expected.

"So." Ben blew out a long breath of air. "This deal isn't just an opportunity for the firm, but an amazing opportunity for you as well. I'm a good guy to impress." He grinned, ensuring we were now both in on the same secret.

"Of course," I said, trying to keep my voice steady. "You can count on me, Ben."

"I wouldn't expect anything less. This one is going to require a Herculean effort from you and your team, but I'm sure you're up to the task."

"Absolutely," I said with more certainty than I felt.

———

Walking back to my office, a whir of emotions was spinning inside me. If I performed well on this deal, I was basically guaranteed the StarCorp secondment. Just thinking about it made me feel like I was levitating from elation. And being involved in an acquisition of this magnitude would definitely bring accolades. I always got a major adrenaline rush whenever my name made the list in New York Law Journal's "Lawyers Working on Billion Dollar Deals." The first time my name appeared, I'd cut out the article and sent it to Mom and Dad, eager to show off my newfound celebrity status. Mom put it in the scrapbook, which was mostly populated with articles showcasing Margaret's athletic achievements. "And your name is in bold!" Mom had cooed.

But, being handed the opportunity to work on this deal also came with the tremendous responsibility not to screw it up. I didn't even want to imagine what would happen if I didn't perform to Ben's standards. His Herculean standards.

"Well?" Sadir called out when I entered the office.

I leaned against the wall, my head still spinning. "You know, when you didn't have the inside track on a big deal being staffed by Ben I really did think that it might be something as benign as the associates committee."

"Yeah, sorry about lying to you, Mackenzie." He nodded somberly. "I already heard through the grapevine that Ben was staffing a monster deal. I just had to give you some hope, though. It's like putting a blindfold over someone's eyes before they're about to be executed," he explained. "You just have to do that for a person. It's the humane thing to do."

I snickered and flopped down in my chair. "He did say it was an honor to be put on this deal—a *reward* for earlier work."

"Well, welcome to the pie eating contest . . . where the only prize is *more pie*."

4

I FUMBLED WITH MY pad of paper and nervously entered conference room 23A—the largest one in the office, usually reserved for impressing clients. The last time I was here was for the "coffee taste test party" when I was a summer associate. The events coordinator had lined up ten types of coffee from around the world, including a rare bean flown in from the Coffee Expo that retailed for $80 a cup. A coffee sommelier walked us through the different types as we sipped samples and munched on pastries from Payard. But the only offerings today were thermoses of Starbucks and pastries from the cafeteria.

Anxiously tugging at the hem of my skirt, I took a deep breath as my body flooded with adrenaline. When Ben told me to attend the kick-off meeting I'd nodded dutifully, hoping he wouldn't notice the flush creeping across my neck. Normally only partners or senior associates attend kick-off meetings, so for Ben to bestow the honor on a mid-level associate was unusual. It felt like an invitation to the inner circle of F&D royalty, sending my heart rate sky high.

Senior associates from all practice groups buzzed anxiously around the overgrown mahogany table running the length of the room with leather chairs tucked neatly under it. Knowing there wouldn't be enough seats for everyone, I perched on a credenza off to the side—it was career suicide to do otherwise. The most senior lawyers get the seats. Always. I've seen women so pregnant they look ready to pop standing, not wanting to break this unspoken code of conduct. Even the order of email addresses in a CC line of an email is supposed to be arranged according to seniority, starting with the most senior partner and ending with the most junior associate. Some partners won't even read emails if their name isn't in the pole position.

The air felt charged with power and influence. The grandness of the room, with its wall-to-wall windows, the imposing Empire State Building looming in the distance, and the grey suits practically oozing testosterone, gave me the sense that I'd just stepped onto the set of *Wall Street*. At any minute Gordon Gekko would appear and announce, "Greed is good."

Sitting here (okay, perched here) I felt like I'd made it to the big leagues. I could almost hear Carly Simon's "Let the River Run," playing, while I stood in my corner office, smiling triumphantly. Despite being a small cog in a big wheel, and even knowing that this deal would engulf my life, I couldn't suppress my smile.

Surreptitiously, I looked around the room. The key partners in every department were here. There was Ron Richards, head of the Labor and Employment Department and self-described "unions' worst nightmare." Alongside him stood Anthony Booth, head of the Real Estate Department, the oldest partner at sixty-seven, refusing retirement and leveraging his many loyal clients to prevent it. Steven Burrows, head of the Intellectual Property Department, was there too. He'd earned the nickname "Seven" because of an acceptance speech he gave during an awards dinner for The Top 40 Lawyers Under 40, announcing that his greatest accomplishment did not relate to his practice, but instead was when he engaged in all seven deadly sins in one day. Scott Kesler, head of the Environmental Law Department, had even made an appearance. He was responsible for figuring out how our clients could avoid any law enacted to protect the environment. Finally, there was Anton Waldorf, head of the Tax Department, best known around the firm for berating a pregnant associate, bringing her to tears and then telling her the tears were the reason the firm hated breeders. He was also one of the highest paid partners in the entire firm, which just reinforces the theory that there is an inverse relationship between money and mental stability.

Numerous junior associates in other departments would learn their Friday night fate following this meeting. They would have to make the same call to their friends that I had to make an hour ago. Kim was disappointed I'd be missing out on 90's movie trivia night, but I promised her I'd have six months of free evenings when I landed the StarCorp secondment.

The collective breath of everyone in the conference room was held when Vincent Krieder swaggered in. If F&D had an organizational chart of partners, Vincent would be the box at the top. Not only was he a four corner partner in the corporate department, but Vincent was the grand poobah. The mere presence of Vincent in this meeting confirmed the tremendous importance of the deal to the firm.

Vincent came up behind Ben, setting both hands on his shoulders for a three second massage. "Ready for this?" He took his seat at the head of the large table without waiting for an answer. "Welcome, gentlemen . . . ladies." He looked around the room, taking us each in, his voice commanding immediate attention. "Happy Friday, everybody," he added dryly. "This is a big one, guys . . . big." He paused for effect. "You all know that Pegasus lost two key public pension investment funds when they purchased Lexington Group, the largest ammunition company in the country. It was —" He paused. "Well, let's just call it unfortunate timing."

Heads nodded somberly all around. I'd learned from Google that two days after Pegasus had purchased the Lexington Group their bestselling assault rifle had been the weapon of choice in a mass shooting. To make matters worse, the Lexington Group took to Twitter and fired off a fairly objectionable tweet about the right to bear arms. It was a public relations disaster for Pegasus.

"And now they need to scrub their image. The pension investment funds that invest large amounts of money in private equity funds like Pegasus have publicly stated they are going to pay closer attention to what their money is being used to purchase. Who the fuck knows why?" Vincent threw his hands up. A few chuckles ensued.

"We need to negotiate and sign a binding purchase agreement with Highlander Hotels in time for Pegasus's annual general meeting, which is February 28th so they can announce the acquisition to the investors. And they need the deal to close before their fiscal year ends, which is the end of May."

Partners around the table furrowed their brows.

Vincent grasped his chin and thought for a moment. "Now, in terms of the client's wants and their expectations—they said they WANT this deal to happen so I told them to EXPECT it to be expensive." More chuckles. "In terms of what we actually *know*—it's limited."

"Ain't that the truth," Anton Waldorf quipped, grabbing a strawberry Danish from the platter of shiny baked goods laid out for the meeting.

Vincent gave Anton the finger. With so many egos in one room, it didn't take long for the grandstanding to begin.

"Okay, here is what we know, other than that Waldorf is an asshole." He continued to fill us in on the details as I furiously scribbled notes.

Vincent laid his palms flat against the conference room table and slowly slid them back and forth, a tiny smirk breaking across his face. "They want this, guys—let me be crystal clear about that. Cost is not an issue. If you are in the shower *thinking* about this deal, bill it. If you are away from your desk, but have a Highlander document on your computer screen, bill it."

"If you're fucking your mistress in a Highlander Hotel, bill it," Waldorf called out. I mentally rolled my eyes. The only shocking thing about his statement was how unshocked everyone in the room was.

"You get the idea." Vincent slapped the table and stood up. "Let's get this done and our year is set." With that, the big guns filed out of the room, leaving us peons to follow behind them.

———

"Well, you look surprisingly happy for someone who just told me she'll have no life for the next six months." Jason entered my office and passed me a white plastic bag.

"What's this?" I peeked inside.

"A chopped salad from Toasties and a black and white cookie," he confirmed. "I knew you wouldn't be able to make it out for lunch and I didn't want you starving."

"How did you know that I was just debating whether the stale granola bar in my drawer could substitute for lunch?" I kicked off my shoes, crossed my legs in my chair, and began digging in.

"Because I know how you get when you're focused on something." He grinned.

I did have a tendency to throw myself into my tasks. Kim used to refer to me as "Rocky" when I would study for my final exams. "It's like you disappear into the Russian mountains, training for weeks," she'd teased. "And when you come back you have this crazy focus, like the Eye of the Tiger." The description always made me laugh, but whenever I got an A I did picture myself at the top of the steps of the Philadelphia Museum of Art, pumping my fists triumphantly.

"You know me too well," I replied, beaming.

"And it's because I know you so well that I can recognize that worried look in your eyes." He wagged his finger at me. "The one you get when you think you're in over your head. Trust me, you're going to do an amazing job and Ben is going to be begging you to take that secondment. I mean, out of everyone he could've picked, Ben chose *you* to work on the biggest deal in the firm. I'd take that as a pretty good sign that you're capable." He gave me a quick wink. I'd always found winking cheesy, but Jason managed to do it in a way that was endearing.

"Ben did sound pretty ominous about the work load with this one." I chewed on the side of my fingernail. "He actually used the word 'Herculean.'"

Jason burst out laughing. "Ben sure has a flare for drama."

"That's nothing. Apparently he told the first years this was going to be a marathon and to stay hydrated." I rolled my eyes.

Jason hooted and slapped his leg. Now he had me laughing too. I could feel the anxiety draining from my body.

"So." He cocked an eyebrow. "I take it this means you aren't going to be able to make it to my cousin's wedding?"

I grimaced. "When is that again?"

"In three weeks . . . " he trailed off.

"I'm sorry," I said, looking contrite. Canceled plans were the norm in Biglaw, but it was still tough to see Jason's disappointed expression. "You know I would try to get the time off if I could, but I need to knock it out of the park with this one. Chances to land a career opportunity like the StarCorp secondment just don't come along every day."

"Neither do family weddings." Jason flashed that killer smile that I love. He knew that all social plans we made always had an asterisk attached—work dependent. He just wanted to make me squirm a little longer.

"I could see if I could get away for a day," I lobbed, hoping he wouldn't take me up on the offer.

"Don't worry about the wedding." Jason rubbed my shoulders. "It's not even a cousin that I particularly like. You focus on being Hercules." He pinched my bicep playfully. "And impressing Mr. Dramatic."

I put my hand over his. What had I ever done in my life to deserve such a sweet, understanding boyfriend? Whatever it was, I was grateful I'd done it. "I really am sorry I have to miss it," I murmured.

He pressed his mouth right next to my ear and whispered. "Don't worry. You totally got this."

5

"Okay." I looked around the table, feeling puffed up because I was the most senior associate in the room. It was our first meeting in the "war room"—a conference room on the thirtieth floor that was reserved indefinitely for "Project Mojo," the codename given for the deal. As first year associates, Gavin Shin, Patrick O'Shea, and Sheldon Laurie were too junior to attend the kick-off meeting, so I was responsible for filling them in on what happened and doling out the specific duties. When Ben had referred to the first years as my "team" I had the sudden realization that I'd never had a team before. Sadir was right—I was moving up in the world.

I had worked with each of my team members before, so I had a good idea what to expect. Gavin was the oldest of the three, having taken off two years between college and law school to figure out what he wanted to do. This made him hungry to catch up for lost time, so he worked around the clock to prove that he should be considered better than his peers. He always jumped at the opportunity to have face time with a partner and was often the last one to leave the office. Rumor had it his work ethic was fueled by his pesky cocaine habit which quickly became obvious to anyone who worked with him.

Sheldon was the polar opposite. He was a devout Mormon, whose work was always meticulous. His attention to detail would have been enviable if there was no timeline, but on this deal it was going to be irritating. Last time I worked with him it took him *five* hours to review one supply agreement. Then he came to my office distressed that the contract contained a lot of grammatical errors. I had to explain to him that the quality of drafting was not an issue for us. Our responsibility was solely to summarize it, but he looked at me like a Labrador trying to understand his master, cocking his head from one side to the other in confusion. In Sheldon's world his job included editing previously executed contracts. So, despite my explanation and plea to work faster, his summary included a long list of supposed grammatical errors in the contract, all of which were insignificant.

Patrick, on the other hand, was a barrel-chested, quick-witted Irish Catholic from Boston who always said he didn't have time for bullshit. And to Patrick, *everything* was bullshit. You need him to revise his work? Bullshit! The cafeteria is out of fried chicken? Bullshit! It's raining? Bullshit! I couldn't give him the responsibility of coordinating the paralegals or giving instructions to the specialists because I knew he'd come across as brash and aggressive, thereby creating more problems than it was worth. But his work quality was better than Gavin's and quicker than Sheldon's, so that made him my favorite.

Grasping my hands in front of me, sitting ramrod straight, I mustered my best power-commanding tone. "Highlander Hotels has thousands of corporate documents, contracts, and policies relating to their hotels around the world and each one has to be reviewed. They're posting the documents in an online data room and for confidentiality reasons they're not permitting us to print them. So, we'll work from this checklist." I slid three copies of the 177-page stapled checklist across the table.

"Holy crap," Patrick muttered, flipping through the pages.

"I know it's a lot of work, but I'm really going to need your one hundred percent on it," I said in a tone I hoped was motivating rather than pleading. "So, let's get started." Taking a deep breath, I flipped open the first page of the checklist.

———

Two weeks into our efforts, Ben called the first status meeting. Reviewing my notes one final time before I headed to Ben's office, a tiny smile played at my lips. I'd been up for twenty-six hours straight. My eyes were burning and my deodorant had long since ceased to be effective. I hadn't consumed anything but coffee and Diet Coke, but that wasn't why I felt light headed. I was dizzy with excitement. After reviewing one tediously boring contract after another, I'd come across my own version of a smoking gun.

I squinted at the clock on my computer. *9:55 A.M.* Five minutes to freshen up. I swiped a handiwipe under my arms, ran a brush through my hair, and popped a breath mint. After a futile attempt to dab out a grease stain on my skirt, I picked up my notes and headed down the corridor to Ben's office, mentally giving myself one final pep talk.

Ben looked well rested and freshly showered as he waved me in from behind his polished desk. I felt a pang of embarrassment, but hoped my unkempt appearance communicated my level of commitment. Maybe this was what he meant by going "above and beyond."

I handed Ben the due diligence checklist so he could get an idea of the dent we'd put in the work load. He ran his eyes over it, expressionless, then put it down and launched into a list of outstanding items he wanted me to attend to. I scratched feverishly on my notepad. He was adding a lot of work to what already felt like a bottomless pit.

"So." He blew out a long breath, leaning back in his chair. "Any red flags in the due diligence I should know about?"

I cleared my throat. "Yes, actually I found something that may be of interest to you."

His lips pressed into a thin, impatient line.

"Ben?" A sharp voice trilled through the office.

I looked up to see Sarah standing in the doorway. She was wearing another one of her flawlessly pressed, fitted black suits, and a pair of blood-red stilettos.

"You wanted to see me?" she said, in crisp, precise diction.

"Yes." Ben perked up as he waved her inside. "Take a seat. We're just about done here." He gestured with his chin towards me.

"Great." Sarah flashed a Cheshire smile as she sauntered over to the chair beside me. Her eyes swept over me and I was suddenly very aware of my greasy hair sticking to the back of my neck.

I shifted uncomfortably in my seat, hoping Ben had the good sense not to mention the StarCorp secondment. I knew from Sadir that Sarah had been passed over for the secondment two years ago, the position going to a well-connected associate who had the good fortune of being related to the CEO of a big client. If Sarah caught wind that I was in the running for the secondment this year that would be akin to painting a giant target on my back and handing her a gun.

"What was your question, Mackenzie?" Ben asked distractedly as he watched Sarah lean back in her chair and cross her toned legs. I couldn't help but wonder if she was going to pull a Sharon Stone right before my eyes. She did have a way of carrying herself in the office that seemed to be the perfect balance of offering herself up a silver platter while still maintaining professionalism. She laughed a little louder at men's jokes, lingered with eye contact and strategic lip licking but, annoyingly, she still spoke with authority and proficiency.

I looked down at my notepad, doing my best to ignore the flush that was creeping up my neck. "Well, Highlander gets all of its bedding from Southern Hospitality, the company that owns the Blissful Bed Collection, pursuant to a five year supply contract they have in place. The contract is set to expire at the end of March and so far I haven't come across any plans to renew. So —"

Ben waved his hand dismissively, interrupting me. "That's not noteworthy. With a company of their size supply contracts can fall through the cracks. Just make a note of it in the diligence memo." He tossed me back the diligence checklist.

Out of the corner of my eye I could see the side of Sarah's thin lips curl up into a smirk. I wanted to reach over and wipe the smug look off her face.

"This supply contract is particularly important, though." I continued, a slight shake in my voice. "Highlander just spent two hundred million dollars on an advertising campaign centered around the fact that every one of their hotels is furnished by Blissful Beds. If they let the supply contract expire, they'll have to dump the whole campaign which would be a big hit. Our client would be stuck with a bill for a new ad campaign."

A small smile crept across Ben's face. His expression reminded me of a parent watching a kindergarten graduation.

I took a deep breath. "I think we should make the renegotiation of the Southern Hospitality supply contract a condition to closing."

Ben was nodding approvingly now, as though I had passed some test. "You're absolutely right, Mackenzie. Great catch." He scratched a note onto his legal pad. "Go ahead and add that to the draft of the purchase agreement."

"Will do." I tossed a satisfied smile in Sarah's direction on my way out. *How you like me now?*

As soon as I got back to my office, I closed the door and did a happy Snoopy dance. Jason was right. I totally got this.

6

I PUSHED OPEN MY office door, nearly hitting Sadir, who was sprawled out on the floor, looking like a corpse and smelling like one that had been there for days.

"Mackenzie!" Sadir jumped to his feet. "Shit, is it morning already?" He snorted and snuffled as he raked his sleeve across his nose. Then he rubbed his bloodshot eyes and attempted to smooth down his hair, which was sticking up after being mushed against a pile of files used as a makeshift pillow.

"Yuuuup. Morning time," I answered with a hint of annoyance, placing my bag on the floor, slipping off my coat and hanging it on the back of the door before taking a seat at my desk. I was used to Sadir sleeping in the office, but this morning I found the sight a little . . . repulsive.

"Looong night." He let out a guttural sigh, stumbling to his seat. "Reallllly long night." I could tell he wanted me to press for details, but I wasn't going to take the bait. My mind was hazy from sleep deprivation and all I really wanted was to sip my latte and peacefully do some online shopping. Clicking open Outlook, I could hear Sadir running through his morning routine on the other side of the partition—eye drops, mouthwash swished ten times and spat out in the garbage can, and two spritzes of cologne. I knew what was coming next.

"Hey, did you hear the latest?" He popped his head over the partition.

"Nope," I answered disinterestedly, scrolling through my email. Every morning Sadir offered up what he referred to as "the latest," which gave the sense that he had some juicy tidbit of gossip, when in reality it was just the information he'd gathered on who was working on what, what deals had died, or whether one of F&D's clients was in the *Wall Street Journal* that day. None of it fell into the category of "the latest," but that didn't stop Sadir.

"There's a new deal being staffed. Wanna know the partner?" He paused before drawing out the name dramatically. "Saul Siever. Some poor associates will be sucked into his vortex of craziness today."

"Really? That sucks." I continued my daily script of responding enough not to be rude, but not enough to encourage him—then my mind caught up to what he'd just said. "Wait." I suddenly felt my insides cramp, remembering Saul standing in the elevator when I stepped in at 6 P.M. last night. I was just ducking out for a quick sushi dinner with Jason, a tiny present to myself for enduring the all-nighter and impressing Ben. Saul gave me an angry once-over as I resisted the urge to tell him I would be returning to the office in an hour (and that I'd just come off an all-nighter). Now, I was kicking myself for staying silent because Saul Siever, the craziest partner at F&D, thinks he saw me leave the office for the day before seven. In Biglaw that was akin to pulling the trigger four times in a game of Russian roulette, knowing you had two pulls left and one was the bullet. "*Who's* staffing a new deal?" I stood up slowly, my heart pounding.

Before Sadir could answer, my desk phone trilled, filling our small office with a sound that I was certain got louder and louder with each ring. I took a moment to steel myself before I looked, but still felt like the wind had been knocked out of me when I saw the name on the caller ID: SAUL SIEVER.

Sadir's eyes were wide. "Aren't you going to get it?"

I nodded, saying a silent prayer that Saul had simply dialed the wrong extension, and tentatively picked up the phone.

"Come see me. I need you to do something for me," the voice on the other end snarled, almost unintelligibly. Then he hung up. There was no "Hello, this is Saul Siever. Can you come to my office, please?" Not even a chance for me to respond with an, "Okay, on my way." Just dead air.

I felt my throat close up. After a moment of listening to the deafening silence, I pulled the receiver away and noticed my fingernails were digging into my palm, as I death-clutched that phone like it was the last piece of solid ground and if I let go I'd be washed away.

"Well?" Sadir looked at me expectantly.

Without responding, I fumbled around my messy desk frantically, picked up a legal pad, and hustled down the corridor of filing cabinets towards Saul's corner office. There was no way I could work on a deal with Saul simultaneously with the Highlander deal. Ben specifically asked me to commit one hundred percent of my time. *Just tell Saul you're too swamped to take on anything more*, I told myself firmly. I had two years of dealing with partners under my belt and knew what to expect: impatience, ingratitude, edginess, and the occasional threat of violence. I considered myself such an expert in the Biglaw partner personality that I could've tapped into my BA in psychology and written a book: *Fragile Male Egos with Napoleon Complexes and No Idea of Limits* by Mackenzie Corbett. Surely that meant I could handle Saul.

51

As I approached the corner office I could hear Saul's voice raised, presumably on a conference call. "Listen, these motherfuckers think a buyout is their only fucking choice. That's crystal fucking clear." I stopped outside the door, suddenly too afraid to knock or go in. I felt like I had bricks in my shoes, unable to put one foot in front of the other. *Is this what it feels like to be paralyzed with fear?*

Anna Perez, Saul's latest secretary, glanced up from her computer. "You gotta show no fear, hon—just knock and go in." She pointed a long, animal-printed fingernail at Saul's door. I'm sure she was used to the sight of tentative associates making their first trip to see The Godfather. I grinned tightly and nodded. Taking a deep breath, I lifted my hand and knocked.

"Yeah?" Saul barked. I cautiously put my hand on the door handle, looked at Anna, who gave me a confirmatory nod, and pushed the door open.

Saul's office was the size of a small apartment; its sweeping view stretched all the way up from Midtown to the tip of Central Park. In the middle of the room was an imposing desk, roughly the size of a large dining room table. Seated behind it, in an elevated chair that reminded me of a throne, was Saul. Pasty-faced and balding, he looked like the type of person that must have been stuffed in a locker multiple times in high school. He was skinny, with no muscle tone, and had a scrunched-up face that reminded me of a weasel. His dress shirt was so wrinkled it looked like it had been balled up on the floor before he picked it up, dusted it off, and put it on. He had two deep furrows between his eyebrows, the kind that implant themselves on a face after a lifetime of scowling, and his few wisps of hair flew crazily on his head. He glared up from his phone, regarded me with a mixture of disdain and contempt, then returned his focus to the call.

I took this as my cue and removed the pile of files resting on the chair across from him and sat down. Immediately, I felt like I was Alice in Wonderland, having just eaten the pill that made me smaller. I thought for a moment that it was the large, intimidating office that made me feel this way. Then I realized my seat was about six inches lower than Saul's. The whole thing was designed to make me look and feel tiny. On the plus side, if you could call it that, my chair did afford the most amazing panoramic view of the park—you could see all the way up to the reservoir, not that Saul seemed to notice. He spent most of the day with his back to the view.

"We need them to continue to think their ship is sinking and we're the last fucking life boat," the voice on the other end of the speaker phone blared. "The last thing we need is any fucking media leaks making the stock go up giving these imbeciles a shred of hope."

Sitting in on my first conference call, I'd been surprised at how much the clients swore. These were educated, grown men (and occasionally women), but they used the word "fuck" with the frequency most people reserved for adjectives. It was like being on a playground with a bunch of fifth graders who had just learned their first swear words. "Fuck" was used as a noun, a verb, and sometimes even a preposition. Some of the combinations they put together didn't even make sense. "The fucking guy's a fucking shit ass fuck." "The cock-sucking draft they sent us was fucking fucked." Not exactly the most articulate way of describing things from these so-called titans of business. But our clients were large hedge funds and the people that worked there were known for being gritty and unrelenting. These were not people that came from old money, living off trust funds. No, these were guys who started with nothing and climbed, one hand over the other, all the way to the top, making millions in the process. Even though they had more money than ninety-nine percent of the population, they still had huge chips on their shoulders and rarely uttered a sentence without adding "fuck," "shit," "asshole," or some combination of the three.

I was experiencing the strangest feeling sitting in Saul's office. It was like being in a haunted house—I could almost feel the souls of former associates that Saul had crushed lingering around me. I shivered as I picked up my pen. Taking notes of this call was the least I could do for the unfortunate associate who would have to replace me on this deal when I told Saul I was too busy with Highlander.

"I hear you. I hear you." Saul leaned into the speaker phone, nodding impatiently. "I can assure you this place is like Area 51. Nothing ever leaks. Look, I gotta bounce. We'll get started and circle back tomorrow night." He slammed his finger down on the "end call" button as the other line rang, and scribbled something down on a yellow sticky note.

53

I looked down at my notes. "Buyout. Confidential. Motivated seller—sinking ship." The details of the transaction must have been discussed before I arrived. These notes were not going to be a big help when I passed them on.

"I assume you got all that." His tone was almost accusatory.

I cleared my throat. "Unfortunately, Saul, I don't think I'm going to be able to help on this transaction. I'm working on the Highlander deal and Ben said that it would take up one hundred percent of my time." I tried to keep my tone even, but I noticed a tiny shake in my voice.

Saul folded his arms across his chest, glaring at me. His expression was unreadable and I briefly wondered if he was sizing me up to see if he could take me. Then, as if I hadn't even spoken, he said,

"The relevant documents are on my secretary's desk. Copy them and get up to speed. Get me a bid letter and document request list by tonight." He returned his attention to his computer, signaling the end of our conversation.

Back in my office, I pressed the heels of my palms hard against my eyes. How was I possibly going to balance surviving a Saul deal with impressing Ben? And why weren't there any other associates on the deal? A small deal usually had at least two corporate associates working on it. A large deal could have more than ten assigned. It was one thing to be on a deal with Saul—that was bad enough, but to be the ONLY one on the deal with him? That meant no buffer between me and Saul. I'd be the only one for him to abuse.

I picked up the phone and called the one person who could help. Jason might sympathize, but not being in the corporate department, he had no idea of the implications of being put on a deal with Saul. The partners in the Trusts department might as well have been Birkenstock wearing, tie-dye clad, dreadlocked, hacky sack–playing hippies sitting around holding hands around a campfire singing kumbaya compared to the partners in the corporate department.

"Nooooooo! Oh, man, you're screwed—he's going to eat you alive!" Alex wailed.

I sighed impatiently into the phone. "I've worked for Maxwell before, remember?" Maxwell was certainly no picnic. He believed associates should be treated like soldiers and routinely employed the tricks of psychological warfare he'd learned during his ten years in the Israeli army. Except instead of trying to gain information from a prisoner of war or get an enemy to surrender, he used these tactics to get his associates to work harder, stay later, and never EVER make a mistake.

"Please," Alex scoffed. "Maxwell is a kitten compared to Saul."

I suppressed a shudder. "Okay, then fill me in on what I need to know before working for him."

"Let's see. Well, he likes to drink the tears of sobbing associates."

"Ha, ha. You know what I mean. Like, he's best to deal with in the morning, he'll freak out if you don't print out his documents double-sided . . . " I tried to tap into my repertoire of partner idiosyncrasies.

"Doesn't want you to refer to him by his first name? Doesn't want you to eat meat while working for him? You know, just one of those strange quirks that all partners seem to have . . . anything like that?"

He cleared his throat and lowered his voice. "Listen, and understand. Saul is out there. He can't be bargained with, he can't be reasoned with, he doesn't feel pity, or remorse, or fear. And he absolutely will not stop, ever, until you are dead."

Had Alex lost his mind? After a beat of silence I remembered. "Umm . . . is that a line from *Terminator 2*?"

"Yes, but it is surprisingly appropriate in this situation."

"As helpful as your 90's movie knowledge has been . . . " My tone was clipped.

"Okay, okay . . . " His voice softened. "Listen, Mac, the only advice I can really give you is to repeat the following in your head: 'sticks and stones may break my bones, but names will never hurt me.'"

Not helpful. At all.

I flipped through the pile of documents that Saul had provided and tried to make some sense of them. No matter how many times I looked at them, though, they still looked like a random compilation of corporate documents from various companies. There was an organizational chart of the employees for an entity called Falcon Mobility Inc., a few directors' resolutions, and the bylaws of various entities. Were they subsidiaries of Falcon Mobility Inc.? It was impossible to tell. There was nothing in the documents to indicate which company was making the bid, what they were bidding on, or what the proposed terms were intended to be. And I would need to know whether our client was purchasing the stock or the assets. That detail was crucial to drafting a document request list.

I felt like I'd been dropped in the middle of the Sahara without a compass. Saul knew I'd only been there for the end of the call, and his directions had been so sparse, I'd just assumed the background material would be in the documents he provided.

I called Anna, hoping that she'd inadvertently missed a few documents. I really, really didn't want to go back to Saul with questions if there was any way I could track down the information myself. That would be like handing him a loaded gun and helping him point it at my own head. Anna confirmed she'd given me everything she had and I hung up the phone, knowing I'd hit a dead end. "Shit, I'm screwed! Day one of working with Saul and I'm already screwed," I exclaimed aloud, burying my face in my hands.

Sadir leapt up from his seat. "He's thrown something at you or threatened to fire you ALREADY?" he asked excitedly.

"No," I responded softly, feeling a bit embarrassed about my theatrics. Saul hadn't done *anything* to me yet. "He just . . . he's put me on this deal which I have *no* time for and he hasn't given me enough information to do what he wants. And by not enough information, I mean he's given me like, NO information." I dejectedly flipped through the documents again.

"So . . . ask the senior associate on the deal for more information," Sadir replied, sitting back down, clearly disappointed that I didn't have a Saul torture story for his collection.

"That's the worst paaaart," I whined. "There isn't another associate—it's just me!"

"Oh, man, you've got no buffer? You really ARE screwed. There's no way to avoid failure in that situation."

I slumped back in my chair, sulking. *What did I do to deserve this?* I wondered, filling with self-pity. It had to be karma. I must have been a terrible person in a previous life. Maybe Attila the Hun. Why else would I deserve my present fate?

"I'm going to go grab a sandwich." Sadir stood up and grabbed his coat off the back of his chair. "There's no use sulking about your situation, Mackenzie. It just . . . it is what it is." He shrugged.

It is what it is. I had grown to hate that expression. That, and "it's the nature of the beast." Leave it to the legal profession to overuse two expressions which essentially amount to saying "you have no control over your life, so don't try and do anything about it, just suck it up and take it."

I'm building this up too much in my head, I thought as I typed out the email to Saul. *I've dealt with difficult partners before.*

I reviewed my email three times, proofing it for errors and ensuring I'd asked everything I needed to know in the most succinct way possible. Finally I hit send. Staring at my inbox, I exhaled a long breath. The only thing left to do was wait for a response.

———

Ten minutes later I heard someone thundering down the hallway. *Is there some kind of emergency?* I wondered, as I stood up to see what was going on. Then there he was. Saul. He gripped both sides of the door frame, his eyes blazing, breathing heavily.

Partners *never* visited associates' offices. I stared at him, stunned.

"What the hell do you think you're doing? This deal is under a STRICT Chinese Wall. A fucking CHINESE WALL." Spit was flying from his mouth. "You put the name of the target company in the email, you stupid shit."

I stood at my desk, in shock, the burn of mortification creeping up my neck. I swallowed hard. "I . . . ummm . . . you . . . ." I sputtered as I reached down, fumbling to gather the documents his secretary had provided me.

He lurched forward a few steps, pointing his finger at me. "Are you an idiot? Are you an idiot? Are you a God-damned fucking IDIOT?" His voice rose higher with each repeated question until he was shrieking. "A Chinese Wall means you NEVER refer to the buyer or seller by anything other than their fucking codenames. I should FIRE you right here." He waved his hands wildly. "And what the fuck would possess you to send ME that email instead of asking Sarah your questions," he said through clenched teeth. "I'm running six MULTIBILLION dollar deals. I don't have time to answer your God-damned questions." He inhaled deeply through his nose and pointed his finger at me again. "NEVER . . . YOU . . . NEVER AGAIN!" And then he was gone.

Thirty seconds later, I heard him slam his office door so hard that the walls shook all the way down the hall. I had never witnessed that kind of unmitigated rage, and it was directed at ME. Thankful that I had the office to myself, I closed the door and held onto the handle to steady myself as I tried not to hyperventilate. *Keep it together, Mackenzie. Keep it together, Mackenzie*, I repeated to myself.

I blinked back tears. *Okay, what do I do now?* I let out a long breath, sat back down, and picked up the phone. With my hands shaking, I dialed Sarah's extension.

————

"Oh, Mackenzie—I was wondering when I'd hear from you. I couldn't make the conference call with Saul earlier because I was at a meeting out of the office. I figured you'd just touch base with me after. What'd I miss?" she asked disinterestedly. I could hear her clicking away at her keys over the speakerphone.

I was stunned. There was a still, beating silence before I found my voice. "Uh, Sarah . . ." I cleared my throat. "I didn't even know you were on the deal, so I didn't know I was *supposed* to contact you." I could feel my anger rising.

"Well, didn't you ASK Saul who was on the deal team?" she asked condescendingly. "I mean, you're not new here anymore. You should really know the proper questions to ask by now. You shouldn't need your *mentor* to help you with that!" She gave a brief snort of laughter.

58

"Sarah." I pressed my fingers into my brow bone. I've never considered myself a violent person, but what I wanted to say to her was, "the mere sound of your voice nearly sends me into a murderous rage and I am *this* close to coming down to your office, leaping across your desk, and poking your eyes out with your bobby pins." *No! Be above it, Mackenzie! You're a bigger person than that!* Taking a deep breath, I forged ahead. "I need some details of the proposed transaction to draft the documents that Saul requested. He just informed me I should be addressing my questions to you." I tried to sound professional and calm as my heart rate returned to normal. I'd plot her death later. Right now, there was work to do.

"I just heard him seriously unloading on someone. That was you?" She was still enjoying toying with me. Then, in a sickeningly innocent tone, she added, "Didn't you read the email I sent you earlier?"

I quickly scanned my inbox. Every email was opened and reviewed. There was no way I could have missed an email from Sarah. I balled up my fists, digging my nails into my palms in frustration. "I never received an email from you, Sarah," I said tightly. "You didn't send it."

"Huh . . . I could have sworn I sent it to you. Strange. Anyway, our client Doberman Partners wants to buy Falcon Mobility Inc. and take it private. I just re-sent the email to you, so review what I sent and prepare the documents Saul requested. You should have enough information now. Let me know if you have any questions," she added breezily. "Oh, and make sure you send them to me for review before they go to Saul. We don't want another blow-up."

Click.

My blood was boiling when I opened her email. There, below Sarah's infuriating "see below," was Saul's email to Sarah instructing her to send me the documents and bring me up to speed. At bottom of the email, in bold, all caps Saul had written CLIENT WANTS CHINESE WALL STANDARDS IN PLACE. BUYER = ALPHA, SELLER = OMEGA, TRANSACTION = PROJECT MONTAUK ON ALL DOCUMENTS AND COMMUNICATION.

"You have got to be freaking kidding me." I blew out a long breath. And the fun was only just beginning.

7

THE DRIVER DEPOSITED ME outside of my building. I signed the voucher and made my way inside. It was midnight, the earliest I'd returned home since I'd been put on the Highlander deal.

The past week had passed in a round-the-clock haze of work and verbal abuse. Saul didn't like a day to pass without releasing his aggression, sort of like how some people can't get through the day without their morning coffee. Sometimes it was a seemingly rhetorical email like "ARE YOU STUPID?" "WHY THE FUCK WOULD YOU THINK THAT?" "DID YOU EVEN GRADUATE FROM LAW SCHOOL?" (He wrote his emails in all caps, which had the effect of making you feel like he was yelling at you, even when he was nowhere near you.) Other times it was contradictory, rhetorical emails like "IS THERE A REASON YOU HAVEN'T SENT ME THE SUMMARY?" followed by "WHY THE FUCK ARE YOU SEND-ING ME THIS?" when I sent him the summary. Those were fun.

Then there were the phone calls. "This is not what I fucking asked for!" he'd screech so loudly I'd have to hold the receiver away from my ear until the line went dead. He clearly didn't have the time to fill me in on what was *wrong* with the work I'd given him or explain what he *had* asked for. I was always at a loss as to how to handle those calls. Should I have called him back and politely said, "We must have got cut off, Saul. You were saying?" Or maybe spoken to him in his own language with something like, "Well, what *did* you fucking ask for?"

But Saul's all caps email tirades and phone calls didn't compare to witnessing his terror in person. Above all, I dreaded the "come to my office" email. That meant he wanted to personally witness your reaction to his torture. He wasn't going to be satisfied with just hearing your voice crack over the phone or picturing your face drop as you read his offensive email. No, when he demanded to see you face to face you knew there would be yelling and humiliation. It would almost certainly be enough to ruin your entire day *and* keep you up all night. And today he'd been out for blood.

"You need to get your shit together," Sarah had hissed at me as we both scurried out of Saul's office, fleeing a particularly scathing fit over my misplaced comma. "You are making too many mistakes. Go home and go to sleep," she'd commanded. From anyone else it would've sounded like thoughtful advice. From Sarah, it was a direct order. So I did as I was told.

"Evening." Eddie gave me a nod when I entered the lobby of my apartment building. I'd come to know Eddie Esposito better than I knew any of the other doormen. He was your typical New Yorker— a Bronx native with a mess of gelled black hair who was quick to dispense advice on where to find the best coffee, or complain about the Yankees. He worked twelve hour shifts, 8 P.M. until 8 A.M., which meant he was the first person I said hello to in the morning and usually the last person I saw in the evening.

"Hi, Eddie." I gave a wan smile.

"Another late night, Mackenzie?"

"Uh huh," I sighed, readjusting my messenger bag on my shoulder. I was too tired to speak in full sentences, let alone actual words.

He blew out a large puff of air and shook his head in disbelief. "There's gotta be an easier way. There's just gotta be."

"Goodnight, Eddie," I called out without turning around, avoiding his stare and my own reflection in the mirrored lobby on my way to the elevator.

"'Night, Mackenzie. Get some rest," I heard him say as I punched the button for the tenth floor.

I closed my eyes and leaned against the elevator wall. Even in my semi-awake state I could still recall with perfect clarity the first time I walked through the doors of the Death Star, dressed in the interview suit I'd borrowed from Kim. The sound of my heels click-clacking in the high ceilinged lobby had made me feel like I was one of the Wall Street power players, on my way up to a conference room to say things like "My client says 'No deal!,'" slamming my fist down on the table for effect. *Click clack, click clack.* "Only the best are invited to interview here," the intense looking woman from Human Resources informed me in the same tone actresses use when uttering the line, "It's an honor just to be nominated." She'd led me down a winding corridor, past walls of filing cabinets and the sound of whirring printers. "Your interview is with Phil Sirett, the head of the Litigation group," she'd whispered, raising her brows with significance as I nodded, looking appropriately impressed. We stopped abruptly in front of a huge, stark office. "Here we are! Phil, this is Mackenzie, your four o'clock," she'd sing-songed, before turning and giving me a final wave. Behind a spotless, clutter-free desk sat a grey-haired man, peering down at my resume through glasses perched on the tip of his nose. Without looking up, he gestured for me to sit down in the hard wooden chair across from his desk. It was at this point that I thought I might throw up. Instinctively, I knew this would be a doozy.

A minute of silence ensued, while Phil finished reading my resume. I sat ramrod straight in the chair, legs crossed, hands folded in my lap, poised and ready. Scanning his office for any common ground I could casually bring up in conversation, I came up dry. The walls were bare, the impeccably organized book shelves housed three-inch black binders arranged alphabetically, and the only thing on the huge desk other than three perfectly aligned stacks of papers with color-coded sticky tabs was a carefully arranged rubber band ball. Everything, right down to the carpet, was precise and immaculate. It looked like the meeting place for an OCD support group.

Finally, he spoke. "You have an impressive resume, Mackenzie—top five percent of your class, Associate Editor of the Georgetown Law Journal, pro bono work, and first place in the Moot Court Competition. Impressive."

I smiled in a way I hoped was modest but confident. "Thank you, Phil, I —"

Before I had a chance to finish my sentence, he waved his hand, cutting me off. "But a lot of impressive resumes walk through my door. Yours is nothing unique. Do you know I interviewed a guy today who won an Olympic gold medal? It was in equestrian, which isn't really a sport, but that's beside the point. The point is that everyone is qualified. Everyone has an Olympic gold medal these days now that they've added sports like horse jumping. But we don't need someone working at F&D that expects a horse to do all the work while he gets a gold medal. You get my point?"

I nodded, thankful that my resume did not include an Olympic gold medal.

"But enough about horses. Why should I hire you?"

"As you'll see from my resume," I began the little monologue I'd rehearsed all morning—about how I'd worked throughout college and law school, what I'd learned from volunteering at the free legal clinic, why I was excited to work at a firm as prestigious as F&D—but was abruptly interrupted by Phil's sudden coughing fit.

"Are you . . . um . . . are you okay?" I asked as he coughed and sputtered. As if on cue, Phil's secretary swept into the office, two tall glasses of ice water in hand. Stone faced, she passed one to Phil and one to me.

"Thank you." I took the glass, grateful for the moment to regroup my thoughts and wipe the sweat from my brow.

Phil gulped down the water, which thankfully put an end to the coughing. "What we're looking for," he began distractedly while rooting through his bottom drawer, locating a coaster, and placing it carefully on his desk. "What we're looking for is something extra." He placed his water on top of the coaster and stared into it like a crystal ball.

"Yes, of course —" I tried for a second time to get a word in, but was waved away impatiently.

"Do you know how this firm started, Mackenzie?" My heart rate quickened. I hadn't expected to be quizzed on the history of the firm. I racked my mind for anything I could remember from the website, but Phil didn't wait for an answer. "This firm first opened its doors in 1948 with a small group of lawyers dedicated to providing advice and expertise on the highest levels." Relieved, I sat back in my chair and listened.

Fifteen minutes later, he was still droning on in this vein, while I was trying to maintain my most interested expression, despite the sweating water glass still in my hands. I wanted to put it down, but judging from the immaculate condition of Phil's cherry wood antique desk, he wouldn't react kindly to a water mark. And with Phil barely pausing between sentences, there was no opportunity to interrupt and request a coaster. Besides, if I did somehow manage to get a word in, I wanted to use what little time I had to sell myself. So, I held onto the glass, surreptitiously drying my hands on the bottom of my skirt.

"And so, for nearly seventy years, we have achieved extraordinary results following the ambitious vision of our founders. Well." He exhaled a long breath that he had seemingly been holding for the past half hour. "Looks like our time's up. Nice meeting you . . . " He glanced down at my resume before adding, "Mackenzie." He stood abruptly, walked from behind his desk, and rather than shaking my hand, reached for the glass of water. "I'll take that now."

"Oh, um . . . thank you," I stuttered, handing it to him, confused.

He lifted a pile of papers and slid a coaster out from underneath. As he set down my glass on the coaster, I noticed a tiny grin playing at his lips. "You know, Mackenzie, you could have just asked me for a coaster."

I could feel my face flush from embarrassment as I silently berated myself for not speaking up.

"But if you had done that," he continued, "it would mean you expect to be coddled. Or you could've put the glass down directly on my desk, but what kind of Neanderthal would put a water glass down on an antique?" He gently patted his desk like a favorite pet. "So you solved the problem yourself."

I nodded, no longer bothering to try to squeeze a word in edgewise. At this point I was utterly confused about what was happening, and now was not the time to open my mouth.

"And you had to sacrifice your own comfort level in the process," he added, emphasizing the word "sacrifice." By the way he was talking about this glass of water you would think I'd held onto a three hundred pound weight for the duration of the interview. Placing his hand on my shoulder, he burrowed his gaze into mine. "Anyone can come in here and drivel on about how she'll be willing to work hard and sacrifice for the good of the firm. What sets a person apart, what makes her unique," he paused dramatically, "is when she *shows* me." He raised his eyebrows meaningfully before adding a brisk, "Good day, Mackenzie."

My head was spinning when I walked out of the Death Star. I wasn't sure if I'd just been a rat in some bizarre psychological experiment that Phil had dreamt up while polishing his desk or how he'd managed to form such a generous opinion of me when I hadn't strung together more than three words, but it didn't matter. I knew the job was mine. In that moment, I felt like I'd finally reached the top of the mountain I'd spent years climbing. I'd never been happier.

There's gotta be an easier way. Unfortunately you're wrong, Eddie. Hard work and sacrifice is the only way.

I flicked on the light in my bedroom. Jason yanked a pillow across his eyes.

"Sorry!" I whispered. "I thought you were staying at your place tonight."

"I wanted to see you," he murmured, lifting the duvet welcomingly. "Eddie let me up." I climbed in, happy to have my spot already warmed. It was as though he'd known I needed him here tonight even though I hadn't known it myself. He rolled back over and I could hear his deep rhythmic breathing within minutes.

I envied Jason's ability to fall asleep so easily. My whole body ached with exhaustion, but my mind was still racing. *How many documents are left on the checklist? Is there a more efficient way to divvy up the work load?* After multiple attempts to calm my thoughts proved futile, I rubbed my eyes, got out of bed, and padded through the living room into the kitchen. I rooted through my cupboards for my last tea bag, plopped it in a mug full of microwaved hot water and leaned against the counter waiting for the Sleepytime herbal tea to live up to its promise.

My living room was bathed in the glow from my laptop, reminding me I hadn't emailed Mom in a while. I carried my mug over to my makeshift workspace, cluttered with coffee mugs, sticky notes, and a legal pad containing some Falcon deal notes. A brief nightmare flashed to my mind where Saul suddenly appeared for a surprise clean desk policy inspection, the way a sergeant inspects a soldier's barracks. I slipped the legal pad in the drawer. Better safe than sorry.

Swiping my finger across the touchpad, I peered at my computer screen in confusion. It was signed on to my work portal, but I hadn't done any work from home in a few days. It was uncharacteristic of me to leave my laptop powered on, let alone forget to sign out. Definitive proof that I needed a good night's sleep. I fired off a quick email to Mom, signed off, and shut my laptop, congratulating myself for crossing off one last to-do before the day was done.

I padded back to my bed, climbed in next to Jason, and tried once more to quiet my racing mind, to no avail. *Maybe some cleansing yoga breaths would help.*

There was a time when I thought yoga was a ridiculous trend—as if breathing, which your body does involuntarily, and twisting yourself into positions your body was never meant to be in would somehow reduce anxiety and be a good workout. But in our freshman year Kim dragged me to a class as part of her "I'm trying new things" kick after her latest break-up. We giggled the whole way through as the Hare Krishna–looking yogi instructed us to breathe and visualize our throats as a garden hose, with each breath passing through like a trickle of water. "That makes me want to pee," Kim joked, ignoring the glares. But even though we mocked it, we were amazed how good we felt afterward. We've been converts ever since, but I hadn't been to a class in months.

Inhale though your nose. Pull the breath in. I instructed myself. *Now hold it. No, wait . . . am I supposed to hold it? Or breathe it out like a garden hose? I remember something about using my diaphragm.* Shit, I really needed a refresher. Does adding "go to yoga class" to my to-do list negate the whole relaxation aspect of it? Sometime around one in the morning, I abandoned my yoga attempts, absentmindedly checked my BlackBerry one last time, curled into Jason, and finally fell asleep. Namaste.

Five glorious hours of sleep later, I rolled over and fumbled around my nightstand for my BlackBerry. Nearly knocking over a glass of water that I was unsure how long had been there, I finally located it and typed in my password. Scanning my inbox, a wave of choking panic suddenly washed over me. Ben had emailed at 2:14 A.M. He needed to see a summary of the supply agreement between Serta Mattresses and Highlander Hotels. ASAP.

Oh, fuckity fuck. It was like someone threw a bucket of ice water on me. "ASAP" was the absolute kiss of death in Biglaw. No matter how quickly you respond, it is never ASAP enough. Judging from the tone of Ben's email, he fully expected that I should be in the office, able to fill his request immediately.

The large red numbers on my clock—*6:35 a.m.*—seemed to be screaming at me as I leapt out of bed, bolstered by the huge shot of adrenaline.

"Is everything okay?" Jason croaked, his sleepy eyes squinting at the light.

"Fine, fine, everything's fine," I said breathlessly, as I threw on some clothes and ran a brush through my hair.

"Didn't you just get here?" Eddie called out as I flew through the lobby. I was in a cab, on my way to the office, in seven minutes flat.

The trip to Midtown was pure agony. I leaned forward, peering out the windshield, willing the gridlocked traffic to move faster. How could this many people possibly all be going in the same direction? Wasn't it the driver's JOB to know the quickest route? How can I be expected to do my job when this guy can't do his? I glared at the driver, who was tapping his thumbs against the steering wheel to the beat of a song on the radio looking like he had all the time in the world. My stomach churned with frustration. *Come on, buddy, come on, buddy—Drive! Step on it!*

Seeing the light turn yellow I subconsciously pressed my foot on an imaginary gas pedal. But instead of speeding up, Mr. Safety did something I've never seen a New York taxi driver do—he stopped at a yellow light. Bubbling over with aggravation, I could barely keep still in my seat. "I'll get out here," I barked to the driver two blocks away from the F&D offices. The meter read $10.80, but I threw a $20 bill into the front seat and dashed towards the office and into a closing elevator where I manically pounded the buttons in an effort to make the doors close faster. Catching my breath, I pulled my Black-Berry out of my pocket to see if Ben had emailed again. No email. Maybe there was still time.

I located the document in the data room, summarized it, and sent it to Ben by 7:57 A.M. It was the best I could do. Staring at the sent email, I breathed deeply, trying to get my heart rate to return to normal. *Good enough*, I reassured myself, leaning over to open my snack drawer, searching for a breakfast bar in the mix of empty wrappers. *Good enough*. It was only then that I looked down and realized the boots I'd put on in my haste didn't even match. One brown, one black. Not even close.

———

One hour later, Ben sent me an email asking me to come to his office immediately. The face-to-face was never, ever a good sign. That meant they needed to reassert their authority by reprimanding you and witnessing the look of deference and remorse on your face. Knowing that, I put on a pair of matching shoes from the stack underneath my desk and, like a soldier that straightens his uniform before heading out over the trenches and into the battlefield, I smoothed my hands over my pencil skirt, brushed my hair, and headed down the hall to face my fate.

When I arrived at his office, Ben was sitting behind his desk with his phone pressed to his ear, looking tense. Seeing me standing hesitantly at the door way, he gestured for me to come in and close the door.

Uggg. Not the closed door. An even worse sign. I shut the door and tentatively sat down, bending my head as if readying myself for the guillotine.

I could tell from the tone of his voice it had to be his wife on the line. "Do we really need a six burner oven with a warming tray?" Ben asked, impatiently. The Russian heiress was redecorating apparently. "Okay, you're right. I could see where that would come in handy."

Pause. "HOW much?" Pause. "I understand, you're right, quality is expensive." He gave me a tight smile. "Right, right . . . okay . . . love you too . . . bye, bye." He hung up the receiver and turned his attention towards me.

"Mackenzie, I'm extremely disappointed in your response time," he opened with, in a completely different tone than he'd just been using with his wife. "I needed to read that summary before the 8 A.M. conference call. You left me completely unprepared. COMPLETELY unprepared," he repeated. "I specifically said I needed it ASAP. What the hell happened? Were you *asleep*?" The tone of his voice and look on his face indicated he couldn't imagine anything less appropriate to be doing at 2 A.M.

I waited a beat, hoping the question was rhetorical, but he was clearly waiting for a response. The truth was when Sarah told me to go home and sleep, that sounded rational. Wasn't rational thought what separated us from the animals? But I didn't think a discussion about anthropology would have gone over too well. I was going to have to come clean and admit my dirty deed—that yes, I was asleep at 2:14 A.M. "Ssssorry, I didn't realize that you would need anything more last night so I . . . I . . . fell asleep."

The apology slipped out before I could help it. You'll never find a man saying "I'm sorry" to his boss—it would make him appear weak. But women did it all the time. I once worked with a woman who started all of her sentences with an apology. "*Sorry, I have a question.*" "*Sorry, I'm going for lunch.*" "*Sorry, do you have the time?*" It was really annoying and I was trying to eliminate the word from my professional vocabulary. "Sorry" wasn't a word spoken in Biglaw.

Ben glared at me as if there could never be enough apologies for the misunderstanding. For him, there was simply no reason for your BlackBerry to go unanswered. Ever. "I had my BlackBerry on vibrate," I continued, "but I must have slept through it." Okay, that was a lie, but I was grasping for a life preserver.

"Do you realize what the Highlander deal is? Do you realize what an opportunity it is for this firm? For *you*?"

"Of course I—"

70

"When I agreed to let you work on the Saul deal, I thought I made it clear that it could not interfere with your responsibilities on *this* deal."

When he *agreed* to let me? It sounded like Ben was referencing a conversation that never actually occurred. I certainly would never have jockeyed to work with Saul. I had no idea what he was talking about, so I fell back on some advice Sadir had given me on my first day at F&D—when in doubt, nod remorsefully.

"I thought you understood the timeline with this deal, but apparently not, so let me be crystal clear. We require your full commitment in order to get this done. We ALL need to make personal sacrifices. Sometimes that means not sleeping when we want to."

I felt as if he'd just punched me in the gut. There are a lot of things I wanted to do—go for coffee with a friend, have a meal outside of the office, maybe go to the gym or pick up my dry cleaning, but I hadn't done any of that because of this deal.

"It won't happen again," I said firmly, finally disarming his assault.

"Well, it had better not. Look, you have to be available when I need you. At *any* time. That doesn't mean that you need to be in the *office* all the time," he added, with a tone that I'm sure he thought was reassuring. "You just need to have your BlackBerry on you."

"Your wife's on the phone," Ben's secretary called out from her cubicle, thankfully knocking Ben off his soapbox. "She needs your credit card number." Ben winced and picked up the receiver.

"Yeah," he said impatiently. I took it as my cue to leave and slunk back to my office, leaving him to negotiate the cost of kitchen appliances.

71

———

Painfully aware that I needed to brush up on my relaxation techniques if I was going to survive the next few months, I ducked out of the office at 7 P.M. for a one hour Vinyasa yoga class, leaving my BlackBerry on vibrate, of course.

"Exhale in the mountain pose . . . inhale stretch up . . . exhale down into a forward bend . . . remember your breath . . . " the yogi purred.

"So it was Sarah who told you to go home for the night?" Kim whispered, moving into her forward bend. We were situated in our favorite spot (back row in the far corner) where the buzz of the heater drowned our whispers out.

"Yeah, she said that I needed the sleep. It was kind of novel hearing something come out of her mouth that I actually agreed with." I'd filled Kim in on the way over about my reprimanding at the hands of Ben this morning. It was selective disclosure, of course. I couldn't give her the details of the transaction, but described my recent highs and lows in my quest of making a good impression.

"And Sarah was in his office when you had that great moment when you wowed Ben?"

"Yes! It made the moment even sweeter."

"Inhale and step the left leg back . . . exhale back into downward dog."

I did as the yogi instructed and the gnawing pain in my permanently tense shoulders lessened. It felt so good to be working out again. I hadn't exercised since before the Highlander deal (unless you count running out of Saul's office in fear). The pocket of my Lululemon pants buzzed, so I took a quick glance at my BlackBerry, ignoring the yogi's stern glare, before returning it to the zippered pocket on my way into downward dog.

"But why was Sarah in Ben's office? Is it possible he's considering her for the secondment too?" Kim raised her eyebrows, giving a significant look.

Caught off guard, I lost my balance and nearly face planted into the mat. I'd been so laser focused on impressing Ben, I hadn't even considered my competition. In my mind, Sarah had already had her chance to earn StarCorp and now her time had passed. I rooted my hands and feet on the mat and pushed my torso into the air. This was quickly spiraling into the least Zen yoga class ever.

"Forget I said that," Kim interjected before I could answer, inhaling forward into the push up position. "That job is yours for the taking. Nobody works harder than you, Rocky."

I smiled, but couldn't help thinking about the fluorescent lights that still glowed on the twenty-seventh floor of Death Star whenever I left for the night. No matter how hard you worked, someone else always worked harder.

8

THE BEST PIECE OF advice I received in law school came from my roommate, who'd spent a summer working in Biglaw a year before I did. "The one thing you should never do is cry," she'd warned. "The men who work in Biglaw are offended by human weakness." I'd snickered, but late that night I quietly Googled ways to prevent yourself from crying. "Create a slightly painful sensation to redirect your attention," the article from Glamour suggested. "That way your mind focuses on physical pain rather than an external stressor." I remember looking in the mirror that night while biting the inside of my cheek, ensuring it was an innocuous method to keep myself from letting the tears flow. Since then I've only had to enlist the method a few times, but today the inside of my mouth was chewed raw.

"You got off easy, Mackenzie." Sadir popped his head over the partition.

"Easy?" I repeated in astonishment, my voice shaky from the latest tirade I'd just endured in Saul's office. "How do you figure?"

I thought I'd finally gotten used to Saul's yelling, the way someone with a backache gets used to dull, constant pain. Today he'd upped the ante, though, ripping up the document I'd spent hours drafting into tiny pieces, while screeching "REDO IT! REDO IT! REDO IT!" I'd never seen anything like it. His entire face and neck were crimson red, except for the purple vein throbbing in his forehead, as he scattered the tiny pieces around his office wildly. He looked completely unhinged. Thankfully, my primal survival instincts took over and I slowly edged out of his office backward, not taking my eyes off him for fear of him throwing something at the back of my head on the way out. I had quietly returned to my office, not mentioning what had just happened with Saul, but I wouldn't have been surprised if Sadir had been crouched down behind some inconspicuous planter watching the entire scene.

"Well." Sadir cleared his throat, readying himself to dispense his perceived wisdom. "Last year Saul took a document Russ Tornelli drafted, crumpled it up, tossed it into his trash can and lit it on FIRE. Then he ordered Russ to remove the burning trash can from his office immediately. Poor Russ." Sadir stifled a chuckle. "He ran so fast down the hall, burning trash can in hand." He mimed the actions, holding an imaginary trash can in his hand and waddling around the office. Sadir was always at his most animated when telling a story about associate torture. "He ran all the way to the bathroom and threw the can in the shower." Sadir dramatically threw his imaginary trash can. "He totally drenched himself. Had to walk out of that bathroom looking like a dog that had been hosed down for picking at trash." He snorted and laughed at the memory.

My eyes widened in horror.

"So, yeah, consider yourself lucky." Sadir sat back down and began pecking away at his keyboard, leaving me to mull that over.

More troubling than the fact that Saul had just torn up my document was that Sadir was starting to make sense to me. When I'd first met him, his point of view always sounded so negative and depressing, but now I wondered if he'd adopted that mentality in order to survive here. Maybe Sadir had started out energetic and eager to please too.

Am I going to end up just like him? I pictured myself, the female version of Sadir, sulky and objectionable with an extra fifteen pounds of Seamless dinners on my frame, dispensing my cynical wisdom to the next crop of incoming associates. Was I going to wind up with the same personal hygiene deficits too? It was too horrible to imagine.

Thankfully, my nightmare was interrupted by a thick Long Island accent. "Knawwwk, knawwk!"

"Hi, Rita," I sighed dejectedly. I knew she was checking in on me, just like she did after all of Saul's public tongue lashings. She was like a mother bear protecting her cubs, not that "motherly" is the first word that would come to mind when looking at her. She was a petite woman in her early forties with long, bleached blonde hair that, judging from her dark roots, hadn't been colored for a few months. Her skin tone can only be described as "tanning salon brown" and today she was showing off her thin, muscular legs in a micro-mini leather skirt. And despite what it said in the "managing your secretary" section of the Lawyer's Manual, she was not the type of secretary that would tolerate being "managed."

"I'm sorry, hon," she said softly, putting her hand on my shoulder. My eyes prickled with tears. Her simple sympathetic gesture penetrated the emotionally detached wall I was struggling to preserve. I was beginning to feel like a wishbone, with Saul and Ben tugging violently on opposite sides. Any minute I was going to snap.

"Don't let it baw-tha you. He's just an asshole."

I swallowed hard, trying to dislodge the lump in my throat, and nodded in agreement.

"Listen, do ya guys wanna a piece of Sherry's birthday cake?" She tried to put some cheeriness into her tone. "There's lots left."

"We celebrate birthdays around here? Since when?" Sadir responded as he stood up to take her up on her offer.

"Not you lawyahs because you guys will nevah pony up for cake." She rubbed her thumb back and forth against her four fingers. "You're all too cheap. Make all that money and you're still all cheap."

"You could go broke with all the solicited donations around here," Sadir replied as he headed out the door for his slice of free birthday cake.

"Pfffffffff . . . cheap ass," Rita muttered after him. She turned back to me. "Mackenzie, cake?"

"Sure. Why not?" I grabbed a ten dollar bill from my wallet and handed it to Rita to donate to the communal cake fund and followed Sadir out the door to Rita's cubicle. Nothing a piece of cake can't fix.

———

"Lucky?" Jason repeated in amazement.

"That's what Sadir said—consider myself lucky that he ONLY tore up my document rather than burning it."

Jason and I were perched on my couch digging into General Tso's chicken and chow mein. I'd planned on working late to finish up a document I was working on for Sarah, before I delved back into Saul's operating agreement and Ben's due diligence, but when I did a lap of the floor at eleven, all three of their offices were darkened. I knew I had to seize the opportunity to get out of there, unnoticed, and spend some time with Jason. I deserved it after the day I'd endured. So, at eleven thirty I ordered my Seamless meal (I was allowed to expense $40 for dinner—enough for two with leftovers), slipped my BlackBerry in my pocket, and hoped I wouldn't hear from anyone until the morning. Sitting in the Town Car on my way uptown to meet Jason with a bag of greasy Chinese food beside me, I silently congratulated myself for not crying and for holding onto my last shred of dignity by resisting the urge to bend down and pick up the shreds of paper on my way out of Saul's office.

"Wow. That guy is a sociopath masquerading as a lawyer." Jason exhaled a tiny snort and speared a piece of chicken before passing the take-out box to me.

"And you should've seen how crazy he looked! Completely insane." I shook my head in disbelief, picturing his deranged, crimson face. "Unfortunately for me, the inmates are running the asylum at F&D."

"In your department they sure are." Jason snickered.

"Speaking of inmates, have you seen my BlackBerry?" My eyes darted around, suddenly fearful that I would miss an email from Ben demanding an immediate response. Saul may be making me lose my mind, but I wouldn't let him cost me the secondment too.

"Oh yeah, it's right here." Jason picked it up off the side table and peered down. "No new emails," he reported before tossing it to me.

"How did it get all the way over there?"

A funny look flickered across his face. "I just needed to text Alex when you were in the bathroom."

"Why didn't you use yours?"

"My battery was dead and I didn't think using yours would be a problem. Is that okay?" He drew out the word "okay" in a tone that was uncharacteristically condescending.

"Of course. I know you two can't go more than a minute without contact." I tried to lighten the mood that suddenly prickled with an inexplicable hostility.

"Very funny." He grinned, squeezing my hand. "So are you going to tell me anything about this mystery deal other than Saul's atrocities?" He jammed a forkful of chow mein noodles into his mouth and passed the container to me.

"I wish I could, but you know the rules of the Chinese Wall. I can't utter a word to anyone that isn't working on the deal. I even have to use codenames in internal emails. It's all very James Bond."

"Ah, okay, Double O Seven."

"Hey, haven't you heard 'loose lips sink ships'?" I teased, pointing my chopstick at him.

"Only in times of war, Mac." He winked.

"Well, if word gets out that this company is being purchased and the stock price runs up there's a good chance Saul will start a war."

"Are you're worried I'm going to pick up my direct line to Reuters and leak the news?" He smirked.

"Hey, I don't make the rules, I just follow them."

"My little Girl Scout." He rubbed my knee. "Either that or you have a God complex and just love knowing what's going to happen before the rest of the world does."

"Ha, ha," I responded dryly, but there was some truth to what Jason said. One of my favorite parts of the job was being part of a select inner circle of knowledge. The first time I worked on a high-profile deal was thrilling. Billions of dollars at stake meant the business media was hungry for details. *Is Keystone Foods for Sale?* was splashed on the business section of national papers, flooding me with a giddy jolt of pleasure. I, Mackenzie Corbett, was in on a secret that not even reporters from the *Wall Street Journal* were privy to. But now I was more concerned with avoiding the wrath of Saul than the thrills of a secret.

"I know you want to follow the rules, but I'm just worried you're keeping it all bottled up. I can see the stress on your face, Mac. You can't take it all so seriously."

I nodded thoughtfully. Jason's laid back attitude towards life had always been appealing to me. He was the tranquil Yin to my over-anxious Yang. But sitting there, watching him chew his food without a care in the world, I felt a twinge of resentment. Jason was always relaxed, like he was living a life of leisure, which, when I thought about it, he was. His father had founded the Kermode Company, the world's largest maker of GPS units, and made millions in the process. His parents gave him everything he wanted, he didn't have to choose a college based on how much scholarship money they offered, and he got this job through his father's connections. His life had been a series of easy choices. He never wasted time grappling with which path to take like I've always done. He simply selected the path of least resistance, purposely creating an undemanding, uncomplicated life. His BlackBerry battery was dead, yet he wasn't the slightest bit concerned. I, on the other hand, would break out into the shakes if my BlackBerry was out of my sight.

"Well, I can't exactly take my one source of income lightly," I responded in my best passive aggressive voice.

Before Jason could reply, a familiar buzzing sound filled the room. A look of uncertainty flashed across his face, but only for a second. "Ah ha!" He put the take-out container down and began rooting through the coat draped across the arm of the couch. "I knew it was around here somewhere."

"I thought your battery was dead." I peered over his shoulder as he pulled his BlackBerry out of the inside pocket.

He shrugged. "I tried calling it earlier to find it, but it didn't ring. I figured the battery must be dead. I guess I'd just left it on vibrate and couldn't hear it. " He did a quick check before stuffing it back in his coat pocket. "Enough talk about BlackBerries for one night." He pulled me towards him and nuzzled my neck. "Listen, I've been thinking," his sleepy voice growled in my ear. "We should make this official."

"This?" I giggled.

He pulled his head back to look me in the eyes. "This." He gestured to each of us with his chin. "Let's move in together."

"Really?" My heart rate sped up.

"With the way you've been working, it just makes sense. That way there'll be a reason I'm camping out on your couch waiting for you."

For a moment my mind whirred through the possibilities—falling asleep and waking up together every day, not having to worry about which apartment we were staying at each night, or whose stuff was where.

"Where would we live?" I asked. Jason hated my neighborhood, preferring to live near the action of the East Village instead.

He shrugged. "You could move in to my place."

"But my lease . . . " I trailed off.

"Geez, this is like pulling teeth." His tone was light, but I detected an irritated edge to it. "When does your lease end?"

"April."

"Then we can do it in April." He rubbed his hand along my back, giving me goose bumps. "And we can pick a new place. Our place."

A wide smile broke across my face. "Our place" had a very nice ring to it. Any momentary hesitation I felt floated away and excitement took its place. "Let's do it," I gushed, nodding enthusiastically. "Let's move in together in April."

Jason pulled me close, his tired eyes crinkling into a smile. I inhaled the scent of him, thinking I soon would have the pleasure of sleeping beside him every night. "April can't come fast enough," he murmured.

Before I shut my eyes for the night I did one final email check. Seeing no work emails, I scrolled through my outgoing texts out of curiosity, but never did find the text that Jason had sent to Alex.

9

I TOOK A SWIG of my vodka soda and picked up my BlackBerry to check the time. *10:28.* Kim was now twenty-eight minutes late. *Typical*, I thought, leaning back on the black leather chair and scanning the bar. I hadn't even wanted to go out tonight, but Kim insisted. And just as I always have, I cracked under the pressure of her persuasion. This usually resulted in a round robin of "just one more bar" as we followed her latest band-member boyfriend, but tonight it meant sitting at a loud bar in Midtown when I'd rather be home sleeping.

"Do you want another, hon?" the waitress asked, pointing at my glass of melted ice.

"Sorry, sorry, sorry!" Kim breezed up beside me. "You know how I am with the whole being on time thing." Like the cable guy, when Kim gives you a time to meet, it should be considered an estimate. Knowing my friend too well, I'd thought about staying at the office until ten to finish up some work, but in Biglaw if you squander an opportunity to leave the office, the chance might not come along again.

"If we'd said 10:30 then you'd be early," I quipped, standing up to give her a quick hug.

"We'll have two of those," Kim instructed the waitress, nodding at my empty glass and slipping off her coat.

"So." She flopped down into the chair across from me. "I've been calling and calling you."

"Sorry, work has been crazy."

"Well, I've been dying to fill you in on the meet-and-greet with Quinn's family."

"Right!" I felt a pang of guilt realizing I didn't even know the monumental parent meeting had already occurred. "How did it go?"

The waitress materialized, setting our drinks down in front of us. Kim took a thirsty gulp before answering. "Well, you'll be happy to know that he doesn't have a wife, children, or secretly live with his mother."

"All good things. Check. Check. Check."

She stirred her drink, a tiny grin playing at her lips. "He was super sweet, Mac. He kept worrying he was overwhelming me. Which, I have to admit, meeting the entire family at once was a bit intimidating. I felt like the Bachelor on hometown date."

I laughed.

"But it was actually fun. Surprisingly. His family was really excited to meet me. They said Quinn never brings girls home."

"Aw. He was just waiting for the one."

"You're such a helpless romantic." She flicked her straw at me. "Oh, and you know that school fundraiser I've been organizing?"

I nodded.

"Quinn convinced his brother to do the music for it. And you're not going to believe this, but Quinn actually signed up to be one of the volunteer cooks."

"A volunteer cook? Could he be any more in love with you?"

"It's for a good cause!" She leaned over and slapped my knee.

"Yeah, you." I smiled. "Well, I think we can put it bed—he's a keeper."

"Speaking of bed, how are things with your man, anyway? I haven't heard anything about him in a while."

"Sneaky little segue," I said wryly.

She did a mock bow of her head, clearly pleased with herself.

I considered for a moment whether I wanted to tell Kim about the mystery of the supposedly dead BlackBerry battery the other night. Kim and I had always shared the nitty-gritty about our love lives with each other, down to every last cringe-inducing detail, but I was hesitant. I knew what Kim thought of Jason. "Isn't he a little . . .

generic?" she'd asked after I brought Jason out for drinks one night to meet her. "Like he's been computer generated or something?" Then she pried for what exactly it was that I saw in him. I believe her exact words were, "Is he the male version of the sexy librarian—like, he sheds his boring, stuffy exterior and becomes a mad man in the bedroom?" (In the interest of full disclosure, the answer to that was no.) Jason wasn't a big fan of hers either, calling her boisterous, unfiltered personality "a social liability." So, my best friend and my boyfriend hadn't exactly hit it off initially, but once Jason and I started getting serious Kim made an effort keep any negative comments to herself. Unfortunately, Kim had a horrible poker face. Whenever Jason was around I could practically see the thought bubble over her head: "Please don't let my best friend marry this dud." If I revealed any unease now, I knew she'd go in for the kill.

"Things are really good." I took a sip of my drink, avoiding eye contact.

"Really?" Kim regarded me skeptically.

"Yeah." I paused, stirring my drink. "Actually, we're moving in together," I said casually, bracing myself for her disapproval. I wasn't going to tell her tonight, knowing she would try to talk me out of it, but now was as good a time as any to face the firing squad.

She started to cough, seemingly choking on her drink. Putting her glass down, she pounded her chest with her fist, her eyes watering. "Sorry, wrong pipe," she croaked before clearing her throat. "When?"

"April."

She gave a puzzled look. "Why April? Why not now?"

"That's when my lease runs out."

Kim took a careful sip and set down her drink. "Waiting for your lease to run out . . . interesting."

"Look, I know you aren't his biggest fan, but —"

"It's not that," she interrupted. "I admit, I think there's someone else out there who's a better fit for you, but that isn't the point. The point is, I don't think *you* want to move in with him."

I gave an exaggerated eye roll. "Okay, that might work with your preschoolers. 'Little Johnny, I don't think you *want* to hit little Susie, do you?'" I mimicked, patting her hand with mine. "But it's not going to work on me. I really *do* want to move in with him. We're just thinking about it practically, that's all."

Kim's blue eyes regarded me calmly. "Don't you want a guy who makes you want to bust out of your super achiever mode and do something totally spontaneous?"

I snorted. "You know I don't."

She sat back in her seat, readying herself to dispense her armchair analysis. "Look, I've known you for nine years, Mac. I know you're a rule follower and blah blah blah, but if you really wanted to move in with Jason, you wouldn't think twice. You'd jump."

I felt a flutter of annoyance. "Please, this is *me* we're talking about. You remember how I wouldn't even break my cell phone contract even though I really wanted to get the new iPhone and only AT&T had it? I stayed with my crappy Verizon phone for the full two years just so I wouldn't have to terminate the contract early. The fact that I'm waiting out my lease before moving in with him doesn't prove anything."

84

She looked amused. "You do realize you just compared your relationship to a mobile device, don't you?"

"Hey, the new iPhone isn't just a mobile device—it's a *revolutionary* product."

Kim threw her head back and laughed.

That was when I saw her. She was sitting in the back corner of the bar, the type of secluded spot that celebrities pick to canoodle and not be spotted by the paparazzi. "Oh my God," I hissed, slumping down into my chair.

Kim gave a puzzled look.

"It's HER. Sarah."

Never one for subtlety, Kim whipped around and scanned the room. "Where?"

"Shhhh! Turn back around. I can't believe she's here. I thought she never left the office."

"Well, where did you think she slept?" Kim's mouth twitched with humor.

"I don't know. A coffin in her office when she's not feasting on the undead? Cover me — I don't want her to see me." I positioned myself perfectly with Kim as my shield and peered with morbid curiosity. "It looks like she's waiting for someone. Oh my God, I'm dying to see the guy who would date that cold fish."

"Poor guy." Kim tsked.

"And she has a . . . " I squinted to get a better look. "You're not going to believe this. There's a file on the table. Sarah brought a work file on a date. That's how weird she is!"

Sarah looked up from the BlackBerry she'd been furiously pecking on and locked eyes with me.

"Shit," I whispered anxiously, averting my eyes. "I've been spotted."

"Really? But you were being so subtle," Kim said sarcastically.

"Ha, ha." I peered at Kim over my empty glass, which was now substituting as my cover.

I turned my attention back to Sarah just as she was ducking out a side door. I didn't see what she did with the file, making me wonder if I'd really even seen it or if I'd just been incapable of picturing Sarah without work in her hand. "She left. She just up and left as soon as she saw me." I eyed the door curiously. "Isn't that crazy?"

"Well, some would say that channeling Nancy Drew is kinda crazy." Kim lifted her eyebrows at me.

I snorted. "Okay, point taken. That woman just brings out the crazy in me."

"Forget about her." Kim waved her hand airily. "She's a nonentity."

"You're right." I sighed. "Look at you getting all wise in your old age."

"You bring the brains, I'll bring the wisdom." She raised her glass, clinking mine.

"Okay, tell me more about Quinn's family." I leaned back in my chair and willed myself to listen, but I couldn't shake the sight of Sarah's facial expression when we locked eyes. It looked like she'd been caught with her hand in the cookie jar.

10

WALKING INTO MY OFFICE at 6 A.M. Monday morning, Venti dark roast in hand, I was wishing I could just inject the caffeine right into my veins. It would be so much more efficient that way. Monday mornings were the absolute worst part of my week. Saul wanted everyone working on the deal—paralegals, tax and intellectual property specialists, Sarah, and me—to meet every Monday morning at 7 A.M. to discuss the status of the deal. I'd asked Sadir why Saul would schedule a non-essential meeting for 7 A.M. when it could just as easily be held at 3 P.M. "For the same reason a dog licks his own balls—because he can," Sadir had responded, shrugging like the answer was obvious. The meetings were always merciless and vicious. Personally, I think he called the meetings because he wanted to start the week off by publicly castrating all the men in the room and reducing the women to tears. So, every Monday morning I arrived at work before most people woke up to prepare for a thirty minute hazing courtesy of Saul. My only goal was to minimize the bloodbath.

I put my cup of Starbucks' finest down on my desk, marveling how quiet it was. Sadir wasn't in yet, meaning no aggressive pecking on keys, no frustrated grumbles. I could get used to this. I flopped down on my swivel chair and attempted to mentally prepare for the day ahead. But my brief moment of serenity came to an abrupt end when I saw the headline on WSJ.com.

Falcon Mobility Exploring Sale of Company, Says Source

Founders of Falcon Mobility Inc. are exploring a sale of their shares in the company, the third largest smartphone company, a source familiar with the matter said.

Talks of the possible deal have been going on the past two weeks, the source told the *Wall Street Journal*, declining to be named because the matter isn't yet public.

Attempts to contact a company spokesman were unsuccessful.

My stomach lurched up to my throat. "Holy shit," I croaked. Today's bloodbath was going to be gruesome.

———

"Well, I'm sure you've all fucking seen it." Saul slammed a folded newspaper against the large mahogany table. "Someone has fucking Paul Revered this thing all over Wall Street and now Falcon stock is up eighteen percent. EIGHTEEN FUCKING PERCENT," he shrieked. "Can anybody tell me what that means? I'll tell you what the fuck it means. It means we have to sign this deal before those little fuckwits get it in their minds that they can seek out a bigger price. Before they think they can play hardball. Or worse. Worse." The room fell silent for what felt like an hour but was probably only about thirty seconds before Saul continued. "The boost makes them think they don't need to sell to our client and instead can keep this company afloat themselves. Because if that happens then we'll all be left sitting here with our dicks in our hands."

I squeezed my eyes shut in a desperate attempt to remove that visual.

"Now that the news is out, we need to move even more aggressively on this. Time is of the essence. Everything is due NOW." Saul slammed his small paper cup on the conference room table, splashing hot coffee on his file folder and the Intellectual Property associate who'd made the tragic mistake of taking the seat beside him.

"Mackenzie, did you tell the specialists to get you their summaries TODAY?" Everyone in the conference room turned their attention to me.

"Specialists" is a term used by corporate lawyers to refer to any other type of lawyer that specializes in a particular area of law—Tax, Intellectual Property, Employment, Real Estate—if you weren't in the group structuring the deal (the corporate group) you were simply referred to as a "specialist." One of my roles on the deal, other than Saul's personal punching bag, was to compile summaries of the contracts the specialists reviewed during their due diligence.

"I thought you wanted their summaries by Wednesday," I managed, trying to stay calm. That's what Saul said in last Monday's meeting and everyone in the room knew it. No one, of course, would openly agree with me.

"I . . . told . . . you . . . " His voice dropped to a whisper. "I . . . told . . . you . . . " A flush crept up Saul's neck as he pounded his knuckles against his skull in frustration. He started to stomp his feet furiously on the ground, like a spoiled child throwing a fit, before shrieking, "MONDAY! MONDAY! MONDAY! I TOLD YOU TO EMAIL THE SPECIALISTS AND TELL THEM MONDAY!" His jaw was twitching with petulance. "NOT WEDNESDAY! Now we're two days off schedule thanks to your fucking INCOMPETENCE! You are fucking INCOMPETENT! Do you even KNOW that? Or are you too fucking STUPID?"

I tried to hold myself perfectly still, not wanting to let everyone see me tremble. The whole room prickled with awkwardness. It wasn't until that moment that I truly appreciated the wisdom of Alex's advice: *sticks and stones may break my bones, but names will never hurt me.* I opened my mouth to speak, to say something to defend myself, but Saul held up his hand for silence.

"Mackenzie, tell me that YOUR summaries are at least done. Tell me that you did SOMETHING right." My face burned with humiliation. Everyone averted their eyes in the interest of preserving my dignity. We received two new boxes of contracts to review late last night. He *knew* there was no way my summaries were done. He just wasn't ready for my public reprimanding to be over. Like a cat playing with a half-dead mouse, he was relishing my suffering. He wasn't going to be satisfied until I was a red-faced, stammering, teary-eyed mess, but I wasn't going to give him the satisfaction.

I bit the inside of my cheek and blinked back the tears trembling on the brink of my lashes. "I can have the summaries for you tomorrow," I said with as much confidence as I could muster.

"Tomorrow, tomorrow," he mimicked in high-pitched tone, with his face contorted as if he smelled something bad. His wispy comb-over stood straight up and his glasses sat noticeably crooked on his face, making him look deranged. "We're on a fucking TIMELINE here, people. Why can't any of you morons grasp that?" He shut his eyes tightly, shook his head, and turned his attention to Sarah, his next victim.

Sarah held up better than I did under Saul's barrage. He was clearly worn out from his full blown fit and it was as if someone had finally given him the lollipop he'd been wailing for. She got one or two "what the fucks" and there might have been a "fuckwit" thrown in, but the shrieking, red-faced toddler had been placated.

When Saul was finally done picking us off one by one like target practice, I grabbed my legal pad with trembling hands and, with as much poise as I could gather, filed out of the conference room, looking down at the floor in an effort to avoid any eye contact. I headed for the one true place of refuge in the firm—the bathroom.

After peeking under the stalls to make sure I was the only one there, I pushed open a stall door and sat down on the toilet. Being verbally disemboweled on a daily basis was starting to break me. Clearly my parents had done me a great disservice, because my conflict-free upbringing had not—in any conceivable way—prepared me for working in Biglaw. Maybe if there had been more yelling in my home I would have been able to withstand Saul's assault. I leaned forward and put my face in my hands. It was burning hot. *I can't handle this anymore*, I thought, my eyes filling with tears. Because I was alone in the bathroom, I didn't bother to fight them.

11

"I COME BEARING CAFFEINE." Alex stepped into my office, two Venti sized Starbucks cups in hand. "I figured you weren't going to feel up to our daily Starbucks exodus today." He handed me a cup and flopped down on the chair across from mine.

"You could hear the bloodbath all the way down in your office?" I wrapped my hands around the hot cup, savoring the feeling of comfort. I'd made good use of the makeshift medicine cabinet stashed in my drawers—a few drops of Visine in my red-rimmed eyes, concealer on my blotchy cheeks, two Advil for my aching head—so I was at least looking okay on the outside.

"Well, I heard the word 'fuckwits' being thrown around. Fuckwits is never a good sign. It probably went something like this." He put down his cup, mussed his hair, and proceeded to do a spot-on impression of Saul's deranged rant, complete with the scrunched-up, constipated look on his face.

"You are getting way too good at that," I giggled. And just like that, the giant knot in my stomach dissolved. Thank God for Alex. In the sea of crazy that was the corporate department, he was a life vest.

"I've had plenty of exposure to my subject," he reminded me.

"Lucky you." I sighed. "Hey, did you get a text from my phone on Friday night?" I asked in a tone that I hoped sounded casual.

"Uhhh . . . no. Should I have?"

"No, I was just wondering." I shook my head, suppressing a flutter of unease. "Forget it. Long story." I took a gulp of my latte. "Hey, what's in this? It's delicious."

"Two shakes of vanilla powder, one shake cinnamon, and a half a packet of Sugar in the Raw. It's my secret recipe." He looked pleased with himself.

I raised my eyebrows.

"What?"

"I have a hunch you're taking the credit for someone else's handiwork." I pointed to the name "Jessica" scrolled across the cup above a phone number and "call me!"

Alex waved his hand, but I noticed the faintest blush. "I perfected that deliciousness myself. I happen to have been a barista in college, Little Miss Skeptic. Some of us had to work in school, you know."

"I was one of those someones too, don't forget."

"Yah, I always forget you don't have a trust fund. You're just gonna marry one."

"Hey!" I flicked the rubber band I'd been fiddling with at him.

"Hey yourself." He ducked, laughing. "You and Jason will have adorable little trust fund babies." He took a long gulp of his latte. "You want my advice?"

"On marrying into Jason's trust fund?" I eyeballed him over my cup.

"No, on Saul."

"Well, I've already learned the value of the 'sticks and stones' tip, so shoot."

"Here's what you have to do. Treat these Monday morning meetings like a tornado watch. Get in a crouched position with your head down and shield your head with your arms." He bent his arms over his head as if shielding himself from a punch.

I laughed as he bobbed back and forth like a boxer. It felt so good to laugh about Saul's rage rather than cry.

"No, seriously! It's the only way to deal with him."

I leaned back in my chair. "You think his next step is physical violence?"

"No, no, no. Listen, it's your *optimism* that's making you miserable. You're always *expecting* things to go well. It's sweet, Mac, but it's a mistake. When I work for Saul I just *assume* that any time I have any interaction with him it will result in him loudly berating me. That way, when he doesn't, I feel relieved and grateful. Happy, even. You need to stop thinking that you might actually get out of those meetings without abuse. Go into them anticipating the worst and maybe you'll feel thankful from time to time when you manage to avoid any carnage."

I nodded slowly and considered that for a minute. "That's actually good advice," I said. "Depressing . . . but good."

"It's the Tao of Alex." He grinned, lifting his coffee cup to toast me.

———

On Friday I was enjoying a rare moment of reprieve and doing some online shopping, wondering if I could find a good pair of work shoes that doubled as going out shoes. I hated wasting time going home to change. Not that I was actually doing a lot of going out lately, but, like a Biglaw Boy Scout, I wanted to be prepared. After Saul's diatribe in the Monday morning meeting, things started looking up. With Patrick, Gavin, and Sheldon ripping through the due diligence, we were reviewing the documents faster than Highlander was providing them. This meant I could stay on top of Saul's daily demands. I didn't dare expect a Saturday off—that would be the old, foolishly optimistic me—but I was getting some free time, allowing me to slowly recover emotionally. I'd even managed to return to my routine of grabbing lunch with Jason and Alex. They'd welcomed me back to the land of lunch outside the office by treating me at my favorite sushi hole in the wall. We'd stuffed our faces with spicy tuna rolls and the large knot in my stomach uncoiled just a little bit. All I needed now was some retail therapy and I would feel like myself again.

93

I was idly scrolling through Saks' new arrivals, wondering whether I could justify spending six hundred dollars on a pair of shoes, when a voice interrupted my thoughts.

"We need you in Dallas."

I looked up and saw Sarah hovering in my doorway. "We need you in Dallas," she repeated casually, as if the task were routine. "How soon can you get there?"

I gazed at her like a deer caught in headlights, leaving the Saks website open on my screen. "Um . . . Dallas? What do you mean?"

"What I *mean* is how soon can you get to the airport and fly to Dallas?" she asked impatiently. "It turns out the target company has a bunch of highly confidential documents we haven't seen. Apparently they think they're too voluminous to copy or make available online." She paused briefly to roll her eyes at the apparent ignorance. "So someone will have to go to Dallas to review them. That someone is you, Mackenzie." She pointed at me with both hands like I'd won a prize.

"They're willing to keep their offices open all weekend so if you work efficiently you'll be back in time for the Monday morning meeting. I'm sure Saul will want a status update about your review. I'd go, but someone's gotta stay here and man the fort." She paused just long enough for me to see she wasn't even trying to suppress her smile. She was clearly delighted that I was the one who would have to provide all the information to Saul. I was the messenger and everyone knows what happens to the messenger. "Anyway, it looks like you have plenty of time on your hands." She motioned to my computer screen, displaying a pair of red patent peep toe Jil Sander shoes. Price tag: $579. "Those look really cheap by the way." She turned on her heel and sauntered away.

94

I sat still in my chair, a string of expletives lodged in my throat. My dislike for Sarah had evolved into full blown loathing. I hated everything about her. I hated the wisp of bangs that fell over her eyebrows, the overly shiny gloss she smeared on her lips, how tightly she cinched her pants with her belt. There really was no giving this woman the benefit of the doubt—she was a total bitch. Maintaining the sanity to restrain myself from running down to her office, throwing myself across her desk, and grabbing her skinny little neck might just require full blown therapy—forget *retail.*

———

"Riiiita," I whined as I approached her cubicle, using the same tone as I did with my mother when I needed help with a problem. Rita might as well have been my mom given how much time we spent together lately. And, like Mom, she was always telling me I needed to get more sleep . . . or wear more under-eye concealer. "You look like ya' have two black eyes," she'd say. "You're the post-ah child for why they make conceal-ah!"

She couldn't understand that no amount of makeup was going to camouflage the dark bags I was carrying around these days, but she was my sounding board when I needed to complain about the lawyers I was working for. She'd murmur, "What an asshole!" and I'd return the favor by listening to her complain about her latest deadbeat boyfriend, giving an equally emphatic, "What an asshole!"

Rita had two children, by two different fathers. She claimed she wanted to settle down, but that all the good ones were taken. That didn't stop her from continuously looking, though. Singles events, night clubs, bars—all the worst places in New York to find men—Rita was there. "My son's fath-ah looked just like Mario Lopez," she'd say as she pointed to her little boy's school picture pinned up on the wall of her cubicle. "I want to find a guy that looks just like him who isn't such an asshole." Looks didn't appear to be a big factor in her selection process, though. She'd hooked up with Freddie Pearson, the partner with the gross habit of picking his nose whenever he was nervous (which was anytime a member of the opposite sex was around). "He took me back to his place, which was HUGE! And right on Pawwk Avenue," she'd told me the day after their first hookup. "Terrible in bed, but I could put up with that if I got to live in that apawt-ment." Unfortunately for Rita (or fortunately), things never progressed any further than that. "Guess he just doesn't think I'm 'marriage material'" she'd said with air quotes, without the slightest bit of self-pity in her voice.

"Yeeeess, hon?" Rita responded as she continued filing her nails. She was starting her Friday afternoon beauty routine early, which included doing her nails, putting her hair in large rollers and applying her "going out" makeup, all while simultaneously answering the phone and typing up documents. All this in preparation for another Friday night out with her sister, both of them hunting for a husband.

The first time I saw her sitting at her desk with pink foam rollers in her hair I did a double-take, but now it was just a reminder that it was Friday afternoon. Even Sadir knew the beauty routine. "Geez, is it Friday already?" he'd ask on his way into our office, passing Rita's desk, noting the one indicator we both had that the weekend was upon us. There was a certain comfort for us in the routine.

I glanced down at the color of polish she was applying today— *Burlesque Show, Red.* She only wore that color when it had been a long dry spell. Poor Rita. "Pretty." I gestured to the bottle of nail polish.

"Yah—cross your fing-ahs it works and gets me some action. What can I do for ya?" Rita cut to the chase.

"I need to go to Dallas. Apparently, ASAP. " I let out a big, exhausted sigh. "Can you find me a flight? It's for Project Montauk."

"Working all weekend again?" She shook her head in disbelief. No matter how long Rita worked at F&D she was always surprised that lawyers had to work on the weekends. "Lemme guess . . ." She lowered her voice to a stage whisper. "The Ice Queen?"

I nodded, looking over my shoulder, hoping people walking by didn't overhear our conversation.

She scrunched up her face in disgust. "That bitch! Someone really needs to dislodge that huge stick up her butt. Maybe get her laid or somethin." Rita cackled at her own joke. Now I *really* hoped nobody could hear our conversation. "Leeeet's see . . . " She turned her attention to her computer screen and clicked away with her mouse. "First class, I assume?"

I nodded. Hell, why not? If I had to get on a plane today I might as well be offered something more than peanuts to eat.

"Hm. Hm. Hm." She clicked the keys with her long fingernails "Okay, there's a flight in an hour and a half out of LaGuardia and the next available one isn't until 6 A.M. tomorrow. Which one you want?"

The flight gods were shining on me—I couldn't pack and get out to LaGuardia that quickly, which meant I wasn't going to be able to get to Dallas tonight. "Just a sec. Be right back." I scurried down the hall to Sarah's office to break the news.

"What don't you understand about the word TODAY?" she hissed when I finished the run-down of the flight schedule.

"No, I know, listen—the only available flight today is in an hour and a half, sooo . . ."

"And?" She raised her perfectly shaped eyebrows.

"Aaand that wouldn't give me enough time to pack and make it out to the airport," I reasoned.

She took a deep, exaggerated breath, like I was trying her patience. "Mackenzie, I really don't have time for this amateur act. It's not rocket science—leave now, do not pass go, do not collect two hundred dollars." She waved her hand at me dismissively.

I gave her a puzzled look. Why couldn't she ever give straightforward instructions?

She let out a bigger sigh and shook her head in disgust at my perceived hopelessness. "Get a Town Car. Go to the airport now. Get on the plane." She paused between each instruction like she was explaining something to a five-year old. "Purchase a change of clothes once you're in Dallas and charge it to the client. They *do* have clothes in Dallas, you know."

Well, it sounded pretty easy when she put it that way. Maybe I should have pieced that one together myself, but I still wasn't schooled in the multitude of ways Biglaw lawyers spend their clients' money. I'd charged lots of things to clients—Town Cars, meals, hotels—but never clothes. I guess when their bills are in the millions clients just don't notice a few hundred dollars' worth of clothes. I left her office feeling a little stupid, which was quickly becoming my default feeling after any conversation with Sarah.

Ninety harried minutes later, I sat alone in a plush leather seat in first class, thankful for the lack of BlackBerry service on airplanes. For four blessed hours, I was completely inaccessible and it wasn't my fault. What a luxury. *Maybe I'll get lucky and the runway in Dallas will be backed up.* Never before had I wished for a flight delay so badly.

I pushed my bag underneath the seat in front of me and began thumbing through the airport magazine. I knew I should be doing some work, but I'd never sat in first class before. They actually gave me a drink and a pair of slippers before we even took off! I wanted to savor this moment of peace . . . and I was so tired . . . and the seat was so comfortable . . .

"Gooooood evening, this is your captain speaking," the intercom boomed, startling me awake. Dazed, I lifted my head and rubbed my eyes. "We'll be landing in Dallas in approximately thirty minutes. Please return your seats to the upright position and stow your tray tables . . ."

Landing? I looked around frantically. *I must have slept the whole flight.* "Shit," I hissed and slumped back in my seat. There went my plan of getting any work done on the flight. I raised the shade and peered out the tiny window, hoping to catch a glimpse of the Dallas skyline. Seeing nothing but fields, I leaned forward and squinted towards the windows on the other side. Next to me, a man with dark hair and big brown long-lashed eyes was looking back at me. He must've sat down after I fell asleep. Without intending to, I noticed the dimple on his chin and the faintest five o'clock shadow. He was seriously cute. With his muscular arms, he reminded me of someone famous—Ben Affleck, maybe? Was I still dreaming?

"Rise and shine," he said, smiling.

I smiled back at him flirtatiously. If I was still dreaming I might as well make the most of it.

"You must've been tired—you were out before we even took off." He gazed down at his shoulder. I followed his gaze, but couldn't figure out what he was showing me. It was a nice Zegna shirt he was wearing . . . was he fishing for a compliment? Then it clicked. Oh my God . . . I'd been sleeping on his shoulder. I had fallen asleep on a complete stranger's shoulder! A really cute stranger, but a stranger nonetheless! Oh God, had I snored? Talked in my sleep? Please, please don't let me have drooled!

"Oh, I'm sorry," I stammered awkwardly. "I didn't mean to . . ."

"Raise your seat back, please," the flight attendant interrupted, patting the back of my seat as she walked by.

"Sorry," I repeated, fumbling with the button on the armrest, aware that my cheeks were flaming. "Um . . . I haven't really been sleeping lately. I mean, I *have* been sleeping, but very little. Between work and . . . well, work . . . it just hasn't been my best week." I paused. "Or my best month for that matter," I heard myself saying. "See, I'm working with the reincarnation of the devil which is wreaking havoc on my ability to impress the person I'm trying desperately to impress, my so-called mentor has become the bane of my existence, and getting drenched with rainwater on the way to the airport was the closest I've come to showering in two days." I took a deep breath. It had all come out so fast and completely uncontrolled.

Oh my God, why did I just say all that? Where had my filter gone? Clearly it was still asleep.

He eyed me curiously, and I felt myself turn redder. "I . . . I don't know why I just said all that," I stammered.

"Feel better?" he asked, cocking his head at me.

I nodded.

"Maybe you just needed to get that off your chest. You did seem a little . . ."

I raised my eyebrows, waiting for him to fill in the blank.

"Tense," he finished, smiling. "Lawyer?"

I nodded again. "How'd you know?"

He shrugged. "It just seems to be the one profession where people announce how long it's been since they've showered like it's a badge of honor."

99

I grimaced. He was dead on. Sadir was always pointing out his lack of time to attend to personal hygiene. "Haven't had time to change my suit in seventy-two hours—too busy billing!" he'd exclaim, like it was something to be proud of. Now here I was, doing the same thing.

"If it's making you so miserable, it's probably time to quit."

I frowned. Was I really being chewed out for my chosen profession by some stranger on the plane? Cute stranger, but still. I lifted my chin, trying to hold on to a modicum of dignity. "I'm not miserable. I'm actually very happy, in fact."

"Really?" he asked, in a tone that should be reserved for therapists.

"I'm just going through a bit of a rough patch. But I really love my job. I get to work on deals that affect the financial markets, which in turn affect the world economy. I love it." Who was I kidding? "Love" was a bit strong. "I mean, who really *loves* their job these days?" I chuckled nervously, switching gears. "But I've got a great opportunity to really solidify my future. And I'm sure the hours will become more manageable . . . " I paused to think about what my point was. "I just keep thinking that this is worth sacrificing for . . . and I shouldn't be a quitter . . ." I trailed off. "Frankly, I don't know what I'm thinking these days. I'm way too tired to think."

He stared at me, looking bemused. "Not exactly a great time to be working on very important deals then. And affecting the world economy." A flicker of amusement passed across his face.

I smiled weakly back at him. Touché.

"You have a little . . . " He trailed off, brushing his finger to the side of his mouth. I rubbed the corner of my lips.

Oh God. Dried drool! There was a tiny smile playing at his lips.

I was officially humiliated.

I ran hot water into the tub in the hotel bathroom and stripped off the clothes I'd been wearing for the past twenty-four hours. It was 6 P.M. on Saturday and I'd just finished reviewing the contents of the data room. It took me all night and most of the day, but luckily there had not been as many documents as I'd feared. Sarah had been incorrect—there were board minutes in the data room, but no litigation documents or leases. I emailed her my summaries and a brief overview of the types of documents I'd reviewed, then returned to my hotel room, thinking I would just change, grab my things, and go. I'd asked the driver that picked me up at the Dallas/Fort Worth airport the day before to stop off at the closest department store. He drove about twenty miles before pulling into the parking lot of a huge Neiman Marcus. He waited for me while I went in and picked out a bra, underwear, a shirt, and a skirt. Seven hundred dollars' worth of new clothes to add to my travel expenses. When I returned to the car with my shopping bags in hand I felt like one of those wealthy Park Avenue women who has a car and driver waiting for her while she shops all day. But those women don't have to drive to an office and review documents all night. And I did.

The only sleep I'd had in the past thirty-four hours was my three hour nap on some stranger's shoulder on the plane. My six hundred dollar a night Four Seasons suite, with the California King sleeper bed that Rita joked was big enough for a twenty person orgy, ended up being just a high priced storage area for my luggage. So, when I'd entered the palatial hotel bathroom to retrieve the toiletries I'd bought, I wasn't able to resist the lure of the swimming pool sized whirlpool tub.

I poured in a whole bottle of complimentary body wash and climbed in, letting myself sink down into the luxuriant bubbles. Shutting my eyes, I tried to mentally release the stresses of the day: let go of the email from Saul calling me "useless" because I couldn't attend a meeting in his office in five minutes (due to the fact that I was 2,000 miles away in Dallas per his request); let go of the numerous patronizing emails I'd received in the last twenty-four hours from Sarah; let go of the guilt I felt for not visiting Uncle Nigel in months. Let it alllllllll go. But lying there in the luxurious bathtub, inhaling the smell of calming jasmine, I found myself feeling anything but relaxed. *I should head out to the airport now and get back to New York . . . there's so much to do back at the office . . . but nobody knows where I am right now . . . . I should savor this.* I negotiated with myself. *I should crawl into that comfy bed and savor every grain of sleep I can get. But I can't move. I'm too tired.* I patted the bubbles around me and watched as they softly moved between my fingers, marveling at how foreign it felt to be . . . clean. *When did showering become a luxury rather than a necessity?* I submerged my hair and attempted to clear my thoughts, but my mind kept racing. *Did I really fall asleep on some stranger on the plane? And tell him I hadn't showered for two days? And DROOL on him?* I squeezed my eyes shut, trying desperately to eliminate the memory from my mind. *This is everything I've ever worked for*, I reminded myself, forcing my mind back into super achiever mode. *All I have to do is survive this deal with Saul, get the Highlander deal closed, and the StarCorp secondment will be mine.* I stayed submerged in the tub, staring at the ceiling with my mind racing until the water was cold.

Lifting a large, plush monogrammed towel off the shelf and wrapping myself in the cozy Egyptian cotton, I couldn't avoid my Black-Berry lying near the sink—blinking, blinking, blinking. Taunting me. Knowing that it was going to give me bad news, I picked it up and prepared for the inevitable.

To: Mackenzie Corbett
From: Sarah Clarke

You should have let us know right away that the document production was lacking. We need to see the litigation documents. I will get in touch with Seller's lawyers. Do not leave Dallas until we sort this out.

I had just started to write back when a second email from Sarah popped up on my BlackBerry.

To: Mackenzie Corbett
From: Sarah Clarke

The documents we need to review have been tracked down. They are in a warehouse in their offices in Canada. Take your flight home as booked and plan to go to Edmonton ASAP.

Shit. Shit. Shit.

12

"OH MY GOD—IF I have to work another day for that woman, I'm going to go insane," I complained to Jason, as he stood in my bedroom watching me unpack and repack. I had returned to New York for eight hours—just long enough to wash some clothes, pack for my next trip, and have a fight with Jason.

I'd been surprised to see Jason when I stumbled into my lobby, bone tired and semi-dehydrated from the plane ride. I even stood still for a moment, my mind too fuzzy to process that it was him. But there he was, engaged in a hushed and, what looked like, heated conversation with Eddie. Jason looked equally surprised to see me and frankly so did Eddie, who looked at me like I'd just risen from the grave. In his defense, I probably did look worse than death.

Jason explained he had just come by to pick up some clothes he'd left at my apartment, but Eddie was giving him a hard time about entering my apartment when I wasn't home. This was totally baffling to me because Eddie knew the schedules, significant others, one night stands, and fast food preferences of everyone in the building. He rarely even used the buzzer because he knew who to send up. And he was the type of guy who'd probably send up Jack the Ripper if he slipped him a Benjamin. I wasn't exactly sure when my apartment security had begun rivaling Fort Knox, but Jason whisked me into the elevator before I had the chance to ask Eddie why he'd been so strict.

"She's going to seriously send me to the nut house," I said now, grabbing a handful of socks from my top drawer.

"You and me both if I have to keep hearing about her," he mumbled almost inaudibly, as he picked up an old Cosmopolitan magazine lying beside my bed and thumbed through it.

I stared at him in disbelief. It seemed so selfish that he was picking a fight now, during our brief time together and just as I was being banished from the country for an indeterminate amount of time. I couldn't understand it—Jason had always been loving and considerate, but lately he was dismissive when I needed an empathetic ear. Clearly I was having a rough time here. It wasn't until that moment that I realized how frustrated I'd become with him. I put down the socks I was stuffing into my suitcase, my frustration boiling over in one clipped question. "What's that supposed to mean?"

"All I'm saying is you're not exactly the most fun to be around these days." He threw the magazine on my bed. "I mean, I'm hoping when we move in together your life is a little more . . . " He trailed off, seemingly searching for the right word, before adding "balanced."

"Is that what this is about? Moving in together? Because I have absolutely no idea why Eddie grilled you today."

His forehead creased. "That's not the problem, Mac. Even on the few times we're alone together, your head is somewhere else. You're so caught up in F&D and when you're not working, you're complaining about work. You do realize that I work at the same firm, right?"

"Oh, I'm so sorry—has my complaining been bothering you?" I asked sarcastically, my tone more cutting than intended. "When was the last time you had to work on the weekend? Or the last time you had to pull an all-nighter? We may work at the same firm, but we are living in two completely different worlds! I HAVE to work hard. I don't have a father who can bail me out if I get fired." I could hear my voice growing shrill, but I didn't care. After so many days of quietly stewing with resentment, the yelling felt cathartic.

"Wait." Jason lifted his hand to stop me. "Just stop right there." He looked incredulous. I instantly regretted bringing up his father.

Jason lived under the long shadow of his successful father, who made Kermode a household name. Every time someone asked

"Jason Kermode? As in Kermode GPS?" he was reminded that he would never have the opportunity to blaze his own path. And even if the world didn't point that out to him, his father would. Jason had once confided in me that his biggest fear was never being able to carve out his own identity separate from his father.

"Jason," I started before he cut in.

"I don't know why you seem to carry around this idea that I somehow don't have to work as hard as you do, that I have some sort of inside track. Well, here's a newsflash for you. Just because I don't drink the F&D Kool-Aid doesn't mean I don't work hard. These guys will shit in a bowl and tell you it's ice cream, Mac. You think busting your ass is going to make you more successful, but that's just not how the world works."

"Then please enlighten me. How does it work?" My voice was dripping with sarcasm.

He shook his head and pursed his lips as if trying to physically prevent himself from saying what was really on his mind. After a beat of thoughtful silence he said, "You just assume I'll be at your beck and call, day and night, rearranging any plans I have just to catch a *glimpse* of you."

105

"You know as well as I do that having plans doesn't mean *anything* to those guys. There was an associate who missed his own *honeymoon* last month because he had to work. Do you really think I can say 'oh, sorry, gotta go! I have dinner plans with my boyfriend'?"

He glared at me for a moment. "I think you can take me into consideration, yes."

"It doesn't work like that," I screeched, before taking a deep breath and softening my tone. "In my department you can't just . . . "

He waved his hands, indicating he'd heard enough. "For the love of God, Mac, spare me another one of your 'in the corporate department' lectures. Your department isn't an island, you know. Those of us in other departments do actual work too."

I stared silently, knowing that if I opened my mouth right now it would only be to point out that most nights when he's leaving the office, I have at least five more hours of work ahead of me. Or that I'm the one who hasn't had a weekend off in months. Or that he's never been called a fuckwit by his superior. But my expression must have given me away because his face contorted angrily.

"Okay, okay." He threw his hands up in surrender. "Your work is CLEARLY more stressful than mine! And sooooo much more IMPORTANT. So I should just camp out here." He slumped down on the bed. "You tell me when you can fit me into your busy, important schedule."

"I didn't say that. Now you're just putting words in my mouth!" My voice had turned flustered.

"Newsflash, Mac." He leapt up from the bed, pointing his finger at me angrily. "My work IS stressful and I DO work hard, I just don't BITCH and BITCH and BITCH about it like you do."

"Oh, you don't?" I crossed my arms over my chest, glaring at him.

He raked both hands through his hair, looking exasperated. For a moment we were both silent. I could see his chest rising and falling with each irate breath. I thought that might be the end of it, but then his face contorted again.

"Damn it, Mac," he fumed, grabbing his coat off my bed, not even looking at me on his way out.

"So I should just pretend to be HAPPY that I'm on my way to Edmonton per that she-devil's instructions?" I called, but all I heard was the door slam behind him. "Great," I muttered, closing my suitcase. "Just fucking great."

I stepped out into the cold, November evening and hailed a cab for the airport. Veering across two lanes of traffic and narrowly missing a pedestrian, a taxi stopped in front of me the instant my hand shot up. I guess I'm not the only one who doesn't like to waste time. I got in and sunk down into the grey vinyl seat, simmering with anger and misery as the cab turned on to 96th Street, barreling towards JFK airport. The taxi driver aggressively cut in front of two cars, jarring me back and forth in my seat. I grabbed the passenger handle next to the window, as horns honked loudly around me. Overcome by nausea from the erratic driving, I opened my window, letting in a rush of cold air. I tilted my head back, closed my eyes, and let the wind hit my face, hoping to keep my motion sickness in check.

"Fucking asshole!" The taxi driver rolled down his window and waved his fist menacingly at the driver in front of him.

"Amen," I mumbled, my mind wandering back to Jason. What was the fight even about anyway? Sure, I've been complaining a lot lately, but anyone in my position would be doing the same. Did he really need to bring it up during what amounted to an eight hour layover in New York? Grudgingly, I started to consider his point of view. *I guess I'm not the most pleasant person these days*, I thought, realizing how short I'd been with everyone who crossed my path lately. Just this morning I'd snapped at the Starbucks barista when she asked me to repeat my order, which I'm sure I mumbled the first time. And I was pretty sure I knocked over an old lady in the airport, but there wasn't time to turn around and check. When had I become this harried and agitated? I tried to remember the last time I'd really relaxed. There just wasn't the time. Just as I was analyzing my depleted social life, my phone rang. I exhaled a deep sigh of relief. Jason wasn't going to let me go all the way to Edmonton without talking this out first. This is the guy who didn't get off the phone without saying I love you. Of course, he was going to apologize for picking a fight during our brief time together. I'd already decided I was going to forgive him when I saw that it was Kim calling.

"Hey, are you on your way?" she asked, sounding cheerful. I searched my tired mind to figure out where she thought I would be on my way to. Then it hit me—the season premiere of The Bachelor. Ever since freshman year of college, Kim and I had a ritual. She mixed the drinks, I baked the goodies, and we watched twenty-five desperate, single ladies with biological clocks thumping fight it out for one supposedly desirable, but definitely vacuous, bachelor. Sometimes we did theme nights based on where the episode took place—mai tais and macadamia nut cookies for Hawaii, margaritas and churros for Cancun, or sangria and flan for Spain. Sometimes we played drinking games—a shot every time someone says the word "journey." Our Bachelor nights had seen us through exams, messy break-ups, and broken hearts. We looked forward to them when there was something to celebrate and sought comfort in them when we were feeling down. The newest season of The Bachelor was premiering tonight and I was stuck in this stupid taxi.

"I completely forgot, Kim. I'm really sorry, but I can't come over tonight."

"Seriously?" Her voice was full of disappointment. "You can't bail on the first episode. That's when all the crazies get cut!"

"You won't believe this, but the she-devil has managed to exile me to Edmonton. I'm in a taxi on my way to the airport right now."

"The bitchy mentor? You mean you haven't just told her to screw off by now?"

"You know how bad I am about confrontation! I'm attempting the 'kill her with kindness' method instead."

"Wouldn't a kitchen knife be so much more efficient?"

"Well, then there's the whole murder charge and prison thing to think about." The taxi driver peered at me in the rear view mirror and I flashed a sheepish smile in his direction. No need to call the police, sir. Fantasizing is not a crime.

"I guess I'll have to watch the post-rose ceremony break-downs all alone then." She let out a long sigh. "But if I get drunk and call ABC to apply to be a bachelorette it's on your hands," she said, a note of pique running through her voice.

After assuring her that I would not let that happen, I apologized again and hung up.

I leaned back in my seat, closing my eyes. I started to imagine the plane skidding off the runway and me being knocked into a coma, finally able to catch up on much needed sleep. *Two straight weeks of sleep and I'd be good.* A teeny tiny voice in the back of my mind was telling me that was a tad crazy. A sane person doesn't hope for a plane crash.

My cab screeched to a stop at a red light, sending my Marc Jacobs purse sliding wildly across the seat. I snagged it before it fell into the mysterious sludge on the floor of the taxi. Hugging it against me, I gave silent thanks that we both survived this trip to the airport. The soft leather in my hands conjured up another memory, from earlier this year: It was my sister's birthday and I'd planned on taking the train up to Boston and surprising her. But Russ emailed the deal team on Thursday, letting us know we'd need to be in the office most of the weekend. Wanting to still do something special for Margaret, I'd gone onto Saks.com and picked out a leather Marc Jacobs tote, clicked gift wrap and overnight shipping, relishing the feeling of being able to solve a problem with money. I knew it would be the nicest gift she'd receive. Margaret had parlayed her athletic ability into a full scholarship to Duke, but in her third year she tore her ACL, meaning the funds instantly dried up. Mom and Dad took out a second mortgage on the house so she could graduate. She'd used her bachelor's in education to get a teaching job at the school where Dad was a principal. She'd met her husband Luke there. But with twin five-year old boys on two teachers' salaries, money was tight.

"Mac, this is the most gorgeous thing I've ever seen!" she'd squealed with delight, and then, away from the phone, whispered, "Baby, can you help Evan in the potty? I'll be there in just a minute."

"Is the color okay?" I'd asked, knowing it would be. I'd bought the black one, adhering to her belief that everything goes with black.

"It's perfect!" she'd gushed excitedly. "The leather is as smooth as a baby's butt. And I should know!"

I'd felt a swell of pride hearing the joy in her voice. Somewhere along the way, I think my relentless desire to achieve became less about a desire to outshine her and more that I wanted so badly to succeed for both of us. The life I was living, pursuing the goals I'd set out for myself, was somehow keeping her dreams alive too.

"Which airline, lady?" the driver asked, jarring me back to the present.

"Delta." I hugged my purse tighter. And this was the problem: every time that teeny tiny voice questioned why I stayed in Biglaw, it was silenced and replaced by an overwhelming sense that working in Biglaw was a mark of success—and fear that anything outside Biglaw's doors was failure, a cruddy participation ribbon. The job might be rough, but it was what it was. It was the nature of the beast. So, I sucked it up and boarded my flight to Edmonton.

———

"I'm surprised there's only one of you—there's a lot of boxes here. I'm pretty sure I told the other girl that on the phone," the assistant assigned to look after me fussed as he escorted me through the dungeon-like warehouse to the Falcon storage locker. "Sarah, I think her name was? She said it wouldn't be a problem, so I figured you guys were sending a whole team."

I mentally rolled my eyes. Did she also request that I be locked inside the storage locker without food or water? I wouldn't be surprised.

"Nope, just me." I tried to muster as much friendliness as I could. Four years of college, three years of law school, and the hardest bar exam in the country and this is where I wound up: in a dreary storage locker somewhere close to the Arctic under the direct orders of a sadist. I tried to channel some positive thoughts, but the best I could come up with was *it can't get any worse.*

The assistant pulled the sliding door, revealing the contents of the storage locker. Dozens of boxes were piled up high to the ceiling, each covered with sloppy, black marker notations—"November 2013" or "Contracts 2010." They didn't even appear to be in any particular order. "Ummm . . . these don't all belong to Falcon, do they?"

He nodded. "Yuuuuuup, all Falcon. This just sort of became the repository for the 'where the hell should we stick this box?' boxes. I'm not even really sure what we have in here." His eyes darted around the poorly ventilated locker. "Anyway, let me know if you need anything," he said empathetically and walked away.

I scanned the multiple piles of disorganized banker's boxes in disbelief, realizing I'd been wrong. In Biglaw, it can always get worse.

———

Five days later, boarding the Death Star elevator, two bulging bags in hand, I noticed the grey suit beside me peering at the large bag of M&Ms poking out from under the tissue paper I'd used to hide my wares. I couldn't fault him for being nosey. He was used to seeing people carrying briefcases or having their arms full of files. He was not used to seeing someone carrying bags full of the contents of an entire hotel mini bar. My suite at the Fairmont Hotel in Edmonton had come complete with a ridiculously overpriced, fully stocked mini bar. While digging into a king sized Toblerone bar and a bag of gummy bears that substituted for dinner the first night, it occurred to me that it would be just one more charge that disappeared in the black hole of my mounting travel expenses. This gave me an idea. I did a quick calculation of the total cost of the items in the mini bar—$290. A small price for a multibillion dollar client. So, every night when I returned to my room after twelve hours in the storage locker, I emptied everything out and dumped it all in my suitcase. Like magic, the mini bar was fully restocked every day. After ten days I'd built up a fairly substantial stash. And judging from the weight of my bags, a very heavy stash too.

Lucky for me the button for the twenty-seventh floor had been pressed, giving me a chance to readjust the tissue before any more curious eyes got a peek. I needn't have worried, though. All eyes were already fixed on the flat screen monitor flashing the latest headlines. It had become our only source of news.

"Alec Baldwin to host season finale of Saturday Night Live." Seconds later, "Earthquake in China kills 1689." Whoever added those monitors to elevators is a genius. It removes the awkwardness of standing with someone else in silence and staring at the numbers above the doors as if they will do something more exciting than increase in order.

The elevator stopped on the twenty-third floor and three people filed on, balancing trays of food from the cafeteria. I nodded a groggy hello to Maria, Sarah's secretary, but she avoided my eyes. I'd spoken with Maria many times and she was always friendly, despite the fact that her boss was a witch. Now she was suddenly aloof. Was that pity I detected in her expression? What misery did Sarah have waiting for me? Was she going to send me somewhere else—Siberia perhaps? *You're being paranoid*, I told myself, but Maria managed to look everywhere except in my direction.

When I stepped off the elevator, I'd worked myself into such a flap that I didn't notice Jason walking through the glass doors towards me. His eyes widened.

"Mac, you're here early." He pulled me in and gave me a kiss on the head. It was almost like he'd blanked on where we were—this was more affection than we usually showed at the office. As if realizing his mistake, he pulled away, overcompensating with distance.

"Early? What time is it?" My hands were too occupied to check, but judging from the crowd swelling off the elevator, it was the nine o'clock rush.

"I thought maybe you'd be in later today because of your trip." Something in the way he said "trip" made me wonder if he understood that I hadn't exactly been sipping fruity drinks by a pool.

"No rest for the weary, unfortunately," I sighed. "What are you doing up here on twenty-seven?" It was a rare occurrence that Jason made the trip up to my floor. He always said the corporate partners gave him the heebie jeebies. I didn't blame him. I'd avoid them too if I could.

"I was just going to surprise you with a note in your office. Something to welcome you back." He flashed the adorable grin that could still make me weak in the knees.

A wide smile broke out across my face. When I hadn't heard from Jason while I was in Edmonton, I'd assumed he was still angry. Seeing him now, all the resentment I'd felt before leaving for Edmonton instantly faded away.

"Jason, I'm really sorry about how scattered I've been lately." I reached out to squeeze his hand. "You were right—it *isn't* fair that we're always working around my schedule and —"

The elevator pinged and Maxwell and Russ stepped off, looking harried. Jason and I immediately stood straighter, exuding our best "we're having a professional, work-related conversation" posture as they walked past. When I was sure they were out of ear shot I said, "And I promise I'll take you into consideration from now on. Can I make it up to you? Lunch today—my treat?"

"Can't today." He jammed his hands in his pockets, rocking back on his heels. "Busy day for me unfortunately."

"Maybe tomorrow then?"

"Sure." He nodded. "Tomorrow works." His tone matched his still rigid posture, making me wonder if there was a partner nearby that I hadn't noticed.

"Okay, let's touch base later then." I matched his tone and gave a brisk nod goodbye, unsure if we were now playing off a script for any prying ears. It wasn't until I was halfway down the corridor that it occurred to me that Jason had come from the opposite direction of my office.

13

"Whatcha gawt there?" Rita raised an overly plucked eyebrow curiously as I approached her cubicle.

"Just a little gift for you from Project Montauk," I said, plunking the two bags beside her chair. I flashed a wicked grin before heading into my office.

She opened the bag and let out a whoop. "You're like freakin' Santa Claus!"

Beaming, I felt thankful that I could do something nice for Rita. Lately she'd been the sanest person I came in contact with most days.

"What was that all about?" Sadir grumbled, peering out the door, clearly unfamiliar with joyful sounds in the office.

I shrugged innocently, clicking open my Outlook.

To: Mackenzie Corbett
From: Mom

Hi Honey!

Just a quick reminder that it's Uncle Nigel's retirement party tonight. Dad and I wish we could make the trip, but are thankful you can attend as the Corbett family representative! I haven't heard from you in a while so I know you must be busy—make sure you're getting enough vitamin C! And sleep!

xo Mom

Sleep. Just seeing the word made me want to drift off into a blissful slumber for the next twelve hours, but I shook that fantasy from my mind. There was no way I could miss Uncle Nigel's retirement party. After thirty-five years at his law firm, it would be emotional for him to finally hang it up. I silently promised I would not let work interfere with this and went straight to work planning my escape.

Nine hours later I was in the back seat of a chauffeured Town Car on my way out to Darien, Connecticut. I'd emailed Ben and Sarah on my way out, explaining that I had a family emergency and would be out of reach for a short time this evening. Technically it was a lie—a party probably doesn't qualify as an emergency—but if I missed the party because of work my actions may *result* in a medical emergency. So it was for the best.

Settling in for the forty-five minute ride, the tension in my stomach uncoiled as I let my mind drift to April, when Jason and I would finally move in together. The timing would work out perfectly. A few months after the move in, assuming nothing disastrous happened, I would start the StarCorp secondment, meaning I would have weekends off to enjoy my new set-up. I closed my eyes, feeling drowsy from the soothing bumps in the road and fantasizing about easy Sunday mornings spent in bed, exchanging sections of the paper and munching on heavenly breakfast pastries.

My cell phone blared, forcing me back to the present, and without looking at the caller ID, I knew it would be Mom wanting to confirm that, yes, I was on my way to Uncle Nigel's party and, no, I didn't need Dad to look up directions online for me. It was Mom's belief that anytime I crossed state lines, or left my apartment for that matter, I was going to get lost.

"Are you sure the driver knows where he's going?" Mom fussed.

"Yes, Mom," I replied impatiently. "He has GPS."

"That's not always accurate, you know. Routes change and if he hasn't kept his GPS up to date you could—"

"Mom." I cut off what I knew was the beginning of a horror story about someone who used a GPS that had not been kept up to date. "I won't get lost. If I do I'll call Uncle Nigel," I reassured her in the calmest tone I could manage.

"All right. Well, give him a big hug for me," she said wistfully. "And tell him we'll miss him at Christmas." Aunt Ellen's retirement present to Uncle Nigel was a month long cruise on a tall ship which departed December 20, so Mom wouldn't have her big brother home for the holidays, much to her disappointment.

"I will."

"Thanks for taking the time to do this, Mac. I know you being there will mean a lot to him."

"No problem, Mom," I said softly, wishing it hadn't been so long since I'd visited him. I should have at least called him on September 11, knowing how tough the memories of that terrible day he lost so many co-workers and friends must be every year.

There must have been over a hundred people in Uncle Nigel's house, enjoying the catered affair Aunt Ellen had lovingly planned for him. Friends, work colleagues, and family were there to celebrate his career and wish him the best in his retirement. Somehow I imagined Saul's retirement party a little differently. More like hundreds of lawyers joining hands and singing joyfully, "Ding Dong the Witch Is Dead!" At Uncle Nigel's party, there was love and respect for a man so well liked that the toasts continued for close to an hour.

I didn't dare pull out my BlackBerry during the toasts. It went unchecked for over an hour—a new record. Surreptitiously, I ducked into the study. No new emails—bliss! I lingered for a few minutes in my favorite room in their house. A comfy couch and loveseat surrounded by built-in book shelves gave it the feel of a simpler time when people still read books rather than e-readers. Running my fingers across the gold spines of the legal journals that lined the brimming shelves, I marveled at the methods people used to utilize for legal research. I picked one out and began flipping through it, enchanted with the history. My mind drifted to the Latin phrase etched atop the main entrance of Georgetown Law School. *FIAT JUSTITIA, RUAT COELUM:* "Let justice be done though the heavens fall." It had all sounded so noble. When did it turn into "just get the fucking deal done"?

Two large file boxes, presumably containing the contents of Uncle Nigel's office, sat on a leather-topped writing desk in the corner of the room. A framed photo perched on top caught my eye. Mom, Dad, Uncle Nigel, Margaret, and me—dressed in winter coats, cheeks rosy from the cold, with our arms around each other posing in front of the Twin Towers. A lump swelled in my throat when I picked up the frame and ran my finger across the glass. Even though the picture was taken eighteen years ago, when I closed my eyes I could still feel the anticipation in my stomach when we boarded the high speed elevator that would whisk us to the top of the World Trade Center, so high my ears would pop.

What will everything look like from the 103rd floor? I'd wondered excitedly. But it wasn't the view that had captivated me when I walked into Uncle Nigel's huge corner office. It was the awe-inspiring feeling that I'd been transported into the future. A sleek, wraparound desk sat in the far corner of the room, topped with a laptop computer and a gold-plated kinetic sculpture. To the left sat a plush, black leather couch and a coffee table with a base that doubled as a fish tank, the multicolored fish providing a sharp contrast to the monochromatic color scheme. It was unlike anything my ten-year old self had ever seen.

The way the labyrinthine hallways buzzed with activity and the sharply dressed lawyers walked with purpose made it all seem so important. And when I sat in the high-backed leather chair stationed behind Uncle Nigel's massive desk, I felt . . . triumphant. It was then that I knew what I wanted to be.

"Hey, I thought I'd find you in here," a voice boomed, interrupting my thoughts.

"Oh, hey, Uncle Nigel. Sorry, I just ducked in here to check the old ball and chain." I lifted my BlackBerry in explanation, before changing the subject. "Great party! Aunt Ellen really outdid herself."

"She sure did. Whatcha got there?"

"Oh . . ." I turned the photo around. I felt a slight twinge of awkwardness, wondering if it looked like I'd been snooping.

"That's a great shot, isn't it?" Uncle Nigel plopped down on the couch and let out the satisfied sigh of someone who'd been on his feet for hours. "It's hard to believe that I won't have an office to display it in anymore."

I took a seat next to him, grateful for the moment to talk for a bit, knowing I'd be heading back to the office soon. My foot was fidgeting with nervous energy and my mind was running through my mental to-do list. It was impossible for me to sit still anymore with the constant caffeine rush pulsing through my body.

"It *is* hard to believe," I replied. "Do you think you'll miss it?"

He thought for a moment. "There's a lot of parts I'll miss. But I'm ready."

"Well, I know Aunt Ellen is thrilled."

"She's been waiting for this for *years*." He chuckled. "After 9/11 she used to say, 'if running out of a burning building won't get you to retire, I don't know what will.'"

"I think I've heard that a time or two from her." I smiled. "Why *didn't* you retire back then?" Uncle Nigel had never volunteered much information about that day. I knew he was on the 103rd floor and I knew that he got out, but that was really the extent of it. I'd never worked up the courage to ask him any more than that and he never seemed to want to talk about it. But today felt different. Maybe it was the fact that it was the end of an era for him or that I was a lawyer now too, making us peers rather than mentor and student. Whatever it was, the conversation suddenly felt necessary.

His warm brown eyes reminded me of my mother's. "The truth is, I loved my job. I didn't want to curl up in a ball and live in fear. I wanted to keep doing what I loved."

I felt a pang of longing, wishing I had the same fondness for my job. *It'll get better when I land the StarCorp secondment*, I resolutely told myself.

"But it was hard. Things really changed after that. For everyone."

I nodded. "What was it like that day?" I inquired gently.

His expression looked like he was considering how much to reveal. "Well," he started. "I was in a conference room with ten other attorneys when the first plane hit just before 9 A.M."

My leg stopped fidgeting and my mind stopped racing. It was as if my body's desire to constantly keep moving, to keep myself awake, focused, and ready for the next task, finally subsided. The only thing my body willed me to do was listen.

"I was supposed to be talking to the group about a deposition we were conducting in a week. I stood up to speak and saw this plane coming right towards us. The room was wall to wall windows and it was such a sunny, clear morning you couldn't miss it. In a split second, it hit the other building and a huge fireball came out the other side. I'd never seen anything so massive. It was probably eight stories high and looked like it would envelop our building too. Everything just sort of stopped. A few people ran to the windows to get a closer look before someone yelled 'let's get outta here!' That shook us back to reality and everyone started to move towards the stairways and elevators. They were making announcements over the intercom telling us that our building was safe, to go back to our offices." He shook his head in anger. "A lot of people did, but you know me. I've always had a problem with someone else telling me what I should and shouldn't do. 'A problem with authority' one of my high school teachers called it." He gave a half smile, before a wave of somberness came over his face. "The other partner in my meeting listened to the announcement and went back to his office. We told him to come with us, but he thought we were ridiculous to leave when our building was safe. He said he was too busy to go all the way down, only to be told to come back ten minutes later. He never made it out." Uncle Nigel gazed down at the floor and for a moment I thought he wouldn't be able to continue.

"Some of my colleagues headed to the elevators, but I hated the elevators in that building. They were always having problems so I decided to take the stairs. It was one hundred and three floors, and with my blood pressure I knew it wasn't going to be easy, but I felt I could handle it if I paced myself. I made it down to the fortieth floor before the second plane hit our building. It felt just like an earthquake. The whole building shook and some people screamed. Smoke started filling the stairways at this point and the walls started to crack. It was steaming hot, and people were shoulder to shoulder. Everyone was surprisingly calm, though. No one pushed. Some people were crying and whispering prayers. I'll always remember the piles of shoes we had to step over. People were taking them off and tossing them in the corners. I was just trying to focus on the stairs, but I slipped on a puddle of coffee and fell. A fireman, passing me on his way up the stairs, reached down and pulled me up. 'Be careful, sir,' he said. 'Everyone will make it out.' He was so young." Uncle Nigel's eyes flooded with tears, which he resolutely wiped away.

"I haven't talked about this in a while." He chuckled nervously. "I usually try not to think about it, actually. But it's been on my mind a lot today and I'm thankful you brought it up." He let out a long, weary breath. "I think I really needed to talk about it today. Three people from my morning meeting didn't make it out, you know? And I think about them all the time. And two people from the meeting are here at the party tonight. It was just all so random. It didn't matter if you were young and healthy. Whether you were one of the lucky ones came down to the seemingly meaningless decisions people made."

"I'm thankful you were one of the lucky ones." My eyes prickled with tears.

He squeezed my hand before standing abruptly. He walked over to the desk and began rooting through the box. "Here," he said gently, pulling out a small plastic card and handing it to me. "I used to keep this in my office, but seeing as you are the one with the office now, I think you should have it."

I ran my fingers across the face of the card. It was discolored and tattered, but I could see Uncle Nigel's picture smiling back at me. Even in a photo that resembled a mug shot, he was smiling.

"It's my World Trade Center photo ID. They found hundreds of them in the rubble and returned them to us. I used to keep it in my office. Sort of a reminder of what life is all about."

"Thank you for this," I said, unconsciously holding the card to my heart. "It really means a lot to me." I stood up to give him a hug. "It's your retirement party, though—you're supposed to be *getting* the gifts, not giving them."

He smiled. "I'm just so proud of you, Mac. Everyone is. Thanks for coming out here for all this." He gestured to the sounds of the still bustling party.

"I wouldn't miss it."

"Just don't let it be another *four months* before you come out here again," he teased.

"I won't. Promise." And at the time, I believed it was true.

14

Did I leave the lights on in my office when I left last night? For a brief moment I marveled at how strange it felt to even say it in my mind: *my* office. Sadir had finally moved out into his own office two days ago—long past time for a third year associate, but there'd been a shortage—leaving me the coveted spot by the window. I'd have another officemate in a few weeks when the office shuffle settled, but right now I was relishing having my own space.

I'm certain I turned the lights off and closed the door. I'd gone home around three in the morning to sleep for a few hours, take a shower, and change into my suit of armor. Instinctively, I knew I would need a pick-me-up today, so I'd selected my favorite black, stretch-wool suit with a silk chiffon tank, complemented by beige Louboutin leather pumps. Slung over my shoulder, like a soldier's machine gun, was my leather Alexander Wang flap messenger bag. I was dressed for battle. I might be taking my orders from a sergeant who needed medication to control his anger issues and sharing the barracks with a she-devil, but it didn't matter. In my suit of armor, I *felt* like a lawyer. Invincible.

At the moment, though, wariness crept through my bleary mind. Was someone in there? It was only 8:00 A.M.—too early for Rita to be at work. I quickened my step and charged into my office just as the intruder reached out her arm.

"Mackenzie!" Sarah paused in the act of dropping a marked-up document on my desk. "Look who finally decided to come into work today." I noticed a slight shake in her voice.

"What are you doing in my office, Sarah?" My eyes narrowed.

A strange expression flashed on her face and I swear it was the same one that I'd witnessed when I saw her in the corner of the bar, but it was swiftly replaced with her default expression of indignation. "Giving you this." She held up the clipped pages, marked up in angry red. "My secretary isn't in until nine and the word pro center is jammed—said it will take them five hours to get it back to me—so I need you to turn these changes."

I felt my blood start to simmer. *I will not let her penetrate my suit of armor. I will not let her penetrate my suit of armor.* "I have too much on my plate to do that," I said resolutely.

Her thin lips curled into a smirk. "Well, maybe you don't realize how it works around here, but shit flows downstream." She motioned from herself to me. "These changes need to be inputted this morning. It's for Saul."

"I really don't have time, I have —"

"Mackenzie," she interrupted, waving me away impatiently. "Let me ask you this." Her eyes burrowed into mine and I returned the full force eye contact. "Did you sleep last night?"

"What?"

"Did. You. Sleep. Last. Night." She paused between each word.

I glared at her through my eyebrows, the tension between us so thick you would need a chainsaw to cut it. "Yes," I finally croaked, unclenching my teeth just enough to speak.

"Then you have time." She tossed the document on my desk. And even though the desire to whip off my messenger bag, swing it around like an Olympic decathlete, and hurdle it towards her smug face filled every fiber of my being, I simply followed her with my eyes as she sauntered out of my office.

"Saul's expecting it by eleven," she called on her way out.

I collapsed in my chair, letting out a long, exasperated breath. An odd sensation filled my body, the kind you feel when you think someone was in your house when you weren't there. Scooting my chair up to the keyboard, I vowed I would not let Sarah get to me today, but the heat under my cheeks told me she already had.

———

"This is a great idea." I wrapped my arm through Jason's arm as we made our way across 86th Street towards Central Park.

"Well, it's been a while since you've been outside on a Saturday." He leaned into me, kissing me on the head. "I figured a walk in the park is just what you need."

I'd strategically cleared my Saturday morning to spend some much needed time with Jason. Despite being finished with the document at ten in the evening on Friday, I waited until three in the morning to send Ben a draft of the purchase agreement for his review, knowing that move would buy me a break from the Highlander deal for the day. Ben hated working on Saturdays, thanks to his standing Saturday morning tee time at Scarsdale Country Club. He wouldn't get back to me about the draft until Sunday, leaving my Saturday evening free to catch up on the due diligence in the war room. My moratorium from the Falcon deal, on the other hand, was just luck. I hadn't heard anything from Saul or Sarah since I'd sent them the revised purchase agreement at 11:00 A.M. yesterday, just as Sarah had demanded. Since then it had been eerily silent.

"It is just what I need." I inhaled deeply, basking in the fresh air of freedom. It was one of those beautiful New York City late fall days, the kind that you want to bottle up and store to get you through the winter. It looked like everyone in the entire city was out and about taking advantage of it, pushing baby strollers, carrying shopping bags, riding bikes.

We pushed through the doors of Starbucks. "The usual?" Jason asked and I nodded, marveling in the comfortable feeling of being with someone who knew my usual Starbucks order. Looking at him, so handsome in his perfectly fitted cashmere sweater, my heart overflowed with affection. "You really need to change it up sometime, Mac." He smiled, passing me my extra hot, no foam, nonfat latte.

"You know I'm a creature of habit." I grabbed a cardboard sleeve, slipped it on my cup, and lined it up precisely with the drinking spout before heading back out into the crisp air. I linked my fingers through his and took long gulp of my latte, reveling in the peaceful feeling washing over my body.

"You sure seem happy today. I feel like I have my old girlfriend back now that Saul is off your back."

"He's off my back for now, but knowing Saul he's probably somewhere planning how best to terrorize us in the Monday morning meeting." I pictured Saul in his office, tapping his fingers together like an evil genius and laughing demonically at his twisted plan.

Jason raised a quizzical eyebrow. "Isn't the deal dead?"

"Dead?" I shook my head. "Maybe at an impasse, but I haven't received a pencils down email."

"You haven't?" Jason looked puzzled. "I just figured if you were sprung from the office then the deal must be dead."

"From your lips to God's ears." I gave his hand a light squeeze.

We passed the patch of grass behind the Metropolitan Museum, and I smiled at the sight of a father waving a bubble wand, creating huge bubbles to the joy of his two young sons. "More! More!" they exclaimed.

My mind started to wander. *More. . . .. I wonder if there'll be more diligence that will come in soon . . . maybe even back in Edmonton. Oh God, what if I have to go back and Sarah comes too?* I tried to push the negative thought out of my mind, but I couldn't distract myself from the feeling in the pit of my stomach. Rather than embracing the silence, I was actually starting to worry.

"Well, the break couldn't have come at a better time," Jason said.

"Hmmm?" I murmured distractedly.

"Our anniversary dinner tonight . . . " He trailed off with a meaningful edge to his voice.

"Tonight?" I forced myself back to the present.

"I stuck a note on your computer yesterday. Didn't you see it? I made a reservation at Gramercy Tavern at nine."

I did a quick recalculation of timing. *If I wake up really early tomorrow and hit the ground running, I could have the due diligence memo to Ben by Monday.*

"Sounds perfect." I pulled him close, locking our fingers and leaning in for a kiss. "I bought something I think you'll like which will be perfect for the occasion." I ran my fingers playfully across his chest, thankful for online shopping.

"Mmmm," he groaned.

———

Walking into Gramercy Tavern with Jason's hand on the small of my back, I resolved to put the work stress and recent bickering out of my mind and enjoy an amazing night. I had everything planned—at least in terms of my outfit. I was wearing a super cute red Alice and Olivia sleeveless dress, with matching red, vintage lace bra and panties from La Perla. I was afraid that after spending too much time apart, like we had, we had lost the groove in our relationship, but I was intent on getting it back. Hence the three hundred dollars spent on sexy lingerie. It seemed like Jason had the same desire, because he was completely different than he'd been acting lately—relaxed, attentive, and charming.

"You know who our waiter reminds me of?" He leaned in, whispering slyly.

I snuck a peek at our waiter, now theatrically listing off the specials to the table behind us. "That guy—from that hotel." I wagged my finger at Jason, attempting to conjure up the name.

"Jacques!" Jason rolled his tongue dramatically and I couldn't help laughing. Jacques was the concierge at the hotel where we stayed for Jason's brother's wedding. His brother had married a Southern belle at a beautiful waterfront home in Texas. I'd been worried about attending an event where Jason's entire family would be in attendance, but Jason had assured me the wedding would be low key and everyone would love me. Well, my version of low key and the Kermode version of low key are two different things. His family had rented out an entire 160-room boutique hotel for the out-of-town guests, complete with a concierge named Jacques, who acted as if his greatest joy in life was to please the guests of the hotel. "Please accept this brrrreakfast with our compliments," Jacques had sing-songed, rolling his R's longer than necessary, wheeling in a room-service table a mere ten minutes after we'd arrived. He'd theatrically announced the contents before whisking the silver domed tops off, and gesturing grandly to the most delicious looking bread basket I'd ever laid eyes on. Confident we were appropriately impressed, he then gave a mini bow and excused himself. When we were sure he'd closed the door behind him, we'd looked at each other and dissolved into laughter on the bed.

"Yes!" I slapped my thigh with a laugh. "I haven't thought about Jacques in forever!"

"Jacques would be devastated," Jason tsked. "I'm sure he's thought about *you*, Mac," he deadpanned, his mouth twitching with humor.

"Well, I *have* thought about other parts of that weekend . . . " I entwined my leg with his under the table, slowly working my foot up to his thigh, remembering the mind-blowing sex we'd had. Nothing adds to pleasure like a bottle of expensive champagne from the welcome basket and 800-thread-count Frette sheets. Jason and I barely made it to the wedding. A sizzle of anticipation suddenly coursed through my body. Tonight was going to be good.

"Nuh-uh." Jason shook his head emphatically. "Don't be writing checks you can't cash." There was a devilish glint in his eyes, the same one that always sent a tingle right down to my toes.

"I can cash it after dinner." I smiled coyly, reaching across the table to take hold of his hand. His thumb traced tiny circles on my wrists and our eyes were locked. For a moment we were totally connected, like the past few months hadn't even happened. A minor blip in an otherwise fantastic relationship.

"This is nice," Jason said, breaking the silence. "I've missed you."

"Me too," I murmured, feeling a sense of bliss that was such a departure from my daily routine lately that my body must have sensed something askew. My thoughts suddenly drifted to my Black-Berry sitting in my purse, my pleasurable feelings working like an alarm clock reminding me that I hadn't checked it the whole evening. For most people, keeping their mobile device in their purse rather than on the table during a romantic dinner would help them relax. For me, it triggered nerve-wracking fear and intense anxiety. I glanced down beside me and flinched when I saw it—the blinking red light illuminating the inside of my purse.

Don't check it, Mackenzie, just leave it in your purse, I silently commanded, but my mind started to race. *What if it's Ben? I can't afford to miss another one of his ASAP emails.* "Hold that thought."

I laughed nervously and held up my index finger as I picked up my BlackBerry and clicked on the new message.

To: Mackenzie Corbett
From: Sarah Clarke

The timing on the Falcon transaction has been vastly accelerated. Saul needs you to summarize the indemnity clauses of the last 20 publicly filed purchase agreements in telecommunications industry ASAP. Do NOT send to Saul without my review.

S

"Shit," I whispered, my eyes fixed on the email. I could kill this woman. No jury of my peers would possibly convict me. I slowly lifted my eyes off my BlackBerry, dreading the look that I knew I'd see on Jason's face. "Sorry . . ." I grimaced.

Jason's facial expression fell and it was as if the spell we were both under was suddenly broken. "I thought you said Ben didn't need to see the draft until Monday," he muttered with irritation, grabbing his glass of wine and taking a large gulp while looking anywhere but in my direction.

"It's not for Ben."

Confusion flickered across his face. "A new deal came in on a Saturday night?"

"No, not a new deal. It's the Saul deal."

"Mac, that doesn't make any sense." His tone turned flustered.

"I know. I have no idea why this needs to get done tonight, but you know what he's like." I shook my head with irritation.

"I'm not talking about working on a Saturday night." He stopped short.

"Then I don't get it. Are you upset that I'm leaving our dinner or upset that I'm working for Saul?"

Without answering, he pulled out his BlackBerry and began pecking madly.

127

"What are you doing?"

"I assume we need to get the check?" He hastily looked around for our waiter, without answering my question.

I nodded solemnly and he polished off his glass of wine with purpose. An icy silence descended over the table until our check arrived moments later, and we readied ourselves to leave, skipping the third course of our three-course prix fixe.

Practically jogging after Jason on the way out, I was relieved when he stopped near the subway entrance and turned to face me. I was desperately trying to find the words to explain, but he spoke first. "You can take a cab. I'm going to hop on the train." He shoved his hands in his pockets and stared at the sidewalk.

I wanted him to go back to the way he'd been over dinner, before I checked that stupid thing, but that Jason had left for the evening. I could tell from the look on his face that he wasn't coming back anytime soon either.

"I really *am* sorry about this," I said, stepping closer to him. "I shouldn't even have checked it. It's just . . ." I stopped myself from explaining, for what had to be the hundredth time, that the partners in my department expect you to be available at all times, every day, to answer their emails, and won't tolerate any delay in responding. That I didn't have the option to just leave my BlackBerry in my purse. I knew he wouldn't understand, and frankly I wouldn't have understood either two years ago.

"Make it up to you later?" I offered hopefully.

He mouth twisted as if trying to physically prevent himself from saying what was really on his mind, and, with a curt nod of his head, turned towards the subway entrance.

"Hey!" I called out after him as he descended down the stairs. "Happy anniversary."

He didn't turn around.

———

Monday morning I was sitting at my desk, staring at my computer and munching on a Nutri-Grain bar in between gulps of coffee. I'd worked Saturday night and Sunday on the research and I hadn't seen

Jason since we parted at the subway stairs. I was tired, irritable, and hoping Sarah would leave me alone so I could mentally prepare for the torturous Monday morning meeting, but knew I'd cursed myself by just hoping when, ten minutes later, she appeared at my door.

"Good morning, Mackenzie," she greeted me with a fake smile, twirling a strand of hair around her finger. I looked up from my computer and greeted her with an equally fake smile. The whole room prickled with tension. "The deal is dead," she announced tersely. "Stop all work on it immediately."

"Dead?" I couldn't believe it. I'd sacrificed my whole weekend, not to mention my anniversary with Jason, for nothing? "What happened to the timing of the deal being vastly accelerated?"

"Yeah, turns out Falcon changed their minds and decided to take out a loan instead of selling. Or, as the media reported, they're 'righting the ship themselves.'" She air quoted and rolled her eyes as if it were all too tiring. "Anyhoo," she exhaled loudly, "guess Saul won't be needing that research, so looks like I won't have to review it after all." She paused for a moment, seemingly trying to remember if there was anything else she could do to ruin my day. "Oh—make sure you put in your hours for this deal ASAP. Gotta get the bill out!" With that, she gave me her usual condescending smirk, turned, and click-clacked her way back to her office.

The only people more shocked than me about the Falcon deal dying were the shareholders. *Falcon Mobility Shocker: Buyout Deal Falls Apart; Shares Plummet 22%* screamed the *Wall Street Journal*. The shareholder loss was my gain, though, because now I would be able to devote one hundred percent of my time to Ben's deal, keeping my eyes firmly locked on the prize.

15

PUSHING OPEN THE DOOR to the bathroom on Thursday afternoon, I was hit by a heavy waft of hairspray and perfume. I waved my hand in front of my face in an effort to clear the air to breathe. In the haze and fumes, the secretaries were primping for the F&D holiday party like it was the prom. There were only two times a year the firm opened its wallet and treated the secretaries to an extravagant night out—the holiday party in December and the summer party in August. The rest of the time the firm coffers were strictly reserved for the lawyers.

Merry and bright was not exactly how I was feeling right now. I'd just come back from Ben's office, where, after mustering up the courage, I'd asked if I could go home for a few days for Christmas. I might as well have been Oliver holding out my bowl. *Please sir.*

It was no secret that Biglaw partners did not take kindly to vacation requests. Years back, an associate found a PowerPoint presentation, titled "Associate Communication," on the firm's internal document system, presumably used to teach partners how to interact with associates. The stealthy associate posted it on the legal blog Above the Law for all to see. Slide after slide urged partners to "say 'thank you' and 'good work'" when dealing with associates. One slide suggested that partners "be sensitive to cancelling associates' vacations," reminding them that associates have families too. I remember wondering what kind of adult was so socially inept that he had to be taught to say please and thank you. But clearly Ben had missed the memo because his response was, "This isn't a good time. Can't you just move your vacation?"

I blinked at him. *Ummm . . . not unless I can move the birth of Jesus.* "Well, I'm going for Christmas, so . . . "

"Right, right," Ben interrupted, his tone exasperated from my perceived foolishness. "But Mackenzie, don't you think we *all* would like to see our families over the holidays?" He raised a condescending eyebrow.

The thought occurred to me that very few people in this firm wanted to spend *any* time with their families. If they did, they would stop reviewing a document for the fifth time, hoping to catch a comma out of place, and go home and actually *be with their families.* But of course I didn't say that. I merely nodded remorsefully.

"It's the nature of the beast, Mackenzie," he said before his stern expression softened. "You're doing a great job with Highlander and your hard work is not going unnoticed, but we're coming up on crunch time. Look, I won't require you to cancel your trip altogether, but I'll expect you back bright and early on the 26th, and take a laptop so you can work remotely on Christmas Day. Good?" He flashed what I'm sure he thought was a benevolent smile. In his mind he'd just fulfilled his charitable giving quota for the season.

"Of course," I'd affirmed, biting my lower lip. "Thanks, Ben." *God bless us everyone.*

"What'd ya think, Mackenzie?" Rita called out now, posing with her hands in the air.

I squinted through the heavy fog of aerosol. If her dress were any lower cut I would've seen nipple; if it were any shorter I would've seen butt cheek. Just the look she was going for, I was sure. Rita recently had breast implants and it looked like she was ready to show off her new assets. They'd been large enough before—probably a size C, but she was certain even bigger boobs were the missing link to landing a man.

"No guy evah says, 'I can't get with her—her boobs are too *big*,'" she'd explained, as I signed her sick leave request form for her surgery. When she'd returned to work two weeks later, she came into my office with her twenty-three-year old daughter in tow, both sticking out their chests, smiling proudly. They'd received the mother-daughter special and insisted that I touch them to see how they felt. "Totally natural," Rita's daughter Skyler squealed. I poked the side of one awkwardly as Rita explained how she had to massage them daily to keep them soft. "It's like being forced to play with ya' self!" Rita cackled. Rita wasn't exactly the boundaries type.

I shuffled through the secretaries, avoiding their glares, trying to get closer to Rita. "You look gorgeous!" I lied.

She grinned mischievously. "Every year Freddie and I make out at the holiday party—kinda a tradition," she said, applying her lipstick and smacking her lips together. That was one holiday tradition I really did not want to know about. Not exactly the "leave cookies out for Santa" kind. I wondered if Freddie stopped mid-make-out to pick his nose.

"You going?" Rita asked, thankfully cutting short my visual of her and Freddie. Despite the fact that office festivity was essentially forbidden, everyone was encouraged to attend the annual firm holiday party. "No guests," the invitation instructed, just the firm family—lawyers, paralegals, secretaries, and those on the F&D payroll. I'd attended the party last year and for the most part it was your typical drunken debauchery office party, but there was always some partner trolling for associates who don't have enough work on their plates and hitting them with the dreaded "What are you working on these days?" question. Associates hate this question—it's cloaked in a friendly interest in your life, but really means, "Can I stick you with some tedious weekend due diligence?"

133

"If I ever finish the research Ben gave me." Another lie.

Rita waved her finger at me accusingly. "Nahhhh . . . you're going to skip it and have wild sex with that cute boyfriend of yours instead, aren't you?" She whooped and hooted at her own joke.

"You know me too well," I chuckled, playing along, trying to remember how long it had been since Jason and I even had any kind of sex, let alone wild sex. Lately, we'd fallen into a pretty lackluster routine of cuddling for a few minutes before passing out asleep. That needed to be remedied ASAP. Well, maybe not the going down to his office this minute and doing it on his desk type of ASAP, but tonight at least.

> **Mackenzie:** Wanna blow off the party tonight and have more fun at my place ;)
>
> **Jason:** Ummm . . . do you even have to ask?
>
> **Mackenzie:** See you there at 9!

At 8 P.M. I was huddled in my office, long after Rita and her cohorts had left for the party, when Jason and Alex appeared at my door. "Come on, keener—libations await," Alex announced.

"You're going to have to head over without me. I need to finish this research for Ben." I let out a long exhale, trying to sound particularly overwhelmed. I knew Alex wouldn't accept the "Jason and I need time alone" excuse. For Alex there is no good reason not to take advantage of free booze and food. I gave Jason a significant look, assuring he was in on the ruse.

"Ben? Ben isn't going to read *anything* tonight. He left an hour ago—which means he's been feeding some poor secretary overly strong drinks for, oh . . ." Alex looked at his watch, "the past forty-five minutes in hopes of getting her drunk enough to let him grope her."

"Ew." I made a face. "You're not exactly selling this party to me. I've already had the disgusting visual of Freddie making out with Rita. I don't need you throwing Ben into the mix."

"Threesome with Ben, Rita, and Freddie—kinky, Mac, kinky." Alex looked as though he was contemplating the possibility. "Anyway, no one will read what you produce tonight, so get your ass off that chair and come get drunk with us," he said, shaking my chair. "It's celebration time, in case you're too busy with work to be reading your emails. Our golden handcuffs just got tighter."

The managing partner had sent around the bonus memo a few hours ago, informing us there would be a $10,000 increase in bonuses across the board, and heartfelt thanks from the partners for our dedication and efforts. It had been met by gleeful fist pumps from the associates and promises of a night of hearty celebrating. If it was true that we were selling our souls, it was good to know our souls were worth $10,000 more than they were last year. But I had my own celebration in mind and it didn't involve F&D.

"Look at me!" I gestured up and down at my makeup-free face, my hair desperately in need of a haircut, my wrinkled shirt which I'd done my best to iron, but still looked like I'd slept in it. "Do I really look like I'm dressed for a *party*?" I glanced down at my feet. "Look!" I pointed to my toes visible in my Stuart Weitzman peep toe pumps. "My polish is even chipped!" Using my appearance as one more reason I couldn't go to the party made me realize how much it had slipped. When I had time I really needed to attend to that. *To-do list: 1. Get haircut 2. Pick up dry cleaning 3. Get pedicure.*

"You look as beautiful as you always do." Jason placed his hands on my shoulders, giving me a ten second massage.

Mmmm . . . tonight is going to be good.

"And I think Jason has a lot of work to do too . . . " I trailed off, waiting for Jason to pipe up.

"This guy?" Alex pointed to Jason with an amused expression. "When have you ever known this guy to work late? I think it may even be outlawed in the Trusts department."

I lifted my head and locked eyes with Jason, attempting a silent, coded conversation.

"Could be fun. We do need to celebrate." He shrugged, giving a sheepish half smile.

I shook my head in mock disapproval. He'd fallen prey to the powers of Alex's persuasion.

Jason cleared his throat. "Maybe I'll wait here until Mac is ready and we'll meet—"

"She's ready." Alex stopped him midsentence, waving his hand dismissively. "Even with your laissez faire attitude towards your appearance, which I've been meaning to tell you isn't exactly working for you, you know you still look better than the majority of those horse faces at that party, and you can hide those unsightly toes with a pair of those." He pointed down to the mini shoe closet that had sprung up underneath my desk. "And I know your next excuse is going to be you're too tired, but we can just prop you up 'Weekend at Bernie's' style and stick a drink in your hand."

I had to hand it to him—Alex was persuasive. Even when my decisions were set in stone, he could always convince me otherwise. I couldn't blame Jason for folding too.

"Now up, up!" He gestured towards the door. "Libations await!"

———

Walking into the ballroom of the W Hotel in Midtown, I was overwhelmed by the sheer opulence. Crab legs, shrimp, and lobster tails sat piled high on an ice sculpture, a giant, decorative gingerbread arch marked the way to the dessert room (a whole room filled with every kind of dessert I had ever seen or even dreamed of seeing), and champagne was being poured into elegant towers of glasses. Waitresses were making their way around the room with trays of sushi and cocktail napkins emblazoned with the firm logo. The setting was striking, but the location was selected strategically, of course—close enough to the firm office so that lawyers could easily return to bill more hours after the party.

A waiter passed with a tray of champagne glasses and we each took one. "Bottoms up," Alex called out as we clinked glasses and looked around, taking it all in. The room was crowded, buzzing with conversation, and the dance floor was full. The secretaries and mail staff danced to the beat of the live band enthusiastically, while the associates stood off to the side, drinking and scrolling through their email. A few drunk male partners attempted to dance, seizing their one opportunity to grind up against the secretaries, but it just looked like spastic pelvic motions.

"Well, good to see superfluous over-spending is alive and well in Biglaw." Alex raised his glass in a mock toast.

"Hear, hear." I drained my champagne and put the glass down on the empty table beside us.

"Looks like we need another," Alex announced before weaving through a crowd of paralegals doing shots of Patrón. I watched for a moment with morbid fascination as two of them started dirty dancing, complete with Miley Cyrus-style twerking.

"And he's off!" Jason gestured to the bar, where Alex was surrounded by a group of admiring, giggling girls just as he was at every firm party, and probably every day since he'd grown into his ruggedly handsome good looks.

"If I hear him call them 'fresh meat' one more time I'm going to be sick," I said, glaring at the display. Every year before the new class of first year associates join the firm, a book of their headshots appears in each employee's inbox, with a short bio beside each picture. It was supposed to give us some information about the incoming class so we could call them by name, thus making them feel welcome, but instead its arrival resulted in male lawyers huddling in each other's offices assessing the "fresh meat," as Alex put it. Not exactly the warm, welcoming display HR had in mind.

"Ahhh . . . and it's Monica," Jason pointed out. Monica was the one Alex had deemed the hottest from the headshots. I knew from her bio that she enjoyed traveling, learning new languages, and step aerobics. Seriously—step aerobics. What was this, 1992?

"Guess we won't be hearing from him the rest of the night. Or tomorrow morning for that matter," he joked and I felt a tiny twinge of jealousy. "So," Jason started, switching gears. "Should we plan this vacation?"

137

"Yes—let's." I smiled, turning my attention back to him.

After the anniversary debacle I'd come up with the brilliant idea of taking a vacation together after the Highlander deal was over. "Someplace with no BlackBerry reception," I'd promised, selling the idea to Jason. Did that even exist anymore? I hoped so. I pictured myself lounging in an oversized chair in the sand sipping a fruity cocktail with an umbrella in it, watching Jason surf . . . or snorkel . . . or whatever it is people on vacation do. I could get a tan, forget my troubles, wear something other than boring office clothes. Of course, I knew Jason had his complaints about this relationship lately, and frankly so did I. I wasn't too far gone to notice that things hadn't been the same between us. But a vacation could make that all right. We could finally get to spend some real time together—not just the tail-end of a stressful day. It was exactly what we needed.

We drained another glass of champagne and ran through the details. Should we pick Aruba, Saint Lucia, or the Bahamas? (He thought Saint Lucia, I thought Aruba.) Should we get a suite? (Definitely—preferably with an ocean view.) Should we do all inclusive? (No—we wanted the freedom to try different local restaurants.) Part of the fun of vacations is the anticipation and I was enjoying bringing this trip to life with Jason.

"One more?" Jason pointed down to our empty glasses.

"Sounds good. Let's try one of those red ones." I gestured to the waiter carrying a tray full of festive looking red cocktails garnished with green berries. It was called the "F&D Holiday Cheer," a specialty cocktail designed by the W Hotel's resident mixologist specifically for the party — peach nectar, two kids of rum, pomegranate juice, and club soda. We ordered two from the bartender and headed towards an empty table.

"Be right back," Jason announced, putting the cocktails down on the table and turning to snake through the crowds to the bathroom.

I stood by the table, sipping my F&D Holiday Cheer and swaying to the beat of the music. I was feeling loose from the alcohol when I heard the familiar voice.

"Three olive martini. Got that? THREE. OLIVE. MARTINI." Pause. "Say it back to me then so I know you get it. I don't have the time for you to screw it up," Saul barked from a table right beside me.

I froze, like a gazelle trying to avoid being detected by a stalking cheetah. No. Sudden. Movements.

"Three. Olive. Martini," the waitress responded with a visible eye roll.

"Right: not ONE, not TWO, THREE." Saul held up three fingers condescendingly.

I slunk into myself and started to back away, ensuring I didn't turn my back on my predator. To do so would surely result in an immediate strike.

I need to get out of here, I thought, frantically scanning the room for Jason. I spotted him outside the bathroom animatedly telling a story to a group of associates. Now I just needed to figure out a way to signal him to pull the fire alarm to create a diversion.

"Mackenzie," Saul called out, interrupting my thoughts.

Shit. Should I play dead?

"One of the many corporate junior associates I've seen tonight. Clearly we aren't keeping you guys busy enough." A smattering of spittle hit my cheek as he spoke. I surreptitiously picked up a cocktail napkin to wipe it off, as his eyes wandered to my chest and stayed there. He seemed to have an inability to look me in the eye when he was drunk, and not just because I was two inches taller than him.

"Oh, I won't be staying long—plenty to do back at the office," I responded enthusiastically, unsure if he was being facetious. The last thing I wanted was Saul to think I had any gaps in my time sheet. Gaps that could be filled by his torturous work. The waitress returned with Saul's three olive martini. Not surprisingly, it contained a trio of olives, and likely a huge wad of spit.

"Glad to hear it." He paused to burp and picked up his fresh drink. "Try this for me," he demanded, aggressively placing it down in front of me. "Tell me if it's okay. The last one had way too much fucking vermouth and I'm going to tear that fucking bartender a new asshole if he's done it to me again." For a moment I thought he was joking, but judging from the permanent scowl on his face, I was fairly certain Saul wasn't exactly the joshing type.

139

I tentatively picked up the martini glass and put my lips to the rim. My eyes darted around the room for the waitress, hopeful she'd give me a sign if there was something disgusting in the drink meant for Saul. "It's . . . um . . . it's good," I said, returning the drink to the table and sliding it back to him.

Shooting me a skeptical glare, he picked up the glass and took a hostile gulp. "I'm happy to hear you have other work keeping you busy. I can't fucking stand it when a deal dies on a Friday, making associates idle. Nothing worse than an entire weekend with no billable hours."

"Friday?" I must have misheard. I tried to block out the loud music in the background. The deal hadn't died on Friday—it died on a *Monday*. After the weekend. After the disastrous interrupted anniversary dinner. After I worked on his spur of the moment research request. After I seriously considered clubbing Sarah, Tonya Harding-style. Monday.

"I told Sarah after it died that I wanted everyone's hours posted by Friday evening," he said, ignoring my question. "And I noticed you were the only one who didn't have them in. Not until *Monday*. You too fucking busy to get your hours in?" He glared at me, gulped down the last of his drink, and immediately looked around the room for a waitress.

"I—I didn't know . . . " I stuttered, my brain fried from lack of sleep and, ironically, the F&D Holiday Cheer. "But you requested that research over the weekend . . . " I started to say in confusion, sounding more like I was asking a question than giving an answer.

"What the hell are you talking about, Mackenzie? What fucking research? The fucking deal died on a Friday. Friiiii-daaaay," he repeated, drawing out each syllable condescendingly and I could feel his spittle spray on my face again. "Why the fuck would I ask you to do research on a Saturday?"

Um . . . that's what I was wondering, but like most of Saul's questions, I knew it was a rhetorical one.

He peered down at his empty glass, frowning. "Geez, is it this woman's mission in life not to serve me?" He looked around the room incredulously and marched away towards the bar. I was left standing, mouth gaping open in disbelief, trying to absorb what he'd just said.

————

"Okay, now you're just starting to sound paranoid, Mackenzie," Jason said, removing his coat and collapsing on my couch. We had stayed at the party for about an hour after my run-in with Saul, enough time to down another much-needed drink and fill a plastic bag full of candy from the dessert room (also much needed). I didn't tell Jason about the conversation until we were in the cab on our way back to my apartment, wanting to fully digest what Saul had said and figure out what it meant. "You really think that this girl, who doesn't even really *know* you, wants to get you FIRED?" He grabbed a sour patch kid from the bag and popped it in his mouth. "Why would she do that? Why would she pick on YOU?"

"I know it sounds crazy!" I flopped down on the couch next to him and rummaged through the bag for a chocolate malt ball. "But you don't *know* this girl." My hazy mind suddenly flashed back to the party, and the sight of a hostile, pencil-thin silhouette that stuck out from the group. "Wait, was I having a vodka-fueled hallucination or was the she-devil in the group of associates you were talking to outside the bathroom?"

"Outside the bathroom?" He paused, as if running through mental images from the evening. "Maybe. I don't really remember."

"I didn't realize you two knew each other."

"Yeah. We sat next to each other in a CLE a few weeks ago," he added flippantly, tossing a peanut butter cup into his mouth.

I stared at him bewilderedly.

"Didn't I tell you that?"

I shook my head.

"Oh, I thought I did." He shrugged. "Hey, did you know she's a Columbia alum? She actually chairs the women's alumni association. The youngest woman ever to do that. I remember hearing about her in law school, but I didn't put the pieces together that it was the same Sarah Clarke." He said this with an impressed tone, and I felt my lip curl.

141

Sarah chaired an association dedicated to helping other women? *Oh, right,* I thought, rolling my eyes. *How could I forget her obvious commitment to the whole women's movement?*

"Anyway, from the way you described her, I thought she'd have horns and a tail, but she actually ended up being pretty nice. Even lent me a pen."

"Nice?" I repeated after a pause. "Have you not been listening? The woman *torments* me! Is that what you consider nice?"

"I just mean she didn't seem as bad as you described her." He shrugged.

I could feel a ball of frustration. Sarah tortures me for months, but she goes and lends him a pen and suddenly he thinks she's *nice*? Even if I was being completely irrational in my revulsion for Sarah (which I wasn't), isn't it the job of a boyfriend to dislike everyone

I dislike? Okay, maybe not *everyone*, but certainly the people that strive to make my life miserable.

"Jason, she just INVENTED this research! Saul had absolutely NO idea what I was talking about." I threw my arms up dramatically.

"Mackenzie," Jason started, in a tone that should be reserved for talking someone off the side of an office building. "I saw Saul—he was so drunk he probably had no idea what HE was talking about," he reasoned. "Remember, in Saul's world, days of the week don't matter—to him Friday is interchangeable with Monday. They're all working days, all days that are fit for abusing associates."

He had a point. Hadn't Saul always been wrong about the deadlines he imposed? He'd say Wednesday, but he meant Monday. I guess this didn't have to be any different.

"Why do you always have to be so . . . logical," I mumbled as Jason leaned in for a kiss. I melted into him and completely forgot about Sarah or Saul or anything else but us.

16

I sat at my desk gazing out the window, basking in the last few minutes of peace as the buzz of a new day began outside my door. The view from my office never failed to put me in a good mood, but at daybreak it was really stunning. I loved the way the morning sun glinted off the skyscrapers, making them appear golden, like a gift from the New York City gods for coming into work so early.

"Mackenzie," Rita hissed, padding into my office and closing the door. She looked rough, making me wonder if she was still feeling the effects of the holiday party.

"Morning, Rita." I swiveled my chair towards her, giving her my full attention. "What's up?"

She wrung her hands, looking like a child bringing home a terrible report card. "I gaw-ta ask ya' something."

"Is everything okay?"

"Well, is this firm okay?" She crossed her arms over her chest, raising an accusatory eyebrow. "Because if you law-yahs are running some kinda Ponzi scheme, tell me now so I can get another job."

I looked at her sideways.

She leaned closer and lowered her voice. "A guy came to see Vince today. A guy who looked just like Mr. Clean. You know the guy on the commercials?"

I nodded.

"Anyway, he even had the earring and everything. He said he was from the Securities and Exchange Enforcement Division."

I raised my eyebrows. I have to admit I was somewhat impressed that Rita knew what that was.

"I just finished a book about that crook Bernie Madoff," Rita explained, as if reading my mind. "I like that true crime stuff." She shrugged. "So when I brought them their coffee I made sure I left the door open a crack so I could listen. It wasn't easy with all the phones ringin', but I heard enough." She darted her eyes behind her, as if she was worried someone had followed her into the office. Then, in a voice as soft as she was capable of, she whispered, "Mackenzie, the firm's bein' *investigated*."

"Investigated for what?" I was used to Rita's tendency to exaggerate. She often read the National Enquirer at her desk, regaling me with stories about possible alien encounters and reincarnations. And in her mind, all weather reports were weather *emergencies*.

"He said somethin' about unusual trading on deals F&D has negotiated. Are you guys awwwl gettin' hauled outta here in handcuffs?" Her eyes widened fearfully.

For a moment I enjoyed the wonderful visual of Saul being handcuffed and dragged out of the building, but the worried look in Rita's eyes snapped me back to reality. I mustered my calmest tone. "Rita, nobody is getting hauled out of here in handcuffs. Whenever there's any unusual trading after a deal the SEC approaches everyone involved—all the law firms, the banks, the clients—and asks them to compile a list of people who worked on the deal. All they're doing is generating a list of all the insiders and making sure none of those people did any trading." I'd always thought these types of requests came in a letter rather than a personal visit from the SEC, but I could tell Rita needed to be talked off the ledge, so I didn't mention that.

"So you knew about this visit from Mr. Clean?"

"No, but it's standard practice," I assured her.

She nodded slowly. "I guess that makes sense. I did fig-yah if somethin' shady was goin' on you at least woulda cut me in on it."

"You know I would," I replied, still chuckling at the idea of every F&D lawyer being rounded up by the Feds.

"Good." She grabbed a Diet Coke off of the shelf and popped it open. "You know, it's beginning to look like you're setting up house in here." She gestured to my bookshelves, lined with sixteen cans of Diet Coke and seven bottles of Poland Spring water. My drawers were filled with packets of random condiments—soy sauce, salad dressing, ketchup, pepper. I had six pairs of shoes tucked under my desk and a clean, pressed suit hanging from the hook on the back of my door. Three tubes of lip balm and five handiwipes sat in my paperclip holder for the times during the day that I needed to look presentable, the handiwipes often being a substitute for a shower. If someone had closed the door and locked me in there I probably could have survived for days before I needed to call for help. Weeks if someone would slip a few fruit roll-ups under the door.

"If I roll a bed in here, call Hoarders."

"You workin' late again tonight?"

I nodded.

"How can ya get by on so little sleep, Mac?" I had once wondered the same thing when I'd watched the movie *Wall Street.* How do people keep working if they don't sleep? At some point don't you just tip over? The answer for me so far was no—I had yet to actually cease functioning. Somehow the body keeps going. Maybe it's muscle memory. My body was just doing what it had done thousands of times before—walking, talking, reading. That's the only way I could explain how I was still standing upright when I was this exhausted.

"It'll get better soon," I assured her. *It'll get better soon.*

———

"Okay, how fast are we moving through the supply contracts?" I flipped the page of the due diligence checklist. It was 9 P.M.—dinner time in the war room—but I wanted to multitask, so I asked Patrick to give me a quick update on the due diligence while we waited for our Chinese food to arrive.

"Snail's pace, but it's not our fault," Patrick replied. "They haven't provided most of them yet. They've left placeholders where they should be, but when we click on it, no document."

I nodded, making a note to follow up with the company on the timeframe of when they'd post the rest of the documents.

"Food's here," Gavin announced, lugging three large plastic bags into the war room. We tore into the bags, announcing the contents of each steaming aluminum container we opened as we distributed them across the conference room table. Then we divvied up the twenty cans of soda.

With forty dollars allotted to associates for dinner, we could order whatever type of food we desired and, if we allocated our dinner funds right, there was some left over to stock our office with snacks and drinks. Candy bars, soda, fruit, bags of nuts, boxes of cereal, cookies, granola bars, milk, crackers, cheese and even wine could all be purchased from Seamless. So, if your meal was only fifteen dollars, you threw in ten bottles of water for later. Everyone made sure to take full advantage of the perk, gathering granola bars and Gatorade like they were canned goods that might be needed in an apocalypse. Spend anything less than forty dollars and you were shortchanging yourself.

Of course, with so many Type A personalities in one place, it wasn't long before someone took grocery shopping on Seamless up a notch. Michael Henderson, an entrepreneurial associate in the Finance department, found a way to make a profit from the perk. He would order the least expensive dinner and use the rest of the allocated money on various grocery items to stockpile in his office. Then he'd sell the stockpiled drinks and edibles to other associates for fifty cents apiece. His office became known as "Henderson's Bodega" among the associates and was always open for business. Craving a Twix at 2 A.M.? You just headed down to Henderson's Bodega and dropped fifty cents into the money jar. It was the honor system, but as far as I know, everyone always paid. We wouldn't have ripped off one of our own. At the end of each month Michael would empty the jar and use the money to buy lottery tickets. "I like to refer to it as my 'exit plan,'" he would proudly tell other associates. "One of these days I'm going to hit it big and then 'fuck you, F&D,'" he'd say, sticking up his middle finger. Clearly a man with a dream.

"You know, this war room is like Las Vegas," I observed, filling my plate with chicken and broccoli, steamed dumplings, pork fried rice, and beef chow mein. "There aren't any windows, so you have no idea what time of day it is, and someone keeps bringing you food." Patrick looked around, considering this.

"Nah, Vegas at least has booze. I think it looks more like an insane asylum. It smells like a mix of stale old food and body odor, and I think I see a puddle of drool over there." He gestured to the corner of the mahogany table. "The only thing missing is someone babbling in the corner. Give it a couple hours and Gavin may be doing just that." We all laughed, enjoying our first bites of another Highlander-sponsored dinner in our adopted dining room.

Staring down at my plate of greasy Chinese food, my mind drifted back to the weekend I'd visited Jason during winter break of our final year of law school. I'd taken the bus from D.C. right after my last exam, unable to wait another minute to see him. Jason had offered to pay for an Amtrak ticket, wanting me to have a more comfortable trip, but I declined. My small town sensibilities just couldn't justify the additional hundred dollars for a train ticket when both take you to the same place. But after taking one look at the smelly, rundown bus without any bathroom or food, transporting passengers that looked like they'd escaped from a penitentiary, I would've paid double that amount for a seat that didn't have a pointy spring poking directly into the small of my back. When I finally arrived in Chinatown after my seven hour ordeal at just after eleven in the evening, Jason was waiting for me. He took one look at my frazzled, hungry face and shepherded me to the nearest restaurant. It was just a tiny hole in the wall called Prosperity Dumpling, but I dug into that dim sum with the enthusiasm of someone who'd been adrift at sea for days. We curled up in the corner booth for a couple hours, feasting on dumplings and drinking Tsingtao, joking about making dim sum a weekly ritual when I lived in New York. "Maybe we'll both quit our jobs and write a travel book," Jason teased. "We'll call it *Adventures in Dim Sum*."

I poked at a piece of steamed broccoli, suddenly wanting nothing more than to be at home, snuggled next to Jason. Kim didn't know what she was talking about. Of course I wanted to move in with Jason. I was just being practical about it.

"Did you hear the Wondermart deal died?" Patrick asked, wolfing down his sweet and sour pork and interrupting my thoughts. "Ben was working on that one, so looks like he'll have more time now to micromanage us."

My heart did a little leap. I knew from Sadir's latest that Sarah was working on that deal too.

"Looks like Sarah will have to find another ass to kiss then," Gavin replied in between bites. "She's been stuck to him like gum on the bottom of his shoe."

I could feel my shoulders tense. Gavin was never in the loop with firm gossip. If he was thinking Sarah was sucking up to Ben, he must have witnessed it himself.

"I've got a feeling she's kissing more than just his ass," Patrick snorted.

I choked on my mouthful of chow mein.

"You okay, Mac?"

I nodded, before pounding my chest and taking a swig of Diet Coke. "Fine," I croaked. Visions of Sarah sauntering into Ben's office in her red stilettos filled my mind. Would she really be trying to sleep her way to the top? I rubbed my temples in an attempt to purge the thought from my mind and forced myself to think about it rationally. Ben had entrusted me with the biggest deal in the firm for a reason. I was busting my butt to close that deal. I refused to let Sarah get inside my head and make me doubt myself.

"Hey, where's Sheldon been today?" I asked, seizing the opportunity to change the subject. Sheldon usually didn't eat dinner with us. We'd asked him a few times and he politely declined before confiding in Patrick that he preferred to eat alone. He explained that as a Mormon he believed that mealtime was a time to build up the body, improve endurance, and enhance intellect. A time to treat your body like a temple. I guess seeing us chow down on greasy Chinese food somehow interfered with this goal. But I hadn't seen him since yesterday, which was unusual.

"The computer he was working on is having issues, so he's working back in his office today until IT can come and fix it," Patrick answered, between munches.

Knowing that Sheldon needed constant supervision to make sure he stayed on the right track, I headed down to his office after dinner. We had a lot of documents to slog through and the last thing I wanted was him spending all night reviewing one document and getting bogged down in too much detail. I didn't have time for another summary of the grammatical errors in a contract.

"Hey, Sheldon." I tapped on the door of the office he shared with another junior associate, realizing I'd never actually been in his office. His desk was immaculately clean—not one messy stack of paper. In fact, there wasn't *any* paper on it. Just a cup full of pens and one of those huge ink-blotter desk calendars in the leather holder in the center of his desk. Next to his desk was a large cardboard cut-out of what appeared to be a person.

"Oh!" He popped up from his desk like a jack-in-the-box. "Hi . . . Ma . . . Mackenzie," he stuttered nervously. His face flushed to such a dark shade of red that you would have thought I caught him looking at porn on his computer or something. Which I was sure Sheldon didn't do because I happened to know that his Church forbids it. He told Patrick that all married men at his Church are required to record any sexual urge they have in a diary and meet with a support group weekly to discuss their diary entries. I kid you not. I didn't even want to think about that meeting.

"Ummm . . . what's that?" I asked, pointing to the mysterious cardboard cutout looming beside his desk, praying it wasn't some life-size stripper that would have to be recorded in his diary.

"This? It's a life-size cutout of Abe Lincoln!" he answered excitedly, turning the figure around so I could see. Okaaay . . . this guy was even kookier than I thought. Had I underestimated Sheldon? Was he the type of guy you see on CNN that brings a gun to work and unleashes a spray of bullets on all of us sinners? I could just imagine the interview: *Were there any signs that Sheldon was crazy? Well, let's see, you mean other than the masturbation journal and the giant cardboard Abe Lincoln in his office?*

"What do you think?" Sheldon grinned widely at me. It was the most animated I'd ever seen him.

"Hmmm . . ." I didn't know what to say. I certainly didn't want to be the first one shot if he did end up going postal. I gripped my chin pensively. "I always thought Abe was taller." It was the best I could come up with.

"Wow—good eye, Mackenzie!" He looked at me in astonishment. "Abe actually WAS two inches taller. According to history books . . ."

"Sheldon," I interrupted. I had to know. "Can I ask WHY you have a life-size cutout of Abe Lincoln?"

He looked at me like the answer was obvious. "Not only was Honest Abe a great president, he was also a great lawyer. I couldn't think of anything more inspiring to look at when I come into the office every day." He gazed admiringly at Abe. Looking at Sheldon's devotion to his hero, I couldn't help but envy that he'd managed to find a role model. Sure, he had to look outside of Biglaw and this century for inspiration, but at least he'd found it. Tonight the only thing that inspired me was the dangling carrot of a good night's sleep. Unfortunately for me, it didn't come in a life-size cutout.

———

Two days later, while digging into dinner at my desk (a shrimp salad from the cafeteria salad bar), I finally opened the email from Mom, which I realized with a pang of guilt had been sitting in my inbox, unread, for over a week. Usually Mom thinks some disaster has happened if I don't return a phone call or email within the hour, so I knew she'd be fretting.

To: Mackenzie Corbett
From: Mom

Hi Honey,

We'll pick you up from the train station tomorrow morning. Just let us know what train you'll be on and we'll be there with bells on (Christmas bells!) Ho, Ho, Ho!

xo Mom

Christmas. The word blinked at me from my inbox like a neon sign. Tomorrow was Christmas. I couldn't believe it was here already. I'm one of those people that eagerly anticipates the arrival of Santa in the Macy's Thanksgiving Day parade, ushering in the season. I love Christmas carols, the scent of pine and balsam, and even shopping on Black Friday. This year, though, I'd spent Black Friday fielding angry emails from Saul, and had yet to inhale the scent of a Christmas tree (unless the pine scented air freshener in the bathroom counts). The only carols I'd heard were playing in Starbucks while I impatiently waited for my morning caffeine fix. I couldn't imagine feeling any less festive right now. The one reminder that it even was the holiday season was the eight foot, decorated tree in the lobby that I passed every morning on my way to the elevator and again every evening on my way out. And I wouldn't call it festive as much as I would call it patronizing, like it was saying to me, "Hope I provide you some Christmas joy in your dreary day!" accompanied by a gentle pat on the back.

I reread Mom's email. I found her enthusiasm . . . exhausting. *This is absolutely the worst time to be heading home to visit my family*, I thought. I had so much work to do, and if I wasn't working I'd rather be . . . sleeping.

I wasn't in the mood to answer the questions about my job that would inevitably be posed by neighbors and extended family. "When will you go to court?" (Never, I do corporate law, not litigation.) "Is it really like how it is on TV?" (You mean introducing a piece of evidence at the last minute to save your case and then celebrating with your hard-bodied colleagues at nearby bar? No.) "Can you help my brother get out of jury duty?" (No. And sitting reading the paper all day waiting for your name to be called sounds like heaven to me—he should be thankful.)

But the most irritating question about my job usually came from Mom in the form of something like "Why don't you just tell them you're too *tired* to work that late?" (Because, through decades of peer pressure, lawyers have deemed exhaustion, or any other reason, an inadequate explanation for not working.)

There was no point in saying that to my parents. They'd never get it. How could they? Jobs weren't considered a 24/7 commitment when they were starting their careers. There was no email, no Black-Berries, no way of getting a hold of you when you weren't near a phone. When you left work you knew you were done for the day. They had no concept of the demands of Biglaw, just as I hadn't until I lived it.

I'll take the 6:14 A.M. train Christmas morning, stay Christmas Day, and come back early on the 26th, I reasoned with myself. *Ben couldn't balk at that, could he? I'll barely be there long enough to open presents.* Then it hit me. Presents. I forgot the presents. I couldn't show up without Christmas presents. I looked at the time—7:38 P.M. *Shit, shit, shit!* I grabbed my coat and headed to the only place close to the office that would be open at this time on Christmas Eve—Duane Reade.

I nearly knocked into the automatic doors on my way in. Why do they make those things open so damn slowly? Once inside, my eyes darted around the store frantically as I tried to make a mental list of people I needed to buy for. Knowing that every minute spent shopping was one less minute I would be sleeping tonight, I grabbed a plastic basket from a stack by the door and raced around the aisles, tossing in anything that would be a suitable gift for anyone on my list. *An umbrella—perfect! Isn't Dad always saying he loses his umbrellas?* In the basket it went. Next aisle. *An Oil of Olay gift set—Mom's skin could use some moisturizer, right?* I shrugged and threw it in the basket. Next aisle. A new hair dryer for my sister. *Well, she's always blow drying her hair, right? Like every morning! She probably needs a new hairdryer!* In the basket. Next aisle. Adidas cologne for my brother-in-law. *He's sporty—I'm sure he wants to smell that way.* Next aisle. A stuffed cat in a Santa outfit with the words "Meowy Christmas" printed across the front. *Kids can't get enough stuffed animals, right?* I grabbed two—one for each nephew.

I headed to the line to pay, tossing random bags of Christmas candy in the basket on the way. I could use the candy to fill out the gifts a bit. Everyone likes candy! A box of Hawaiian Punch-flavored candy canes, a bag of red and green sugared gum drops, a foil wrapped chocolate Santa. Perfect. Christmas shopping done in record time.

Exactly twenty-eight minutes after I'd left my office, I was dashing through the lobby at breakneck speed, nearly bowling over a delivery man, causing him to drop his large plastic bags full of Chinese food. "Sorry," I muttered as my shopping bags swung wildly. No time to stop and help. Passing the Christmas tree, I felt it shake its head in disapproval.

Don't you dare judge me, tree, I thought as I stepped into the elevator and repeatedly pressed the button for twenty-seven. *These are perfectly acceptable Christmas gifts.* But still the tree stared, judging. "Screw you, tree," I mumbled, glaring at it as the doors closed.

Back in my office, I flung myself down in my chair and peered into my bag, surveying my purchases. The candy looked like it was from last year. Does candy ever expire? And did I really buy Adidas cologne? Should a company that is known for making something that goes on your feet really be in the fragrance industry? I felt deflated. Piled up together it really did look like a big bag of junk. The stupid tree was right.

"Mackenzie?" I looked up and saw Ben at my door, staring at my bags disapprovingly. "When you're finished with your Christmas shopping, can I see you in my office for a run-down on where we're at with the diligence? I'm leaving for the airport in forty-five minutes." Obviously the moratorium on vacations did not apply to partners.

153

I fumbled with my bags, trying to stuff them underneath the desk. "Of course, Ben. I'll be right there," I answered in my most professional voice.

"You're losing your gumdrops."

"Pardon?"

He gestured to the window behind me, which showed the reflection underneath my desk where one of my bags had toppled over and the large bag of gumdrops was falling out.

"Oh . . . uh . . . thanks." I leaned down to stuff it back into the shopping bag, banging my head on my desk in the process. Popping back up like nothing happened, I gave Ben a tight smile, which he returned and walked away.

I let out a large breath through my pursed lips. Stupid gumdrops. I should have thrown them at the damn tree.

17

I STEPPED OFF THE train at North Station with my laptop in tow. It was Christmas morning and people all around me were gathering their bags full of festively wrapped parcels and slowly making their way off the train. I cringed, picturing my plastic bag full of Duane Reade's finest sitting in my suitcase. They weren't even wrapped.

"Honey, over here!" Mom waved at me over the crowds. I'd almost forgotten how chipper people could be outside of F&D. One look at her cheerful face and my eyes prickled with tears. I didn't realize how much I missed her and Dad until I saw them.

"There's our big city lawyer," Dad boomed, pulling me into a hug.

"Merry Christmas!" Mom chimed.

Being in Dad's embrace felt so comfortable I didn't want to let go. It was like this one element was still frozen in time despite my life surging ahead in New York. With Dad, I was seven years old and problems could still be solved with pizza.

"You look wonderful, honey," Mom gushed as she wrapped her arms around me. "But have you gotten thinner?" She pulled back to survey me, making a disapproving face as she poked my ribs.

"I don't think so, Mom."

"Well, I'll put some meat back on your bones before you leave. I made popcorn balls!" Mom always made my favorite Christmas treat, even though nobody else in the family liked them. And I knew she'd probably cleaned out my old room, put a bowl of my favorite candies on the nightstand, and laid out fresh towels on the bed.

"Thanks, Mom." I smiled, blinking back unexpected tears.

"Let's get outta here," Dad said, putting his arm around me guiding us towards the exit. "Everyone is so excited to see you, and I want to hear all about this glamorous New York City life of yours."

Glamorous? I was definitely going to have to leave some of the messy parts out.

Walking into my childhood home, I inhaled the smell of freshly baked Christmas cookies. My jaw unclenched, my shoulders relaxed, and the knots in the pit of my stomach loosened. I was home. If only there was a way to pipe this smell into my office every day.

"The others don't arrive until two, so we have a few hours. Have you had lunch?" Mom asked, walking towards the kitchen. "I could warm up some lasagna in the microwave. Or if you feel like something lighter I could toast you a bagel." She put her Santa apron over her head and reached behind her back to tie it.

Lunch? I looked at the clock. It was 11:45 A.M. Most days I was lucky if I had time for breakfast by this time.

"Bagel sounds good, Mom." I flung myself down at the kitchen table and watched as Mom buzzed around the kitchen, slicing the bagel, popping it in the toaster, and pulling the cream cheese out of the fridge.

It struck me that my mother put on an apron whenever she entered the kitchen. She was always prepared to whip up a meal, a snack, or just to wipe down the already clean counters. If she had been born at a different time, would she be running a company instead of a household? I wondered if she would be happier, more fulfilled that way. It was hard to tell. Watching her spread the cream cheese on my bagel, humming "*Jingle Bells*," she looked more content than anyone I'd been around in a long time.

She set the bagel down in front of me and gleefully gave me a run-down of our Christmas schedule. "So, everyone arrives at two and we'll do presents and appies then. You'll never believe it, but I managed to track down that video game that Evan asked Santa for." While she launched into a story about befriending the owner of a local toy store, my mind wandered to the stuffed cat I had in my suitcase for Evan. I was already an absentee aunt—what was I thinking, getting him a cheap stuffed cat? An absentee aunt should at least come up big at gift-giving time. *Maybe I'll tuck $100 in with it. Do five-year olds like getting cash?*

I tuned back in just as Mom was wrapping up her victory story. "And when he got the shipment he called me right away and I raced down there to get it. I was actually at a movie and had to leave midway through, but it'll be worth it to see his little eyes light up." She smiled triumphantly.

"That's great, Mom. I didn't really have . . . uhh . . . time to get him anything good. Do you mind if I put my name on the card too?" I didn't want to be crowned World's Worst Aunt this early on in their young lives.

"Of course. No problem, honey." Reading my mind, she added, "it's not the gifts they want from you anyway, so don't worry. Margaret told the boys you'd take them to see the new Muppet movie tomorrow. That'll be better than any gift they'll receive today."

"Mom, I don't have time to do that!" I snapped. Seeing her crushed expression, I took a deep breath and softened my tone. "I'm sorry, but I have to take an early train back to the city tomorrow. Lots to do back at the office!" I forced myself to sound cheery.

157

"You're leaving tomorrow? But you won't even have been home for twenty-four hours. I know you're busy at work, but . . . "

"Well, such is the life of a successful, big city lawyer," Dad called enthusiastically as he entered the kitchen, newspaper in hand, ready to discuss the latest current events with me. Mom turned back to the counter. It seemed like I was disappointing everyone these days. At least Dad understood.

"Have you seen what they are doing with our tax dollars now?" he asked, sitting down and settling in for a debate.

———

"The first thing we need is a glass of wine." Margaret extracted two large wineglasses from the cupboard and set them on the counter.

"I don't remember seeing that in the ingredient list," I snickered as Margaret opened a bottle of pinot grigio and poured two healthy portions.

"Secret ingredient." She grinned, handing me the glass. I silenced my BlackBerry and slid it into my pocket before taking the glass. "All good chefs are drunk when they create their signature dish." She lifted her glass, air toasting mine, and took a long satisfied gulp.

"Well, there's a piece of Food Network trivia I never knew." I leaned back against the counter, surreptitiously examining my sister over my wineglass. Even after having twins, her body still looked like she could model in a fitness magazine. Everything about her was toned and flawless, from her Jessica Alba-esque stomach to her perfectly rounded bum. I was slim, granted, but I was all straight lines and angles. Shape magazine wouldn't exactly be knocking down my door.

"Okay!" Margaret set down her glass, wiped her palms on her jeans, and peered down at the recipe. "How do we make this bad boy?"

"It's my famous gingerbread roll with cinnamon cream." I pointed to the picture in Mom's cookbook. "You'll be in charge of the cinnamon cream and I'll make the roll."

I think I was actually humming as I buzzed around the kitchen, gathering bowls and ingredients. Hearing the familiar clang of pans, inhaling the scents of vanilla, cinnamon, and ginger, I was reminded how much I used to enjoy baking. I loved the feeling of creating something from scratch; measuring out perfect proportions of flour and sugar, sprinkling in new ingredients, changing the taste with a dash of nutmeg. I liked baking cookies until they were golden, their aroma filling the entire house. But I hadn't had the time to bake in . . . I couldn't even remember.

"So how's everything in New York?" Margaret asked, dipping her finger into her concoction and taking a taste.

"Oh, good," I answered breezily. "Everything's good."

"Good? You must be having the time of your life! I'm so envious. I mean, living in New York when you're young enough to enjoy it—the art, the food, the energy." Margaret looked into the distance wistfully for a moment. "Luke and I are *dying* to make it down there to visit you. Maybe when the kids are older . . . ," she trailed off, and began mixing so vigorously I thought the bowl might fall off the counter.

"You should." I nodded enthusiastically, suddenly aware it was the first time Margaret had ever envied something I had. All those years I spent in her shadow, wishing I could be more like her, have her life, and now I was the one with the enviable life. Margaret was right. Living in New York is pretty fantastic. I had everything I've ever wanted. *If I can just get through the next few months*, I thought as I blended the spices into the egg mixture. *Then the Highlander deal will close, I'll get the StarCorp secondment, be on partnership track, and things will fall into place.*

"Cinnamon cream is done!" Margaret announced proudly as I spread batter into the baking sheet.

I put down my spatula and patted her on the back. "I'll just pop the roll into the oven and when it's done we can put it all together."

"I'll be upstairs wrapping presents till then." Margaret started towards the door before taking a few steps back, grabbing her half full wineglass off the counter. "With this." She grinned.

I leaned back against the counter, licking the last bits of gingerbread batter off my fingertips, marveling at how good food tastes when your stomach isn't tied in knots. Delicious smells were wafting from the oven, Christmas carols were softly playing, and the Christmas tree lights were twinkling in the window reflection. I felt just simple and uncomplicated happiness. I picked up my wineglass and let out a long, cleansing exhale.

Bzzzzzzzzzzzzzzzz.

It took me a moment to realize why my pants were suddenly buzzing.

To: Mackenzie Corbett
From: Ben Girardi

Mackenzie,

Vincent's hotel in Mexico doesn't have a printer. Can you Fedex him the latest version of the Highlander purchase agreement and a blackline to the address below. ASAP.

Ben

You have got to be kidding me! I screamed silently. What is it about being a partner that makes a person incapable of completing a simple task, like printing out a document himself? Last winter, Alex had had to trudge out in a blizzard that dumped fourteen inches of snow to personally deliver a sixty-seven page purchase agreement to Vincent because he didn't want the hassle of printing out the document at home.

Surely Vincent can find a printer somewhere around his hotel, I fumed. *And why does he need to see this ASAP? It's not like we're brokering peace in the Middle East—this deal will still get done even if we take one measly day off.* But that "ASAP" shouted at me from the screen. There wasn't time to talk myself down, remind myself that I was here to spend time with my family and that Vincent wouldn't die if he didn't receive the document until tomorrow. I dashed upstairs to sign on to my firm-issued laptop.

Despite multiple attempts with my parents' painfully slow internet connection, I kept getting hit with the same error message. *This username is signed on at another location. Please sign out of your previous session and try again. If you believe you've received this message in error call the Help Desk.*

I could hear laughter coming from the living room, as Dad was telling everyone about his disastrous trip to the mall to Christmas shop. "I was stalking this guy for his parking spot and it turned out he was a security guard patrolling the lot!" His voice boomed. "He thought I was some sort of car thief casing the parking lot!" More whoops of laughter were in the background as I called the help desk.

"For security reasons we can't have employees logged on from multiple locations," the IT operator informed me in a monotone voice.

"I'm not signed in anywhere else," I snapped. "I shut my computer down before I left the office."

She sighed at my perceived stupidity. "It's not your office computer. You're already signed on from an external computer."

"No, I'm *trying* to sign on from an external computer now, but I can't get on. There's no way I can be at two computers." I struggled to use the calmest tone possible, knowing how prickly the help desk can be.

"Okay, I've terminated your previous session," she answered, ignoring me. "So it should work now."

I peered at my computer screen. The error message was gone.

"If you have any problems you can call us back," she said flatly.

"Wait!" This didn't make any sense. "Um, where did the other session originate from?"

"A computer that isn't firm issued. I don't know the exact location."

"Thanks." I hung up the phone and stared at my computer screen. I had the strange sense that something was amiss, but pushed it out of my mind because there was a job to do. I located the latest version, ran a blackline, and attached the documents to an email to the document services department asking them to Fedex them to Vincent and call me when it was done. If I didn't hear back by dinner I was going to have to figure out a way to do this myself. Reluctantly, I turned on Dad's ancient printer, grabbed the mouse, and clicked print. Like most things in my parents' house, the printer should've been replaced years ago, but Dad's thriftiness prevented him from getting rid of anything that was technically still working. I vowed to get them a new one as a belated Christmas gift and scampered down the stairs to the kitchen, just as Mom called out, "What's burning?"

161

"Shit," I hissed, pulling open the oven door as Mom waved a tea towel around the smoke detector. "Shit," I hissed again as I slammed the baking pan onto the stove. "It's ruined." I stared down at my blackened cake roll somberly.

Mom came up behind me and tentatively placed her hands on my shoulders, as if she was afraid I might turn around and attack. "Don't worry about it, honey," she said in a voice barely louder than a whisper. "We have tons of desserts. More than we know what to do with."

Two hours later, everyone was helping Mom clear the table, patting their stomachs and complimenting the delicious dinner. The calm, content feeling I'd enjoyed earlier was completely gone; fretfulness and anxiousness had taken its place. Throughout dinner, I'd kept pulling my BlackBerry out of my pocket underneath the table, willing it to ring and be someone in document services telling me it was taken care of. I barely touched my food, not wanting to add to the brick of stress in my stomach, and couldn't decipher the conversation going on around me, the words just blending together in one loud buzz. I had the distinct feeling that I was outside of the whole scene, like I'd been transported there by the Ghost of Christmas Past, showing me scenes of my family's festivity. *Here you are in Christmas 2015, tethered to your BlackBerry . . . and you burned the gingerbread roll . . .*

"Can you grab the platter of turkey?" Mom gestured to me. "I want to stick it in the fridge." She was balancing a stack of dinner plates in one hand and an unfinished bowl of green beans in the other as I picked up the platter and followed her into the kitchen. I still hadn't heard from anyone in document services. I was going to have to find a place to FedEx the document myself, but I needed to be strategic about it so my parents wouldn't know what I was doing. They would think I was crazy and tell me to relax—that it could wait. They wouldn't understand.

I covered the turkey with Saran Wrap and shuffled some things around in the refrigerator before sliding it in. "Mom, I just have a quick errand I need to run," I said in my best nonchalant tone.

"Now? But I'm going to serve dessert soon," Mom fretted. "Where do you need to go?"

"I'll be back in ten minutes!" I called as I was running out the door, clutching Dad's car keys and the 234 pages I had printed on my parents' painfully slow printer. I didn't dare tell her I was doing work on Christmas Day. It would have broken her heart. Best just to ignore her question completely and come up with an explanation later.

I drove to the nearest FedEx Office branch, hoping it would be open, but when I pulled up all of the lights were turned off. *If you're going to claim you're open all the time, then you should be open ALL THE TIME,* I thought angrily, slapping the steering wheel in frustration. Didn't anyone else *work* besides me? *Okay, what next? Think, Mackenzie, think,* I commanded, rubbing my temples with my index fingers. It had only been a few hours since his email, but I felt as if Ben were sitting in the car next to me, red-faced and angry, shouting, "Send the fucking document NOW!" My BlackBerry buzzed again.

To: Mackenzie Corbett
From: Ben Girardi

Scratch that—Fedex won't be quick enough. Vincent's hotel has
a fax machine. Here is the number 011 223 476 9933. Let me
know when you've sent it.

Ben

A fax machine? What was this, 1988? Frantic, I raced to the neighborhood mini mart, realizing it was the one place close by that
would be open and possibly have a fax machine. *Thank God for the
hardworking small business owners*, I thought as I pulled up to the
parking lot and saw the lights on and a man sitting behind the register. Good people, they are.

"It's a dollar a page." The clerk gestured to the fax machine. "And
that many pages will take a while." He barely looked up from his
magazine. I wondered what tipped him off—the desperate, panicked
look in my eyes, or the fact that I was clutching 234 pages like they
held the answers to the mysteries of the universe.

I threw my credit card down on the counter and handed him my
pile of papers. He didn't move.

"Cash only." He flipped the page of his magazine.

"Shit," I muttered, opening my wallet to assess my cash situation.
I had four singles and a few quarters. "Okay, I just have to go to the
bank machine. Can you start the fax while I go get some cash?"
I flashed a pleading expression. "Someone is waiting beside a fax
machine for this in Mexico. It's really important." I hoped my tone
conveyed the urgency of the situation.

"No. Prepay only," he barked at me without looking up.

Of course.

Fifteen minutes later, after emailing Ben that the fax was on its
way, I returned to the store with a pile of cash and an extremely short
fuse. I slammed the money on the counter. "Okay, start it." Breathing heavily, nostrils flaring, I glowered at him like we were about to

brawl. Not that he noticed—he barely even looked at me. I was having a stare-down with the top of his head.

He put down his magazine and slowly stood up. One by one he leisurely started to pile the pages on the fax. Precious time was ticking away and he was dawdling like it didn't even matter. I drummed my fingers on the counter in frustration "Will take a while. Lots of pages." He said flatly.

Forty-five excruciatingly slow minutes later, I finally got the confirmation that the fax had gone through. "Merry Christmas," the clerk called out as I left the store, the bell on the door ringing as the door slammed behind me.

When I arrived home I found my mom in the kitchen cleaning up the dishes from dessert. "There you are!" she exclaimed, the relief evident in her voice. She put down the dessert plate she was rinsing and wiped her hands on a dishtowel. "Mackenzie, what in the world is going on?"

"What do you mean?" I fiddled with the keys, avoiding her suspicious gaze.

"You just disappeared right after dinner. Is everything okay?"

The concern in her voice made it hard to control the tears brimming in my eyes. For a moment I considered telling her the truth. That everything wasn't okay. That I'd had a caffeine-induced headache for weeks and was pretty sure the burning sensation in my gut was a growing ulcer. That I couldn't remember the last time I'd slept more than three hours in a row or felt the sun on my face. And what I really, desperately needed right now was for her to wrap her arms around me and tell me that I was doing a good job. That it would all be worth it. But of course I couldn't say all that. If Mom knew the hours I was working or the abuse I was enduring she'd insist on coming to New York immediately to take care of me. Or worse, I'd have to return home a failure. I was so, so close to achieving my goals, I couldn't risk Mom's hyper-concern getting in the way. So instead I just blinked back the tears and responded, "Everything's fine, Mom," sounding a little more manically cheery than I meant to. "I just needed to run to the bank."

"The bank?" She wrung her hands. "Are you having money problems, honey?"

"No, Mom! Why would you think that?"

"Well, the presents you gave . . . " she trailed off into an awkward silence.

Oh God. The presents. I'd already erased my family's embarrassing, stumbling "thank yous" from my memory. What was I thinking giving my family that cheap junk? Now poor Mom was undoubtedly wondering if she needed to take out a second mortgage on the house to cover whatever financial mess I'd gotten myself into.

"Mom, I can assure you I'm not having any money problems. Everything is fine. Really. I just needed to zip out to the bank machine because I won't have time to go tomorrow morning. I'm leaving really early," I reminded her.

She nodded, but didn't say anything.

"And Christmas just kinda snuck up on me this year . . ." I mumbled, pulling out a chair from the kitchen table and collapsing onto it.

I could feel her examining me and briefly wondered if this scene was going to play out the same way it always does when Mom thinks there's something wrong: She locks eyes with mine and repeats "Are you suuuure you're okay?" and that's enough to bring on the waterworks and the truth from me. But it didn't happen that way today. Maybe I'd been more convincing than I thought, maybe she was following her natural impulse to avoid conflict, or maybe she was finally letting me figure things out on my own. If she doubted my explanation she bit her tongue.

In the next room, the TV blared, interspersed with hoots of laughter as everyone watched *National Lampoon's Christmas Vacation* for the fifteenth year in a row. My favorite movie of all time.

All I really wanted to do was curl up under a blanket on the couch and laugh along with them. It was even coming up to my favorite part—the part where Eddie kidnaps Clark's boss after Clark tells him the one thing he wants for Christmas is his boss wrapped up with a bow. Cracks me up every time.

"Well." Mom took a deep breath, walked over to the refrigerator, opened the door, and pulled out a plate covered with tinfoil. "We tried to put off dessert until you were back, but after an hour everyone got restless." She popped the plate in the microwave and punched away at the buttons. "I'll just stick this pie in the microwave to warm it up."

I cursed Ben yet again for making me miss out on Mom's apple crumb pie when it was fresh from the oven. I started to fantasize about someone kidnapping him and bringing him here wrapped up in a bow so he could see how his actions affected a family's holiday and learn the error of his ways. Maybe he'd even award me the StarCorp secondment on the spot. It had worked for Chevy Chase.

"Ice cream or whipped cream on top?" Mom asked.

I felt my BlackBerry buzz in my pocket. "Ice cream," I answered distractedly as I pulled it out and surreptitiously checked the message.

To: Mackenzie Corbett
From: Ben Girardi

Thanks.

Ben

Crisis number two thousand eighty-four resolved.

———

The next morning I walked into the kitchen to find Dad at his station at the stove, making his famous pancakes. Mom will defer to Dad for only two types of meals—pancakes and barbeque. After years of making pancakes on Sundays and holidays he has honed his skill into the best pancakes I've ever eaten. In the summer he'll put fresh blueberries in them and it's probably my favorite summer memory— the first blueberry pancake of the season. "You're up early," I said, grabbing a mug out of the cupboard and pouring myself some coffee.

"I couldn't let you go back to New York on an empty stomach."

Dad has never been an emotional guy. Mom showed her love with gushy physical displays and notes left in my lunch box. Dad, on the other hand, was a man of few words. Growing up, getting a "Good job" and a pat on the back from him was as effusive as it got.

That didn't mean he didn't show his love, though. He just showed it through his actions instead. And waking up at 5:30 A.M. to make me breakfast before my 7:22 A.M. train home was a true act of love.

"Where did you disappear to last night?" he asked as he poured a ladle of batter onto the griddle. "It's not like you to miss dessert."

"Just had an errand I needed to run," I responded vaguely.

"Mmm." A sudden, prickly silence filled the room as he stirred the bowl of batter then poured another ladle of batter on the griddle. "Listen." He cleared his throat. "Mom thinks there is something going on that you're . . . uhh . . . not telling her. She said it's not like you to keep disappearing."

I rolled my eyes. Burn one gingerbread roll and skip out on one dessert and suddenly it's a family crisis.

"She seemed to think . . . uhh . . . that I should talk to you about it." Dad's eyes were fixed on the bubbling pancake. "So, is there anything you need to talk about?"

Poor Dad. I think if he could describe his version of hell it would include being forced to utter the sentence "Is there anything you need to talk about?" Don't get me wrong, he doesn't shy away from conversation, but the topic has to be within his realm of comfort— politics, books, sports, TV. Asking an open-ended question that could lead to a talk about feelings—or worse, to tears—would be agonizing for him. If Mom was sending Dad in to do her dirty work now she must think something is really wrong.

167

"Dad, really there's nothing to talk about," I answered in a tone I hoped was reassuring.

"It's not boy trouble, is it?" I noticed the tips of Dad's ears turning bright pink and knew that this moment was just as excruciating for him as it was for me. If he broke out the "Are you using protection?" I was going to have to open the oven and climb in.

"No, Dad! I'm just really busy at work. That's all. I don't know why Mom thinks that's so strange. Geez, I thought you and Mom were happy that I'm a hard worker."

"Of course we are. We *are*," he repeated, looking decidedly more at ease with the direction of the conversation. "And you're still enjoying work, right?"

"Mm hm." I nodded. I don't remember ever telling my parents that I *enjoyed* work, but no use arguing semantics. Besides, in Dad's eyes a job that was paying more than he's ever made would be like winning the lottery on a daily basis. Of course that would be enjoyable.

"Good. I'm glad to hear it." Dad smiled. His work here was done.

"Did you ever get a hold of Uncle Mike?" I asked, trying to change the subject. Uncle Mike was the one sibling of my father's that hadn't been able to make it to Christmas dinner. He'd spent Christmas in Portland with his daughter, Amelia, who had a new job and couldn't get away for Christmas.

"Just talked to him last night, actually. Do you know what Amelia is doing these days?" He pointed the spatula at me. Amelia had always been the rebel of the family, much to the chagrin of her conservative father. When she was seventeen she'd announced that she wasn't going to college because she was going to travel around with her boyfriend's band and play the tambourine. Her parents were distraught and did everything they could to persuade her to go to college, including telling her that they would cut her off financially if she didn't. That didn't sway Amelia, and she spent the next eighteen months on the road with the band until her relationship with the drummer ended and she had to come back to her parents' house, broke. Since then, she'd had about thirteen different jobs, from professional protester to balloon animal artist.

"Joined the circus?" I joked.

"She got a job as a *secretary* for an accountant out in Portland. Can you believe it? *Amelia* working in an office?" He shook his head in disbelief and turned back towards the griddle to flip the pancakes. "Apparently the guy she's working for is a real nut too. He offered to pay well over the market salary for a secretary and he still had the damnedest time filling the position. No one wants to work for him! Which explains why Amelia was able to get the job, I guess." He smiled and piled up four pancakes onto a plate. "The way Uncle Mike explained it, the guy sounds awful. He actually made Amelia work on Christmas Day for absolutely no reason. The guy has no family and nothing better to do."

I pictured my once free-spirited cousin holed up in some dingy office, at the mercy of the ridiculous demands of a Ben clone.

"Anyway, Amelia said she just sat there twiddling her thumbs *all* day. The only thing she did was send a couple faxes. He didn't even need her to be there! Can you believe that? The guy made her miss Christmas with her family when it wasn't even necessary." He shook his head and set the plate of pancakes down in front of me. "Don't worry about your mother. I'll talk to her. Trust me, she and I are thrilled that you've always been so driven. We know how lucky we are," he said, patting me on the back. "Our daughters will never have to work for a jerk like that."

I nodded, poking at the pancakes with my fork. Suddenly I wasn't very hungry.

18

I walked into Vincent's office clutching a fresh legal pad and an expanding file pocket bursting with Highlander transaction documents. Back to life, back to reality. It was a relief to be back in New York after my disheartening trip home. It had been upsetting not to be able to give my family anything they wanted—not my attention, my time, or even a decent gift. At least when I was in New York, I was far away from Mom's concerned looks and my nephews' disappointed faces. I didn't have to expend my energy pretending that work wasn't first and foremost in my mind—here, it was and it was expected to be.

Vincent nodded a greeting in my direction, eyes fixed on his computer screen, as I took a seat on the plush couch off to the side of his desk. It was December 30th and he'd just returned from Mexico. He'd urgently requested a status meeting before he departed for his annual New Year's ski trip to Aspen. God forbid he waste a second of time during his twenty-four hour layover in New York.

Vincent's office was in the opposite corner of the building from Saul's and the interior of his office reflected their differences. Family pictures set in Tiffany platinum frames of various sizes were arranged on the large mahogany book shelf against the far wall: one of a teenage boy with sharp features, pictured at the beach, surf board in hand; a school picture of a girl with braces, with a smile that looked just like her father's; another of Vincent and his wife, dressed up in black tie garb, posing in front of a grand staircase. A mug boasting

"World's Best Dad" sat next to an autographed baseball on the window sill. There was proof of life outside the office—something completely lacking in Saul's office. But, despite the smiling faces staring back at me from the frames, I wasn't fooled.

Every secretary at F&D worked for two lawyers. Rita worked for me and Vincent and, as his secretary, she had to vet every email he received and flag the important ones for him. And not just the work-related emails—EVERY email. "You wouldn't *believe* some of the stuff I've read," she'd whispered to me, after swearing me to secrecy. "Like crazy personal stuff." She went on to tell me that Vincent's current wife, Lynn, was his third wife, but started off as his mistress when he was still married to his second wife, Tina. Apparently Lynn ruthlessly pursued Vincent while he was still married and then made her presence known to Tina at a black tie charity function.

"Can you believe that bitch? Confronting Tina in front of all'ah her friends? I'dah clocked her!" Rita exclaimed while balling her hand into a fist and giving a phantom punch. "Tina got the bettah of Vincent, though." Rita gave a wry chuckle. "Couplah months after the divorce was final she sent Vincent an email saying she was screwin' his best friend and now she finally knows what a REAL orgasm feels like! I flagged the email for Vincent. Figured he should know," she added with a wicked smile.

And it wasn't only Vincent's marriages that were in constant trouble—so were his children. His son, who looked so innocent, tanned, and healthy in the picture in Vincent's office, had recently checked into rehab for cocaine. He was only eighteen and in his first year of college. "The weekend Vincent went ta Vermont to pick 'im up from college and check 'im in, Rhonda, his first wife and the kid's mothah, couldn't pry Vincent away from his BlackBerry. He spent the whole time on the phone doin' conference calls—barely even left his hotel room. What kinda fathah is that? I mean, no wondah the kid has a problem, ya know?"

His daughter, Emma, was in high school now and battling bulimia, Rita explained. Apparently Vincent had emailed Rhonda that Emma must get that from her. "'You never could pass up a donut and now neither can your daughter.' That's what that asshole said to the mothah of his children," Rita said, shaking her head in disgust. "Can you believe that? Deserves to rot in hell." She pantomimed strangling herself with both hands, sticking out her tongue and bugging out her eyes. "Nobody around him is evah happy," she said, shaking her head. "I wouldn't take his life for awwwwll the money in the world. It's not worth it."

"Okay," Vincent said, turning his attention away from his computer and towards Ben, who was sitting in one of the two chairs facing Vincent's desk. The other chair was occupied by a partner in the Finance department. I made myself stop staring at the pictures and gripped my pen, readying myself to take notes. Vincent lifted a paperweight with the words "Trust But Verify" written on it off a pile of papers, picked up the top page, peered at it, frowning, before setting it down in another pile and replacing the paperweight. He clasped his hands and leaned forward on his elbows. "Where are we at?" He looked back and forth at Ben and the finance partner.

"Well, we've got our diligence team plugging away. No deal breakers there." Ben glanced down at the memo I'd painstakingly prepared before shooting me a confirmatory look, as if to say "jump in if I'm wrong." I nodded assent, but couldn't help but wonder if he'd bothered to read my memo. "We are just waiting for your sign-off on latest version of the purchase agreement and we can get that off."

"When did you send me that?" Vincent interrupted, grabbing his mouse and squinting over his glasses at the computer monitor.

"Mackenzie faxed it to you in Mexico." Ben looked over at me again for confirmation and I nodded in agreement.

Vincent scrunched up his face, seemingly trying to bring it to mind, which made me wonder how many faxes he'd made unfortunate junior associates send. "Oh, that?" He chuckled. "I tossed that in the garbage. The ink was too light to read in the sun."

I gritted my teeth.

"Oh, okay." Ben shifted uncomfortably in his seat, clearly annoyed by Vincent's ambivalence. "Mackenzie, do you have the latest draft there?" He gestured towards my pile of documents.

"Right here." I withdrew the document out of the file I'd been clutching and stood up to hand it to Vincent, who peered down at it.

"I'll review this before I head out today. What else?" He turned his attention to the finance partner as I returned to my seat, fuming.

I could hear Dad's voice reverberating in my head. *Our daughters will never have to work for a jerk like that.*

—————

At 8:30 P.M. on New Year's Eve, I was hunkered down at my desk, poking at my tepid lasagna from Seamless when my email pinged.

To: Mackenzie Corbett
From: Jason Kermode

I hope this is the last time we spend New Year's on opposite coasts. I wish I was there ringing in 2016 with you. I'll call you tonight.

1-4-3

Jason had survived his Kermode family Christmas duties in Los Angeles and had texted yesterday to let me know he was headed down to La Jolla to surf. "You have to join me next year," he'd texted. "Next year," I'd promised.

I reread Jason's email three times before I clicked on the picture attached. Jason was standing barefoot on golden sand, blue sea behind him, beach umbrellas billowing in the breeze. It was a post-card setting, but he was giving a thumbs down, jutting his lower lip out in a pout. I smiled in spite of myself. His sun-kissed skin accentuated his toned arms and comfortingly broad shoulders; the saltwater had given his hair a sexy surfer-style wave; and the sunset backdrop somehow made his eyes shine even brighter. *I should be there with him*, my mind whimpered. *Sharing a secluded hammock, his arm wrapped around me as I curl up onto his chest watching the sunset.* I sent back a quick "I miss you too. I'll be in my new home—call me there (aka my office)" then sunk down into my seat miserably.

"I'm kidnapping you, Mackenzie," a voice said, interrupting my pity party.

I looked up to see Alex standing in my doorway. He was wearing dark jeans and a silk and cashmere John Varvatos V-neck. His three quarter length charcoal Hugo Boss wool jacket and beige cashmere scarf completed the outfit. Once again, Alex had nailed the "I'm too cool to put too much thought into what I wear" look perfectly. I noticed the faintest smell of cologne, which meant his New Year's plans certainly did not involve spending the night at the office.

Smiling, I put my fork down, crossed my arms over my chest, and cocked my head inquisitively. "Kidnapping me?"

"I was on my way to a party in the Village when I thought about you sitting here all lonely and mopey in the office. I just couldn't let you wither away here on New Year's Eve. I know you're snowed under"—he gestured towards the pile of documents on my desk—"but I figured you could duck out for a drink. I'll bring you back in an hour—promise." He crossed his heart, flashing an impish grin.

I glanced down at the time, wondering if I would miss Jason's call.

"ONE drink," I emphasized, thankful that I had chosen to wear my skinny jeans to the office today instead of my Lululemon yoga pants. Office dress codes don't apply on weekends and holidays, but I'd decided that stretchy pants would only invite me to stuff myself with candy from the dish on Rita's desk all night. Better to have my skinny jeans on to keep me in check. "But if anyone sees me on the way out I'll have to abort the mission." I grabbed my coat from behind the door, craftily leaving my spare coat on the back of my chair just in case.

"Deal, Captain," he said, giving a salute.

Second Avenue was dense with revelers ringing in the New Year early, so we ducked into the first bar that had an open table and flagged the waitress. Precious moments away from the office had to be used efficiently. Alex ordered a bottle of champagne before I could protest. "You said 'one drink.' Technically that's one drink."

"Only another lawyer would parse the phrase 'one drink.'" I smiled wryly, checking my BlackBerry for the deadly "ASAP" email. Finding none, I positioned it visibly on the table.

"A toast . . . " he said, after the waitress had returned. He picked up his champagne flute, but I was way ahead of him, having already gulped down half the glass.

I involuntarily let out a satisfied "Ahhhhhh." Alex was right—a drink was exactly what I needed right now. Or seven.

He regarded me with amusement. "Easy there, Mac. You're not going to go all 'Leaving Las Vegas' on me tonight, are you?"

"Very funny. I seriously think this job is turning me into an alcoholic. I'm now incapable of drinking slowly. Incapable. And no addiction hotline is going to help me, either. Someone is going to have to come here and pry my fingers off this bottle."

"Well, consider me your enabler then." He grinned and refilled my glass.

I picked up the stem of the glass, studying the bubbles rising to the top and bursting. Somewhere, Kim was karaoke-ing her way into 2016. Margaret was tucking the twins in early and having a quiet night watching the ball drop with Luke, toasting their good fortune. Jason was paddling out to a burgeoning wave. Maybe there really was something to what Eddie had said. "Do you ever think that there's gotta be an easier way?"

Alex smiled, studying me. "Sure. All the time. You?"

I shrugged. "I don't know. Lately I've been wondering."

"Well, if you figure it out, let me know."

The sound of whoops and hollers outside got louder, reminding me that the last few moments of 2015 were ticking away. "Hey, weren't you supposed to be going out with uh . . . " I grasped for the name of Alex's New Year's date. I remembered they'd gone out a couple times, but trying to learn the names of Alex's girlfriends would be an exercise in futility.

"Pammy?"

"Please tell me she doesn't actually refer to herself that way."

"Hey, Pammy happens to be a lawyer," he said. "And no, I'm not supposed to be going out with her tonight."

"Was it the name that ended it?" I grinned.

"You're relentless." He wagged his finger at me. "Nah, I made the mistake of asking her what she wanted out of life."

"Let me guess. World peace?"

"Worse. Her life goal is to meet Beyoncé."

"Noooo!" I slapped the table.

"I kid you not."

"Well, it's good to have a goal." I took a long gulp of champagne. "So how would you answer the same question?"

"Me?" He gave a half smile and, meeting my eyes, opened his mouth, then hesitated. After a beat of silence, his serious expression broke into a sly smile. "You know, just what every guy wants out of life—models and bottles."

"You did NOT just say 'models and bottles.'" I laughed and slapped his arm. "Well, then you and Pammy deserve each other."

"Hey." He raised his hands in surrender. "I've tried to find the right woman. But you're living proof that all the good ones are taken."

The champagne must have really been hitting me, because, for a brief moment, the air around us felt charged and I flashed on what it would feel like to kiss Alex. Blushing, I looked down, hoping he wouldn't notice. Seeing my BlackBerry blinking, I picked it up, my heart quickening when I saw an email from Jason. I felt a shot of guilt, like I was doing something wrong and he'd caught me. I reminded myself it was just a drink with a friend, one who happened to flirt reflexively.

To: Mackenzie Corbett
From: Jason Kermode

I called your office, but must have missed you. When you get home, look in the drawer beside your bed . . . anyone who works on New Year's Eve deserves a pair of Tiffany earrings :-)

Miss you, love you . . . and Happy New Year!

J

I reread the email twice, feeling myself grinning. It wasn't the sparkly earrings waiting for me that was suddenly making me giddy. More than anything, I was touched that he'd taken the time and effort. He may have been miles away, but Jason could still give me butterflies.

"I'm guessing that's not work-related?" Alex inquired.

I shook my head. "Thankfully not."

"Another bottle?" the waitress asked, pointing down at the champagne that, I noticed with slight shock, was nearly finished.

Alex met my eyes and raised his brows in question.

"Wish I could, but I need to get back to the office before I turn into a pumpkin." I fished through my purse and handed my credit card to the waitress. "It's on me."

Alex protested, but I insisted. "I would've been stuck at the office all night if you hadn't dragged me out. And besides, you deserve a drink. You've just broken poor Pammy's heart." Smiling, I signed the bill, gathered my BlackBerry and coat, and took one last swig of celebratory champagne.

"You go ahead," Alex said, gesturing to his BlackBerry. "I texted my friend to meet me here before we head to the party."

"Okay, enjoy. And Happy New Year!" I stood up to leave.

"Hey, Mac?" Alex said.

I turned around.

"You never answered the question."

"What do I want out of life?"

He nodded.

"Just what every woman wants. A good foot massage. And world peace, of course."

"I hope you get both," he said, and smiled softly. "Happy New Year, Mac."

Back in my office, watching the clock turn from 11:59 to 12:00, I thought about the little blue box waiting for me at home, Jason in La Jolla, and how much I wished I was with him.

19

THERE WAS NO REPRIEVE after New Year's. Ben had been right—the timelines were short and the pressure to sign the deal was intense. I did not leave for work and return home on the same day for the entire month of January. The hours were grueling and with work consuming more and more of my time, mere seconds in the day became precious. Everything I did, I did faster to preserve those valued seconds. I walked faster, talked faster, ate faster. I developed daily routines that depended on a split-second rhythm. I walked to the end of the subway platform to be on the car that stopped closest to the exit. I stood close to the door on the train to be one of the first out when it stopped. When anyone wasted one second of my time with what I perceived as careless inefficiency I felt cheated and annoyed: it meant one less second of sleep that night.

A week into the new year, just when I needed it, I got an unexpected treat. Jason surprised me in my office a day earlier than I thought he was supposed to return. When I walked in and saw him standing there behind my desk, I briefly wondered if I was having a sleep-deprived hallucination. "Jason!" I breathed. "You're back."

To my utter shock, without a word, he came around my desk, shut my office door, pulled me into his arms, and kissed me so deeply, so passionately, that I almost tilted right back onto my desk. It was so startling and raw and risky that it was all I could do not to lock my office door and rip his clothes off right there.

"I missed you," he moaned, in between kisses. His hands were all over me, making a trail down my back, then along my hips and around my backside.

"I missed you too," I managed, burying my head in his neck. We were both breathing more and more heavily. The air was so charged that the question was not *if* we were going to have sex, but *where*. I'd never needed it so badly in my life.

"Let's . . . " Jason murmured, his eyes closed, kissing my ear in that way that sends a tingle all the way from my neck to my toes.

And then . . . *Bing!*

My whole body stiffened as the ping of a new email suddenly filled the room.

Fuck. And just like that, the surge of passion receded, like a wave washing back out to sea.

"I hate the sound of that chime." I whimpered, running my fingers through the hair on the back of his head, trying desperately to reclaim the moment. I wanted his lips back where they were, doing what they were doing.

Jason shook his head, seemingly wiping clean the words he'd been about to use to finish his sentence. We were still embracing, but his body language was subdued.

"I've been wearing these, thinking about you." I gestured to my ears, hoping to lighten the mood.

His face suddenly brightened as he gently brushed back my hair. "I have good taste, huh?"

"You sure do." I wrapped my arms around him. I didn't want to ask, but I wondered if he'd changed his stance on not accepting family money. Because if he hadn't, I was probably wearing his entire bonus dangling from my ears, in the only real diamonds I'd ever owned. "They're beautiful," I whispered in his ear. "You didn't need to buy me such an extravagant present, though."

"I know. I just wanted you to know I was thinking about you." He kissed me on the head. "Oh, I almost forgot. I have something else for you." There was a broad smile on his face as he passed me an envelope.

"What's this?"

He shrugged, still smiling. "Open it."

A gasp escaped my mouth when I pulled the check out of the envelope.

Jason rubbed my shoulders. "I know you said you wanted to wait for your lease to run out in April before we move in together, so I figured I'd buy out your lease."

"But," I said slowly. "This is for twenty thousand dollars."

He shrugged. "I threw some money in for the vacation we'll take when you land the StarCorp secondment."

"Jason," I hesitated. "You can't just . . . " I trailed off, unsure how I wanted to finish the sentence. I pressed the check into his hand. "It's so sweet and I appreciate the gesture, but I can't take it."

"Mackenzie!" My intercom blared with Rita's voice. "They need you in the war room."

"I'll be right there," I croaked, still staring into Jason's eyes.

There was a heavy silence before Jason spoke. "Think about it. I know you're busy on this deal, so I won't bug you about it. Just think about it." He put the check back into the envelope and dropped it in my inbox before heading out the door.

———

Sitting at my desk the next morning, I knew I couldn't put it off any longer. It was Friday morning, time to send Ben the weekly status update on our due diligence. My stomach was tight as I pecked away at the keys, drafting an email detailing the impediment we were encountering as we continued our review. Highlander had yet to provide hundreds of necessary documents, including agreements they'd listed on the disclosure schedules of the purchase agreement. Documents that were listed on the disclosure schedules were exceptions to Highlander's representations and warranties contained in the purchase agreement. We definitely needed to review them before our client could sign a binding agreement.

I hit send and braced myself, sensing a shit storm on the horizon.

Two minutes later Ben appeared at my door. He looked surprisingly fresh and well rested in a pressed, navy blue suit. I, on the other hand, was dazed and still dressed in the clothes I'd put on twenty-four hours ago.

"Let me understand this," he started, breathing heavily. "Those fuckers have included documents on the disclosure schedules that they haven't even PROVIDED?" His voice rose with each word, as he reached down and adjusted his testicles. This is the default posture of a Biglaw lawyer—the unconscious crotch grab. They all do it—whatever the time, place, or audience.

No matter how many times I see it, it still puzzles me. I mean, are they checking that they're still there or do testicles really need to be readjusted that frequently? You don't see me adjusting my boobs in public. And, yes, sometimes I'd like to, but I at least show some discretion. Why can't men show the same discretion? More specifically, why couldn't Ben? He was constantly rubbing his balls as if a genie would pop out.

"That's correct," I said, trying to avoid looking at him. He was going in for a real dig, even slightly lifting one of his legs.

"Fucking assholes!" He slapped my door frame. "They're playing with us. Those fuckers are playing with us." Ben always seemed to think everyone was "playing with him," which probably stemmed from the fact that he was constantly playing with *himself*.

"We need an all-hands-on-deck call to discuss this shit with the client. Set it for noon today," he barked, then whirled around and left.

"Will do," I mumbled, conscious that the shit storm was picking up speed.

Three hours later, I was sitting at a conference room table with the firm's top rainmakers. There was always something energizing about an all-hands-on-deck call, but my Biglaw spidey senses told me this one would not end well.

The others began to filter in. Vincent took his seat in front of the triangular speaker phone and turned off the mute button.

"You have F&D," he boomed.

"Okay, Vince. Let's hear what the fuck is going on," Oren, one of the managing partners of Pegasus Partners, the potential buyer of Highlander, responded. "What the fuck is the problem now?"

Vincent took a deep breath and clenched his hands together. "Look, the last round of diligence is moving slower than expected.

We have the manpower to review the documents that are coming in, but the other side is barely dribbling them out to us. We still haven't received what we consider to be the major documents and it's really throwing a wrench in the process."

There was a beat of silence before Oren responded. "Are you fucking kidding me? Seriously. Are you fucking kidding me? What the FUCK?"

"I think the problem is they're running this out of LA and don't have anyone on the ground here who knows what the fuck they're doing." Vincent's voice remained calm.

I added another tick to the five already on my page. Sometimes I kept a running tally of the number of times "fuck" was said on conference calls to keep my mind from wandering, but I usually ended up losing count.

Oren could barely control his rage. "I want someone to get on the FUCKING phone with the fucking CEO and let him know that he needs to send a FUCKING team out to New York, with the documents fucking IN HAND," Oren bellowed. "Documents fucking IN HAND," he repeated. "If they need to rent planes to get their fucking guys to New York, then that's what they need to do. I want those documents in our fucking hands and reviewed by Monday."

The only thing more predictable than the swearing on conference calls is the blatant male posturing. It would have been so much more efficient if they all just put their dicks on the table to see whose was bigger so we could all move on. I looked down at my notes—thirteen ticks so far. Considering we were only a few minutes in, I was on pace to break a record.

"Oren . . ." Vincent started.

"Vince," Oren interrupted. "Listen to me. I don't give a fuck if people EAT, SLEEP, or SHIT before then—these documents will be reviewed by MONDAY. No excuses—life ain't all motherhood and popsicles."

I snickered silently. "Motherhood and popsicles"—that was a new one. It was somewhat entertaining to witness the roles change, with the partners being the ones yelled at. It reminded me of that Bob

Dylan song: *Well, it may be the Devil or it may be the Lord, but you're gonna have to serve somebody.*

Vincent didn't even flinch at Oren's rant—a career spent dealing with these guys had made him immune. He took a deep breath and continued. "Just wanted to make sure you wanted us to take a hard line with these guys, Oren. We have our marching orders now." He looked around the room, ensuring we all understood that this new timeline was a direct order from the client. The shit storm had become a full blown fecal hurricane.

I shook my head in disbelief. I was the lowest person on the totem pole, but it seemed like I was the only one in the room with any sense of reality. Clearly, fear of delivering a reasonable deadline to the client had triumphed over good sense. I tried to imagine what it would be like to be Oren. What would it feel like to be so confident about your place in the world, to feel like you should get whatever you wanted, whenever you wanted it? No matter how you treated people. What gives someone that sense of entitlement? And what would I do if I had it?

To: Mackenzie Corbett
From: Jason Kermode

Are you going to be able to get out before midnight tonight? If not, I'll just head home and see you tomorrow. 1-4-3

To: Jason Kermode
From: Mackenzie Corbett

Midnight would be pushing it, so I'll see you tomorrow instead. Hopefully it will be an earlier night.

1-4-3

Mackenzie: Still at the office? Caffeine break? You still have to see what's in Sheldon's office. Hint . . . it's life sized.

Alex: Still here, but sadly holed up in a conference room with Russ drafting a purchase agreement for Empire Investments. Life sized? I'm intrigued . . .

Mackenzie: Just sent you a purchase agreement from a deal I worked on for Empire Investments a few months ago. Take a look—might help.

20

I DUG THROUGH MY top drawer for my industrial-size bottle of Advil. It had been a week since Oren commanded that no one could eat, sleep, or shit and I'd made a healthy dent in my emergency stash of pain relievers. I popped two in my mouth, chased them with warm Diet Coke, and began scanning my to-do list for the day ahead.

"So what do you think?" Alex asked, walking into my office and flopping down in my guest chair. The bags under his eyes reminded me I wasn't the only one working late nights.

"Of?" I slipped off my shoes and sat cross legged in my chair, thankful for the opportunity to chat.

"Look under your desk." He grinned.

I eyed him curiously and peeked under. "Where did this come from?" I squealed.

Alex held a finger up to his lips. "Keep it down. People aren't used to joyful noises around here." He stood up to close the door before explaining, "I heard Sadir is out of the office today at a closing, so I figured he wouldn't miss his prized foot massager. You have until tomorrow morning to sneak it back in there."

"How did you know that at this very moment I was dying for this?" I was so excited that I clapped. "I'm surprised Sadir doesn't have this thing alarmed." I put my feet on the massager and selected "slow pulse" mode.

He looked pleased. "That contract you sent me was the perfect precedent for the deal I'm working on. You saved me hours of work.

Just figured I'd return the favor. Another late night for the Project Mojo team?"

I nodded. "It seems Ben likes to celebrate his birthday by working all night."

"It was his birthday?"

"Yup, I overheard his kids singing him happy birthday over the speakerphone when I walked by his office. It was like he was hiding from his family or something."

"Well, you would too if you had to go home to that crazy woman."

"True." I nodded, pondering for a moment. "But I thought Ben was actually one of the happier partners."

"Oh, honey." He looked at me in the same way you would look at a sad child who'd just lost her puppy. Alex was the one person in the world who could call a woman "honey" without sounding like a lecherous misogynist or the gay friend in a bad romcom. "Please don't tell me you're still living in the land of gumdrop houses where you actually think that happiness and working in Biglaw are NOT mutually exclusive."

"You really think there's no way to be happy working here?" I asked, eyeballing him curiously.

"Wake up and smell the Prozac, Mackenzie. No one in Biglaw is happy. Not even the guys making the biggest money. We work for morally bankrupt clients who squabble over pedantic bullshit, and the firm throws booze and money at us so we don't notice the fact that we have no personal life."

"Geez, don't try to sugar-coat it for my sake." I snickered. "Well, this isn't Prozac, but it's sure helping." I leaned back, relishing my twelve hour window with the Brookstone X180.

"Just make sure to get it back to Sadir's office by tomorrow morning," he called on his way out.

My day was already looking up. With any luck I would be left alone for the morning so I could review the work done by Gavin last night. Hopefully he wasn't too coked up when he did it. I settled back in my chair and began flipping through the summaries he'd put together.

188

"Knock, knock!" Ben poked his smiling face into my office, his two young daughters in tow, dressed in Girl Scout uniforms. "I've brought a couple of saleswomen who wanted to ask you a question." He looked down eagerly at his fresh-faced girls. "Alyssa, Rachel," he prompted in the friendliest tone I'd heard him use. In sync they sing-songed, "Do you want to buy some Girl Scout cookies?"

"That sounds delicious," I said with as much enthusiasm as I could muster with only a couple hours of sleep and a full day ahead of me. "I'll take two boxes!"

"Oh, I'm sure you could use more than that," Ben responded with a wink. "Alyssa and Rachel are gunning for the lead in their troop for the most cookies sold."

"Yeah, Mariah Williams is in first place right now, but we really, really, *really* want to be first!" Alyssa exclaimed in a voice that veered close to whiny.

I looked down at their eager, determined faces. I felt like I could see into their future—it starts with wanting to sell the most Girl Scout cookies, and the next thing you know it's wanting to bill the most hours. I had to resist the urge to grab them by their little shoulders, look them square in the eyes, and advise them. *You don't always have to strive for the highest dangling carrot. Put down those cookie boxes, girls, and go enjoy your childhood!*

189

"You've convinced me." I gave my best saccharine smile. "I'll take four boxes—two Thin Mints and two Samoas." I hoped the gesture might garner some goodwill from Ben in return.

"See how persuasive you can be, girls! I think I see a career in law in your future," Ben said, giving me another wink while leading Alyssa and Rachel out the door.

"Oh—Ben, did you get a chance to look at those distribution sections I sent you last night?" I asked, seizing my opportunity to get some feedback so I could make any revisions he needed and avoid another late night.

"What distribution sections?" He looked puzzled.

Um, the distribution sections I worked most of the night to get to you because you needed them ASAP? The ones that kept me from getting a decent night's sleep (for the umpteenth time) because you simply *had* to see them? Those distribution sections?

"Oh, yah, yah." Ben clued in, as if reading my mind. "I won't get a chance to look at those today, too much on my plate. You'll need those to keep your energy up, Mackenzie." He pointed to my boxes of cookies. "It's going to be another late night tonight! But make sure you don't eat them all in one sitting or you'll wind up looking like one of the secretaries." He inflated his cheeks like a blowfish and made a face at the giggling girls as he pulled the door shut behind him.

So much for goodwill. Twelve hours and two rows of thin mints later, I was still in my office when I heard the familiar *bing* indicating a new email. Stuffing a cookie into my mouth, I nearly choked when I saw it—an email from Vincent Krieder. An email *directly* to me from Vincent. Vincent *never* directly emailed an associate. Frankly, I was shocked Vincent even knew who I was (even though I'd been in multiple meetings with him, his office was right next to mine, and we shared a secretary). "Junior associates are like Oompa Loompas," Vincent had once drunkenly uttered at the Christmas party. "How am I supposed to tell the difference between them?"

If Vincent was emailing me directly instead of going through Ben, it had to be a major fire drill. Above all, Biglaw associates feared the fire drill. They always had completely unrealistic demands and even more unrealistic deadlines. They're sort of like those reality TV shows that involve ridiculously impossible challenges. *You have four hours to plan a wedding for one hundred guests using the following products . . . a weed whacker, a wicker basket, two chairs, and a tube of lipstick. Go!*

After a year and a half at F&D, I was used to the intensity and insanity that came with the fire drill. At least, I thought I was used to it. I held my breath and clicked on Vincent's email.

To: Mackenzie Corbett
From: Vincent Krieder
FIND THIS NOW

-----------------Forwarded message---------------

To: Vincent Krieder
From: Oren Silverman

Vincent,

Our finance guys have alerted us to a joint venture agreement between Highlander Hotels and WorldRes Europe that we will need to terminate due to antitrust concerns. Is this permissible under the contract?

Oren

My grogginess burned off in a blaze of panic. ASAP didn't exist in Vincent's world. It was NOW. As in "If you're still looking at this email you're already behind." *Oompa loompa doompadee doo, I've got another puzzle for you.*

The joint venture agreements had only been made available at Highlander's lawyers' offices and were not permitted to be photocopied due to their extremely confidential subject matter, so Gavin had spent three days summarizing them in a conference room at the offices of Wexler & Reed. Which meant our only source of information about these agreements was his notes.

Gavin was asleep in his chair when I burst in to his office. "GAVIN!" I went over and shook him.

"Get awwwf!" he groaned. I could tell he was more than just fatigued—he was crashing from whatever high he was on.

"Gavin, where are your notes on the JV agreements you reviewed at Wexler?" I asked clearly and slowly, hoping that would help him understand, but he just stared at me, bleary eyed, and mumbled something incoherent. "Gavin!" I grabbed his shoulders. "Listen. Please." Somehow I mustered my calmest tones. I knew my ass was on the line if I could not get this information to Vincent quickly. Getting through to Gavin was my only hope. "Vincent needs the details of a joint venture agreement you reviewed. Where are your notes?" My eyes darted around his office.

He pointed to a pile on his desk and I frantically started thumbing through it.

"The spiral one, the spiral one," he groaned.

I pulled out the spiral notebook and flipped through it. His hand-writing was atrocious. I couldn't tell which notes were for which agreements. I couldn't even tell if it was English. "Gavin, I need the summary you did for the JV with WorldRes Europe. Can you point to that one?" I asked him in the same tone Margaret uses with Evan when he hides her car keys.

Gavin grabbed the notebook and pointed to a page of scribbles.

I squinted at the page. "Gavin, I have no idea what that says." *Shit! Shit! Shit!* I felt a surge of panic. Then I had an idea. "Okay, Gavin, *you* type your summary into an email for Vincent." I picked up the keyboard, which had been moved off to the side for him to rest his head, and slammed it in front of him. "Like now!" My voice was get-ting louder and more aggravated.

192

Gavin turned to his computer, put his hands on the keyboard, stared at the screen for a moment, and his eyes fell shut.

"GAVIN!" I yelled, as my frustration bubbled over.

"I'm awake, I'm awake." He sat straight up, threw his shoulders back, and started to type. After a few words, his eyes closed again.

I was in full blown panic mode. It was like I could hear a giant clock in my head. "Tick, tick, tick." I was MacGyver and the bomb was about to blow.

Without thinking, I whirled around and grabbed the canister of compressed air from his shelf. It's normally used to dust keyboards by gusting out a hard blast of air to blow out the dust in between the keys. The warning on the side of the canister says not to spray directly on skin, as it can cause frostbite. With the eyes of a crazy person, I turned and pointed the canister at the back of Gavin's neck and pulled.

Pssssssssst. The powerful burst of air startled him awake. *Oompa loompa doompadah dee, if you are wise you'll listen to me.*

He jumped in his chair. "Geez, Mackenzie, what the hell was that?"

There was a time when I treated people with dignity and respect. A time when I would have put a blanket over Gavin so he could sleep it off, checking his breathing every fifteen minutes to make sure he was still okay. Now here I was, using an air canister as a weapon. The way I was morally spiraling out of control, I was going to wind up the F&D "fixer" à la Michael Clayton. But I was so relieved that Gavin was talking in full, comprehensible sentences that it didn't matter what method I was using. The only thing that mattered was that Vincent got his answer ASAP. The ends justified the means.

"I'm just helping you stay awake, Gavin. Now write," I ordered, pointing towards the keyboard. My heart was pounding, my conscience quietly rubbing against my self-preservation.

He sat up straight and began pecking away at the keys as I loomed over him, keeping the air canister strategically pointed at the back of his neck. Anytime his eyes closed I pulled the trigger again. Psssssssssst. "Keep writing, Gavin."

Walking back to my office after Gavin had sent the email to Vincent, my heart rate started to return to normal and my heavy breathing lessened. I silently congratulated myself for getting the job done. My method may have been unconventional, but what choice did I have? I could hear Ben's voice in my mind. *Those who distinguish themselves in my eyes go above and beyond.*

To: Mackenzie Corbett
From: Mom

Hi Honey,

I hope you're taking care of yourself and getting enough sleep. Margaret says she called you at 9 p.m. and you were still in the office—that's too late to be working! Just tell the partners you need your sleep—they'll understand.

xo Mom

To: Mackenzie Corbett
From: Kim Bawolska

Haven't heard from you in a while—everything okay? Do I have
to come down there and physically pry you from your desk? Call
me!!

21

I took a sip of my sparkling water and looked around the restaurant. Barbara Walters was two booths over, and Henry Kravis, founder of the powerhouse private equity firm KKR, was in the booth behind us. I was pretty sure I spotted John Kerry in the corner. The Four Seasons Grill Room was a plethora of white collar pseudo-celebrities. As the restaurant of choice for power-lunchers in New York, the annual income of the lunch crowd was probably bigger than the GDP of a small nation, making it the perfect place to recruit potential candidates to F&D.

"The restaurant selection for the interview lunch is paramount," I remember the Head of Recruiting preaching at the "Successful Recruitment Techniques" seminar last year that I, along with many of my fellow associates, was required to attend. We needed to learn the fine art of courting law students before we could be released into the wild to spread the word about F&D. We were the select "normal ones," I'd realized, looking around at those attending the seminar. They hadn't invited Cheese Boy or the associate that spontaneously fell asleep during conversations. They'd conscripted a select few to fulfill the warm, friendly, female quota that was evidently lacking at the partner level. "We've provided a list of appropriate restaurants in the packet I've passed out." He'd held up the recruiting packet the way an evangelist would hold up a bible. "You'll recognize the names Le Cirque, Four Seasons, and the like. Don't go off the list without consulting me first," he'd warned us before moving on to the last page of the packet, "Be Truthful, but Don't Overshare." "Look," he'd started. "Everyone knows lawyers work long hours, but you don't need to *dwell* on that. Everybody wants to eat the sausage, but nobody wants to see how it's made, if you get my drift." I remember writing that sentence down and underlining it twice, not entirely sure I got his drift.

"So, Spencer, what else can we tell you about F&D?" Ben asked the prospective summer associate he was attempting to woo, bringing me back to the present.

I stabbed at my endive salad with my fork and struggled to focus on the conversation. Normally I would've been thrilled to be treated to a lunch that cost the equivalent of my monthly food budget, but when Ben asked me to join him on a recruiting lunch this morning my first instinct was to decline. With my mile-high to-do list, the last thing I could afford was a two hour lunch. But I quickly realized Ben wasn't asking me, he was telling me. So here I was—having a long lunch while the pile of work sitting on my desk haunted me.

196

Even with the free food, these interview lunches bordered on painful. The recruits always fell into one of three categories: (1) the painfully awkward introvert, whose red face and stuttering makes you even more uncomfortable than him; (2) the pretentious over-achiever who only takes a break from telling you about her list of volunteer work to ask you your thoughts about an obscure court decision she just read about in law school; and (3) the well-con-nected, naturally intelligent frat boy who spent much of law school hung over, but still managed to wind up top of his class. This last guy usually had a Wall Street job lined up, but still wanted to be taken out for a free lunch by each Biglaw firm hungry to recruit him. But the most exasperating part about these lunches wasn't the personalities of the recruits; it was how phony it all was. I was an integral part of preventing people from seeing how the sausage is made, meaning whenever I opened my mouth lies came out. *Yes, the partners are very approachable! Of course pro bono work is always encouraged!* I always felt like I was chanting the mantra of some wacky cult. But it's the circle of life, I suppose—I was fed the lines and now I was feeding them to the next generation.

I put a forkful of salad in my mouth and chewed while looking up at the sparkling chandelier hanging from the cavernous ceiling, blinking my dry eyes in an effort to keep them open.

"Well," Spencer responded. "How would you describe the atmosphere among the associates?" *There's a question straight out of his law school interview brochure*, I thought, sneaking a surreptitious peek at my watch. Spencer fell into category number one, which made the lunch even more excruciating. I chewed fast to clear my mouth to answer, but Ben had already started.

"Our associates are extremely supportive of one another. Other firms may cultivate an overly competitive, 'kill or be killed' environment"—which he air quoted—"but that's not F&D." I nodded in agreement, playing along, and started to tune out his rehearsed answer. "Instead of hoarding the work, our associates look out for each other. In fact, Mackenzie and I are working together on the kind of deal that any corporate lawyer would kill to be involved in. And instead of resenting her for her opportunities, another associate advocated for Mackenzie to work on the two biggest deals in the firm simultaneously."

197

Wait a second. Rewind. What did he just say? Another associate *advocated* for me to be on the deal with Saul? The one that had my ruined my anniversary dinner, jeopardized my chances of impressing Ben, and put my mental stability at risk?

"Wow, sounds like a great opportunity," Mr. Introvert responded eagerly, looking at me. My smile was pasted on my face, and I think there may have been a piece of lettuce dangling from my mouth.

"Yeah," Ben continued. "I was worried Mackenzie had too much on her plate." Ben grabbed my shoulder in praise. "But you balanced both deals handily, just like Sarah said you could."

―――

Back in my office two hours later, my mind was in overdrive. I picked up the phone to call Jason, but after I dialed the first number I hung up. Unloading on him about this now would probably just annoy him and I didn't want another wedge planted between us. I fired off a quick IM to Alex simply saying, "Can you come by?" and waited.

He'd become my personal Buddha when it came to work issues, keeping me grounded and centered. When I was berating myself for crying about a public dressing down at the hands of Saul, it was Alex who explained it was *normal* to cry when someone yells at you. "I'd worry about you if you *didn't* cry — it would mean you've become a robot," he'd reassured me. And when Ben demanded that the deal team pull back-to-back all-nighters to prepare for a contract negotiation meeting after coming off a week when I'd billed over one hundred hours, it was Alex who brought me Advil for my caffeine-induced headaches while patiently reminding me the worst would be over soon, like I was in treatment for some terrible disease. He would know how to handle this. At the very least, he could be a craziness barometer and keep me from going down to Sarah's office and scratching her eyes out.

When I still hadn't heard back an hour later, I called his secretary, who informed me that Alex was out of the office at the Financial Printer. "Said he won't be in all week!" she exclaimed. That explained why I hadn't seen him today. This was the third time Alex had worked on a large stock offering requiring him to be at the Printer, and each time it was akin to falling off the face of the earth. Lawyers, bankers, and clients hunker down in conference rooms of cavernous Financial Printer offices for weeks, sometimes months at a stretch, banging out what will be the final copy of publicly filed documents.

"It's like being in purgatory," Alex said after the first stock offering he worked on, requiring him to spend six weeks at the Financial Printer. "Once you enter, they might as well seal the doors behind you because you'll be there for an eternity." Apparently these Financial Printers have developed ways to keep you from noticing the long wait for the revised proof. "They're staffed with a cast of characters whose only job is to cater to your every whim," Alex explained. "You want a Häagen-Dazs bar at 2 A.M.? Done. Too cold and need a sweater? Someone will run to Saks and buy you one. Need to be entertained while the workers reset the printer for a new proof? Just play a game of billiards or Grand Theft Auto on the sixty inch plasma screen. Not pleased that the Red Bull isn't diet? Then diet Red Bull you'll have!"

It sounded completely bizarre to me, but, as with most perks, it was done to keep you happily working around the clock, giving you no need to stop, fuelling you with as much caffeine and aspartame as you needed, and all of it, of course, charged back to the client. Nothing in Biglaw is free.

With my Buddha stuck in purgatory, I was going to have to handle this latest crisis on my own. I attempted to force myself to concentrate on the director's resolutions I needed to draft. I shook my head. *Focus, focus,* I repeatedly commanded myself, but the lunch conversation kept playing like a movie reel in my head. There was no way Sarah had advocated for me to work on the Saul deal out of the kindness of her heart. Her motives were obvious. She was trying to sabotage my chances with StarCorp.

Six hours of stewing later, at just after eleven o clock, with my director's resolutions nowhere near done, I'd formulated a plan for dealing with Sarah. I'd casually asked Sadir what Sarah was working on these days and he'd launched into a lengthy description of an asset purchase deal that Maxwell was running that was keeping her in the office late every night. I knew Sadir's clandestine data collection on the work habits of his co-workers would come in handy at some point. I decided to wait until after midnight, go down to her office, and confront her face to face. Because of the late hour, there would be fewer curious ears to hear if things got loud, which was a very good possibility. I wasn't going down without a fight. Or at least a catfight.

I took a deep breath and picked up the phone to call Jason on his cell phone. I wasn't going to unload on him, I promised myself. But I'd decided I didn't want to do this without him. He wouldn't be in the office this late, but maybe if I could just hear his voice it would feel like he was here beside me. It went straight to voice mail, which meant there would be no craziness barometer to consult—I was going rogue.

The theme song to Rocky played loudly in my head as I silently rehearsed what I was going to say: "Sarah, I've wanted to give you the benefit of the doubt," *(Risin' up, back on the street; Did my time, took my chances . . .)* "but I now realize that this is personal." *(Went the distance, now I'm back on my feet, just a man and his will to survive . . .)* "And it has to end. Now." *(It's the eye of the tiger, it's the thrill of the fight; Risin' up to the challenge of our rival . . .)* "Because if it doesn't, you're going to have a full blown catfight on your hands." *(And the last known survivor stalks his prey in the night, and he's watching us all with the eye of the tiger!)* Determination was coursing through my veins as I headed down to her office ready to finally have it out with the Ice Queen.

Standing outside her closed office door, I hesitated for a moment. Was this really the right thing to do? Was it really the right time? Maybe I should just do this over the phone or email. Or at least wait until I've run it past an appropriate craziness barometer, rather than the theme song to a 1980s Sylvester Stallone movie. A muffled groan coming from Sarah's office interrupted my self-doubting thoughts.

It sounded like she might have been crying. *Maxwell probably just chewed her out,* I deduced. *Maybe I should come back later.* I turned to leave, but my feet wouldn't let me. *No, I need to do this now! I need to have this out with her or this will never stop.* This is it. I took a deep breath and turned the handle of her office door.

200

My bleary eyes had trouble deciphering exactly what I was looking at—a headful of messy brown hair, the flash of a side of butt cheek. Oh. My. God. There was a naked man on top of Sarah! A naked man! She wasn't moaning from frustration, she was moaning from . . . oh, it was too gross and terrible to think about. I quickly closed the door before I could be noticed.

And then I froze. Time seemed to stand still as my mind caught up to what my eyes had just seen. My heart fluttered in my chest. *I know that hair . . . I know that butt cheek.* I knew with sickening certainty what I had just walked in on. Now my pulse was thumping in my ears. I opened the door again.

"Jason?" I sputtered.

"Mackenzie!" Jason jumped up and attempted to get to his feet, frantically pulling up his pants, which hung down on one ankle. I could feel tears rising up in my eyes. I backed out the door, turned, and quickly started down the hallway.

Oh my God, oh my God, oh my God. I couldn't produce a cohesive thought. Jason. Naked. Sarah.

22

"Mackenzie," Jason called down the hall. I whirled around, flushed with rage.

"You know what, Jason—if you wanted to break up with me, all you had to do was man up and tell me. But cheating on me? With HER? Like this? You have got to be kidding me," I fumed, not caring who heard.

"You were never around," Jason cried. "You can't just expect me to camp out at your apartment, hoping to catch a glimpse of you." He walked towards me, his expression softening. "I wanted to talk to you, I did. I tried . . ."

His words hit me like a slap. "Never around? Never around?" I repeated furiously. "Your little woman in there is the reason I was never around." Then the pieces slowly began to fall into place and the anger started to burn through me. "You . . . you were the reason she wanted me to work with Saul. She was trying to remove me from the picture completely. Did . . . did you *know* about that? Did you two PLAN it? Hell, were you two screwing on my desk when I was away?" The fury in my voice took me by surprise. I noticed Jason flinch.

"Mackenzie," a quiet voice called out behind him. "We didn't plan it. It just happened." I looked over to see Sarah walking towards us, looking disheveled and contrite. I fixed a steely glare in her direction. Adrenaline and humiliation were pulsing through my body. "Sarah, you claim to be committed to your career, but you're just a two-faced bitch out to steal everyone's happiness because you can't find any of your own." With that, I turned away, blinking back the tears that were prickling in my eyes, and ran to the sanctuary of my office.

A massive sense of failure was swelling in my chest. Breathing deeply, I leaned against the wall, slid down to the floor, and buried my face in my hands. I choked back a huge sob. The easiest thing in the world would have been to let the tears flow, but once I started it would be too hard to stop. I rubbed my temples and replayed what I had just seen in my mind. Jason was banging my work nemesis. All the time I wondered why Sarah was out to get me, and now it came into painfully sharp focus: she wanted Jason and had thrown me under the bus to get him. I could hear the "ping, ping, ping" coming from my computer, signaling incoming emails. I suddenly felt nauseous. I needed to get out of there. Using the door handle for support, I got to my feet and opened the door. I peered up and down the hallway to make sure the coast was clear and darted towards the elevator vestibule before I bumped into anyone.

The elevator descended to the ground floor and I burst through the doors onto 56th Street. Tears started to roll down my cheeks as I folded my arms over my stomach and hugged myself. Standing there, in the spot that employees used for smoke breaks, I let the tears flow and didn't even care that my mascara was running or that snot was dripping down my face. Roars of laughter and shouts swelled out of the Pig 'n' Whistle as the door swung open and four men in grey suits spilled out. Even at 12:45 A.M. on a random Tuesday, Midtown was buzzing. Overcome with shock and grief, I staggered to the sidewalk, no longer in control of my movement. Some greater force took over and willed my body to put one foot in front of the other. My voice didn't even sound like my own as I stuck out my hand and yelled, "Taxi!"

———

I don't remember telling the driver where I was going or the ride there or even pushing the third floor button in the elevator. Besides a feeling that my insides were imploding, the next memory I have is the look on Kim's face when she opened the door. Judging from her alarmed expression, I must have looked as bad as I felt.

"Mac, what happened?" Her eyes were filled with concern as I choked on my sobs. "Come here." She pulled me inside, closing the door behind me.

"Is it work?" she asked gently, still holding my hands.

I shook my head.

"Jason?" Her expression was more intense now, anger already welling up on her face.

I nodded, choking back a huge sob. She guided me over to the couch where I plopped down, burying my face in my hands. She wrapped her arms around me, and I realized it was the first time I'd been hugged in weeks. It felt so unbearably good. I let the tears stream down my cheeks as I filled her in on every excruciating detail—the lunch with Ben, the stewing all day, the confrontation, the butt cheek, the humiliation—all of it.

I inhaled a deep, shuddering breath. "I didn't even see this coming, Kim. It wasn't even remotely on my radar."

203

We sat in silence for a moment, Kim seemingly digesting everything I'd just dumped on her. She'd listened quietly, sympathetically, but now she looked like she was trying to find the most sensitive way of breaking something to me. Placing her hand on my knee, she asked gently, "Didn't you know something was up when he didn't even do anything for you tonight, Mac? Flowers, or a gift, or even a phone call?"

I stared at her, perplexed.

"Mackenzie," she said softly. "It was Valentine's Day." Without thinking, I pulled out my BlackBerry to check the date. February 15, 1:15 A.M. A fresh wave of grief washed over me as I collapsed back on the couch, stuffing my BlackBerry back in my pocket. How could I have let my personal life fall so far down my list of priorities that I didn't even notice my boyfriend hadn't bothered to contact me on Valentine's Day? I'd essentially been dumped and completely missed it.

"That fucker," I wailed.

Kim chuckled, nodding. "I know, sweetie." She put her hands on my shoulders and made full force eye contact. "He *is* a fucker, Mac. And you should consider it a good thing that it's over. You just got a Get Out of Jail Free card."

I pulled my knees to my chest. For a moment we were both quiet. "I should just cash that stupid check he gave me," I muttered, breaking the silence.

Kim stared at me, perplexed.

"Mr. Money Bags wrote me a check for twenty thousand dollars back when he wanted me to break my lease and move in with him," I explained.

Kim's eyes widened. "And you still have it?"

I nodded.

"What are you waiting for? Cash that sucker and let's get on a plane!"

I wiped away the tears and managed a smile. "Tempting, but might be a tad drastic in my current condition."

"Fine, but having the chance to take twenty thousand dollars from a boyfriend who you've just caught cheating on you is the dream of every scorned woman."

"I know." I exhaled a shuddery breath.

"Does he have any of his stuff at your apartment?"

"I think so," I answered, realizing I'd been at my apartment so seldom lately that I wouldn't have noticed if he'd already cleaned out his things.

"I'll box it up and drop it off for you. And if you have stuff over there I'll tell him to just chuck it. It's better that way. Trust me. In my experience, the only way to truly end a relationship is to flee like a refugee with nothing but the shirt on your back."

I nodded, wishing it felt as easy as it sounded.

"I can't believe you *finally* went to confront Sarah. I'm proud of you." She patted my knee.

Her name hit my ears with a thud. I'd been so focused on the demise of my relationship and feelings of betrayal and humiliation that I'd completely forgotten there was a face to the other woman. Sarah.

"Kim, how am I going to face her at work without losing my mind?" My voice was small as I hugged my knees, swiping my hands across my eye.

"The question you should be asking is how is she going to face *you*? She screwed someone else's boyfriend in her office on Valentine's Day. I mean, how depraved is that? He obviously doesn't give a shit about her and she knows that. Sarah will always be a lonely old hag screwing another woman's man." She stood up and grabbed a wineglass from the cupboard of her tiny kitchen, raising her eyebrows in a question. She poured me a glass without waiting for an answer. It was then that I realized I wasn't the only one here without a Valentine's date.

"Hey, where's Quinn?" I asked as she handed me my glass.

She took a long, purposeful gulp. "We broke up. About a week ago."

"What? You guys broke up? Why?"

She shrugged, avoiding my stare. "Because guys are assholes—not a big shocker." Her tone was light, but her voice shook. I digested this for a moment, picturing Quinn doing any one of the horrible things guys do to earn the title of "asshole"—lie, cheat (quite familiar with that one now), disrespect, flake out—I just couldn't imagine Quinn doing any of them. He was enamored with Kim. Contrary to what she said, it *was* a shocker. I thought back to all the times in the past I'd seen Kim after she'd had her heart broken by her latest loser boyfriend. There was a certain look about her I could always recognize. It wasn't sad. It was more like defiant. As if she was challenging me to question whether she was *really* fine, as she claimed she was. Studying her now, she looked sad and lonely, almost depressed. Glancing down at the nearly empty bottle of wine on the coffee table, I realized she'd been drinking even before I arrived. My beautiful, dynamic best friend was drinking alone on Valentine's evening. Why didn't she call me? Then it occurred to me: Why didn't she even tell me they broke up?

"Kim, why —"

"Come on," she interrupted, standing up abruptly. "Insomnia Cookies is still open. Let's go drown our sorrows in chocolate chips and peanut butter. And no heart-shaped ones." I could see her bottom lip quivering slightly.

I looked down at the time on her cable box and, like a knee jerking when a doctor's hammer hits, reflexively pulled out my Black-Berry to check my email.

To: Mackenzie Corbett
From: Ben Girardi

Mackenzie,

Where are you? I need you to draft the resolutions for the subsidiaries ASAP.

Ben

What I *should* have done was toss my BlackBerry into my wine-glass, walk to Second Avenue with Kim, and exchange sad break-up tales while letting the chocolate and sugar work their magic. But I didn't do that. Instead, I took a taxi back to the office, because that's the mentality that got me through law school and into this job. Work beckoned, and grudgingly, I answered the call. I think the only person more disappointed than I was that Ben was churning out documents on Valentine's evening was Mrs. Ben Girardi. Somewhere, she was swilling some tequila and popping a Valentine's Day happy pill. I was wishing I had one myself.

To: Mackenzie Corbett
From: Alex Bourque

My secretary said you were looking for me—what's up? I'm stuck in purgatory but thought you'd enjoy this picture of Russ curled up on the floor sleeping in the corner (notice he's clutching a file like a teddy bear). Sweet dreams.

23

I SHIFTED NERVOUSLY IN my seat, checking my watch for the fifth time in five minutes. Why was I so anxious? It was just Alex. We'd met for drinks countless times in the past, just the two of us. But tonight felt different somehow. It had been almost a week since I'd walked in on Jason and Sarah and I hadn't seen Alex in that time. He was still stuck in purgatory so I shouldn't have taken it personally, but I couldn't shake the feeling that he was avoiding me. Not that I'd had much time for chatting anyway. The past week had passed in a robotic haze. I arrived at work every morning at 7 A.M. and worked all day, eating breakfast, lunch, and dinner in my office or the war room. At 2 A.M. I took a Town Car home, had the driver wait outside while I went upstairs to sleep for four hours, shower, and get dressed, then took the waiting car back to work. And the whole routine started again. No need to waste a minute of my time hailing a cab.

It's amazing how much money you can save when you don't pay for any food, transportation, or entertainment. I even expensed my dry cleaning. Lawyers did that all the time when they didn't have time to go home and change. There was a one hour dry cleaner in the basement of the building specifically for that purpose. Technically speaking, I wasn't sleeping in the office, but I still felt I deserved to have the client foot the bill for cleaning my clothes. They were the ones making me sweat. In my new Biglaw reality I was simply utilizing the resources available to me.

My schedule allowed me to hide from pretty much everyone but Patrick, Gavin, and Sheldon. They were the only co-workers I had to face because we were still living like one big dysfunctional family in the war room. We had the occasional fire drill, but I hadn't had to pull out the compressed air canister. Thankfully.

In the light of day I did feel a little guilty about the whole incident. I mean, if you'd told me a year ago I would use an air canister as a motivation tool, I would have thought you were crazy. But it's like those people whose airplane crashed in the Arctic and they ended up eating each other to stay alive. I bet if you'd asked them a year before that, they'd swear that they'd never resort to cannibalism. But they did, and so had I. Gavin never mentioned it. It was just one of those things that happen in the heat of the moment that you don't dare share with outsiders. Like the travelers on that doomed flight, we knew outsiders wouldn't understand. I remember the time Patrick angrily knocked his computer off the table in the war room, sending it tumbling to the ground. He told us all to go fuck ourselves and stormed out before returning calmly thirty minutes later like nothing had happened. Our collective story to IT: the computer fell. Nobody ever talked about the outburst after that. What happens among the deal team stays among the deal team. It was like some code of silence that we all understood. And lucky for me, the air canister incident fell under that umbrella, too.

I knew they'd heard about Jason. How could they not have, with the rumors that were flying around? But they didn't address it, at least not verbally. One night Patrick added a piece of cheesecake to the regular dinner order and solemnly slid it across the table to me. We locked eyes and I nodded a thank you for the conciliatory gesture. And that was that.

Just as I was analyzing how best to handle the whole Jason topic with Alex, I noticed him entering the bar. Spotting me, he smiled and made his way over. I subconsciously smoothed my hair and swiped under my eyes, ensuring they had not morphed into raccoon eyes. "Well, look who's been sprung from purgatory," I joked, standing up to greet him.

"Brought back to life!" He held his hands up triumphantly. "If only for an hour." He hailed the waitress and ordered an Old Fashioned.

"How very Don Draper of you."

"And I plan on knocking it back just as quickly as he does." He flopped into the chair across from mine, looking paler and flabbier than I'd seen him in the past. Spending his days and nights under fluorescent lights, eating greasy dinners topped off with ice cream bars at two in the morning, did not agree with him.

"You'll have to wash it down with some Red Bull if you're headed back to the printers."

"Yeah," Alex responded distractedly, his eyes darting around the room. I was sure he was avoiding meeting my eyes because he didn't know how to broach the Jason topic. He was going to either (a) tell me he had no idea or (b) profusely apologize for keeping Jason's dirty little secret. So long as he didn't throw in something like "bros before hos," I planned on forgiving him.

"Is everything okay?" I prompted.

"Listen, Mac." He blew out a breath of air, his face growing serious. "I saw something today."

"Alex." I held up my hand to stop him. "I already know about Jason and Sarah."

He shook his head. "It's not that. But I promise you I had no idea about that. None. This is about something else." He chewed the side of his thumb.

"Okay." I picked up my glass and took a sip, thankful we weren't going to have to talk about Jason. I'd resolutely decided that there wasn't the option to wallow in my misery. I had enough on my plate to worry about with the signing of Highlander around the corner, and there was no way I was going to let Jason or Sarah or anyone get in the way of that. "What's it about, then?"

He wiped his palms on his pants. He had the pained expression of a police officer knocking on a door at two in the morning, about to break the tragic news that *"there's been an accident."*

My heart was beating fast now.

"My secretary was working on a document for Saul and I saw your name on it."

"Geez, Alex, you scared the crap out of me!" I put my palm to my chest in relief. "I thought you were going to tell me somebody died or you were just fired."

"Well, I'm not but you might be." His voice trembled slightly.

The look on his face was unnerving me. "What are you talking about?"

Alex raked his fingers through his hair. "Mac, what did you mean when you said you wished there was an easier way? On New Year's."

"I have no idea what you're talking about." My tone was stern now. Whatever this was, it was getting irritating.

Alex looked around the room before leaning in conspiratorially. "The document with your name was F&D's response to an SEC inquiry. They wanted a list of employees who had billed time to five different deals."

"Five deals?" The SEC wouldn't ask for a list of insiders from five deals at one time as part of standard practice. That meant they thought there had been insider trading in five different stocks and F&D was counsel on all of them. That was far from standard.

"Mackenzie." Alex dropped his voice to a whisper. "You were the only associate who worked on all five deals."

"Wait a minute. Are you asking me if I've been insider trading?" I asked incredulously.

"I know you wouldn't do that, but at New Year's you said you were looking for an easier way."

"I meant I wanted to work less! I didn't mean I was turning into a real life Gordon Gekko! Geez, Alex, do you know me at all?"

For a moment we were both silent. "I do know you, Mac," Alex finally said, staring down at his glass. "But I also know that Biglaw is like Guantanamo. Nobody comes out of here the same person who went in."

"That may be true, but do you really think I did this? Morphed into a white collar criminal?"

"No!" The crease of worry deepened in his brow. "I saw your name on the paper and it freaked me out, Mac," he said softly. "I think you might be in trouble."

My brain was fuzzy from lack of sleep—there was surely something that I was too slow to understand, something that would make this make sense. "Was there any other associate that worked on all five deals?"

He shook his head, biting his lower lip.

Images of every legal thriller I'd ever read began blurring together—extortion, set-up, arrests, murder. I pressed my fingers to my brow bone to stop my overactive imagination. It was not farfetched to think that if someone picked five deals at random that F&D had acted on in the past year, one associate would've worked on all five. All it showed is that I've worked on a lot of deals. Alex was probably just making a huge deal out of something innocuous. But I was having the same feeling in my gut that I'd ignored for the last month of dating Jason. The feeling that something was off. Really off.

"Do you think I'm being set up or something?" As it came out of my mouth I almost felt embarrassed for sounding so theatrical.

"I have no idea," Alex responded. "But if I were you I'd keep my head down and my eye out for anything unusual."

I nodded. An impossible task in an environment where nothing is normal.

Keeping my head down proved easy as I continued to be snowed under with work for Highlander. But I might have been taking Alex's advice too literally one morning when, on the way back from the coffee room, I almost bumped into a whistling Ben Girardi.

"Glad to see you getting caffeinated — it's going to be a *big* day," he said cheerfully. "We're down to one final point left to negotiate, so it's finally time to get some signatures." He rubbed his hands together gleefully.

"Wow, that's great," I said with as much enthusiasm as my voice was capable of before my morning coffee. I used to imagine the signing of a purchase agreement looking something like this: A CEO outfitted in a $5,000 suit from Savile Row sitting in a cavernous forty-second floor windowed conference room, sterling silver Tiffany pen perched over a signature page, ready to sign and be met with a round of applause by surrounding lawyers and executives. In reality, the lawyers on each side gather the necessary signatures from their respective clients on separate signature pages a few days in advance and when an agreement is finalized, a PDF copy of the signature page is exchanged via email. No pomp, no applause.

I silently decided I'd delegate the signature collecting to Patrick.

"Just one thing." Ben looked around conspiratorially and lowered his voice. "The tax guys had to do some creative structuring for this deal to avoid the regulators." I continued to listen as Ben explained that a new entity had been created to be the purchaser and Stuart Higgins was the only authorized signatory, meaning he was the only one who could sign the purchase agreement.

Even in my pre-caffeinated state my ears perked up. Stuart Higgins, the founder and head of Pegasus Partners, was worth billions and was a notorious recluse. He basically pulled the strings of his company from behind the scenes. Oren, his right-hand man, was the one that people dealt with. Mr. "Nobody can eat, shit, or sleep" was the face of the company; very rarely did anyone deal with Stuart directly. Only a few people that worked at F&D had ever even *seen* him.

"The signature from Stuart can be a little . . . tricky to obtain. I don't want one of the first years given the task. I'm sure they'd fuck something up. I need *you* to do this." Ben paused and looked at me like he was sending me out over the trenches, into an open field surrounded by enemy soldiers. "Probably the best way to get it is to go over there yourself and personally put the signature page in front of him."

I nodded in agreement. "Sure, no problem," I said calmly, like I did that sort of thing all the time. Inside I was bubbling with excitement. Sure, collecting signatures was a menial task, but I was going to be one of the select few that actually got to meet *Stuart Higgins*! A Master of the Universe. The man, the myth, the legend. It was like an actor meeting Marlon Brando or a baseball player meeting Babe Ruth.

"Great, just grab his secretary Carol's number from Rita and make the arrangements with her." He put his hand on my shoulder. "Good luck, Mackenzie."

Out of the trenches, into the battlefield, I went.

———

"Hi Carol, this is Mackenzie calling from F&D." I paused as I heard the clicking of her typing in the background. I took a deep breath and dove in. "The reason I'm calling is I have a signature page that I need to have executed by Mr. Higgins. It's for the Highlander deal. Is there a good time for me to come by and have him sign it?"

I was met with silence, other than the sound of the clicking keys. Rita had warned me that Carol would be difficult. "That woman guards Stuart's schedule like he's the Gawd-damn Prezzie-dant and you're tryin' to find a good time to assassinate him."

"Who did you say you are?" she finally responded in an accusatory tone.

I decided I'd better put it in as simple terms as possible. Short clear sentences. "My name is Mackenzie Corbett. I'm an associate at F&D. I'm working on the Highlander deal and have a document that I need executed by Stuart." I paused for a moment to let that sink in before I continued. "I just want to check with you to determine the best time to come by his office to obtain the signature. It will only take a minute of Stuart's time," I added, trying to sound as cheerful as I could.

Type, type, type. "Well, I don't know how you're going to do that," she responded flatly. I waited a moment for her to expand on that.

Silence.

213

Okay, I'll try this from a different angle. "Is Stuart in the office today?" I asked.

"Nope." Type, type, type.

"Ummm . . . will he be in the office tomorrow?"

"Nope."

I pressed my fingertips into my temples. "Is there any time I can just get a minute with him so he can sign this document? It's the purchase agreement for the Highlander deal—the extremely large and high-profile deal that Pegasus Partners is doing. I only need a minute and I could meet him wherever he is." I stopped just short of pleading.

"Have Oren sign it." As if I wouldn't have thought of that.

After ten minutes of explaining to her in the most patient tones I could muster that the only authorized signatory was Stuart, she finally started to relent.

"Well, Stuart's on a hunting trip. In Michigan. I have to warn you, he does *not* like to be bothered when he is in Michigan. So this better be *important*, McDonald."

I was on the 10:05 A.M. flight from LaGuardia to Detroit Metro. It was a Biglaw first for me—hunting down a client for a signature—but I was no longer fazed by the extravagant steps taken to coddle millionaires. In this case, billionaires. Because if there was one thing Biglaw had taught me, it was that the more important a person becomes, the less capable he is of completing a simple task on his own.

"Unless someone goes out there and physically puts the fucking page in front of him, we'll never get it," Ben had explained. And that someone was me, McDonald Corbett. From the Detroit Metro airport, I took a Town Car out to Hoist Lakes, a remote hunting area in southern Michigan. Seven hours after I'd called Carol, I was pulling up to Bearhurst Lodge, Stuart's enormous log cabin, secluded from civilization deep in the dense woods.

It looked like the kind of place where the Unabomber might live, if the Unabomber had been a billionaire. Security cameras lined the narrow driveway leading up to a cedar log home large enough to be mistaken for a hotel. But despite the opulence, it still had the same kind of vibe as the isolated shack you see on the news after they've found twenty-five bodies buried on the property—it was creepy.

"He'll be hunting until dinner time. You are to wait for him in the sitting room," Carol's email had instructed. Now, standing here in front of the menacing house wondering what (or who) was buried underneath it, her email reminded me of the beginning of a bad horror movie.

The camouflage-clad man that opened the door led me to the cavernous sitting room. "You can wait in here," he muttered, gesturing towards the couch. His moustache was so bushy I couldn't even see his lips move when he talked. I wondered how he even ate with that thing hanging down over his mouth. I sat uneasily on the brown leather couch as he turned on his heel to leave. "Stuart will be back at dusk," he called ominously on his way out of the room.

I sat stiffly on the edge of the couch, barely daring to breathe until I could only faintly hear his thudding footsteps. I looked down at my watch. *5 p.m.* Sitting there, surrounded by rifles and mounted heads of various animals, my mind started to race. *When exactly is dusk this time of year. 6 P.M.? And does dusk mean twilight or sunset or the time in between? And why would you use the term "dusk" instead of just saying a time? Oh God, am I going to make it out of here alive?*

I glanced around the room. Dead animals were everywhere—four huge bearskin rugs were spread out on the floor; there was a lamp shade that I was pretty sure was real zebra skin; and scattered around the room were full-sized stuffed wolves, each with its teeth bared, looking like it had won the man-beast battle when it had clearly lost. My eyes stopped on the deer's butt that was mounted above the glass-top table with the wooden bald eagle base. A butt? He mounted a butt? Why would you mount a butt? I mean, mounting an animal *head* as some sort of trophy I get. Not my thing, but I understand it. You went eye to eye with the beast and that was what you had to show for it. Mounting an ass? That was a new one to me.

I took a break from staring at carcasses to check my BlackBerry. I drew a sharp breath in when I saw what was waiting for me in my inbox.

To: Mackenzie Corbett
From: Ben Girardi

We need to get that signature from Stuart ASAP—Highlander is getting antsy and we're worried they're going to pull out. They won't accept a PDF—original signature page only. Get the signature and get back to the office.

I felt like my throat was closing up from stress. This whole deal, months of work, was now sitting on my shoulders. It was either triumphantly return to the office, signature in hand, or wind up mounted on the wall of Stuart's study. I stared at the looming, oak grandfather clock, watching the second hand tick away precious time, and prayed dusk was soon.

Finally, an excruciating hour later, a man entered the room. He was dressed head to toe in camouflage, with a vest that had at least twenty zippers, and tall black boots that he tucked his pants into. Any skin that was exposed was covered with what looked like black shoe polish. He was still carrying his rifle.

Was I going to be met with enemy fire? I stood up and stuck out my hand. "Hello, I'm Mackenzie," I said, my voice shaking. I was hoping he would introduce himself in turn, as I had no idea if he was Stuart Higgins or one of the other gun-wielding men I'd seen wandering around outside. Instead, he stared at my hand, turned his back to me, and went to sit in the large zebra-print arm chair in the corner of the room, furthest from where I was sitting.

I hesitantly sat back down on the couch. Maybe he doesn't like to be touched? Or spoken to directly? I was going to have to play this carefully. I waited a minute before starting. "Umm . . . I've just come here to get the purchase agreement for Highlander Hotels executed." Nothing.

Maybe he was deaf? Surely Ben would have mentioned that.

Unable to deal with the uncomfortable silence, I plodded forward. "Carol said she'd let you know that I was coming. Umm . . . I'm sure you know that the purchase agreement has been negotiated for the Highlander Hotels deal and it's ready to be signed . . . uh . . . by yyyou," I stuttered.

Ignoring me, he slowly reached his hand up to his head, grasped a small tuft of hair with his thumb and forefinger and started to twist the tuft back and forth. When that chunk of hair resembled a dreadlock, he moved onto the next chunk of hair. He kept his eyes fixed on the floor.

Okaaaay. I guess this is Stuart Higgins. This is the man, the myth, the legend. I had heard Stuart was quirky, but this was a bit more than quirky—it was downright strange. *I'll just wait for him to talk to me,* I swiftly decided. We sat there in silence, as his fingers moved from one tuft of hair to the next.

Tick, tick, tick, the clock seemed to be screaming as my Black-Berry blinked manically.

When he finally spoke, about half of his head had been twisted into tiny dreadlocks. "Are you going to give me the document?" he asked, in a barely audible voice with his eyes still fixed on the floor.

"Oh, yes!" I popped up and grabbed the file that was sitting on the table in front of me. "I just need one signature, right next to the red 'sign here' tab." I walked across the room and placed the folder, open to the page, on the small wooden table in front of him. I clicked open a pen and placed it on top of the opened document. I stood there for a second trying to look relaxed as I waited for him to scroll his signature, but it just felt like awkward hovering so I returned to my seat.

He slid the document to the side of the table, leaned over, and crunched his left hand into a fist. I probably would have been scared that I was about to be punched if he wasn't so . . . weak looking. Even in his camouflage and wielding a rifle he looked like a white Steve Urkel. He even had the pronounced hunch. He placed his other hand on the table, palm open to the clenched fist, and proceeded to tap the clenched fist as if it were a ball. Then he moved his palm-open hand to the other side and tapped the fist back. He was playing tennis with his hands. His face broke into a grin as he followed the "ball" back and forth with his eyes.

Well, now I've seen everything. I did my best to look away, feeling like I was interrupting a private game. But glancing at him through the corner of my eye, I couldn't stop wondering how this guy had managed to make billions of dollars, make hundreds of people under him millionaires, have teams of lawyers grovel over him, and become a titan of industry. Gordon Gekko, this was not.

217

I thought back to the group of strange kids I'd known in high school. Where were they now? Probably running billion dollar companies somewhere.

After a few minutes, Stuart stopped his tennis game, picked up the pen, clicked it open and closed for another few minutes, looking at it with the fascination of someone who was looking at a pen for the first time, then finally signed the document. Acting as if putting the pen down too forcefully might detonate an explosive, he very tentatively placed the pen on the file folder and gently put his hand on top of it, resting it there for a minute. Then he stood up and, without a word or a glance in my direction, walked out of the room.

Awash with relief, I leaned back on the couch and exhaled.

———

Standing in the copy room six hours later, my body limp from my adrenaline roller coaster, I felt like I was going to pass out. But the finish line was so close I could taste it. I just needed to make a copy of Stuart's signature page before delivering the original to Highlander's lawyers. Unfortunately for me, the simple act of operating a copy machine was proving to be overwhelming. It was a task that a secretary would normally attend to, but after the work I'd gone through to get that signature, I didn't want it out of my sight. With my mind half asleep, I pulled the signature page out of the folder, slid it onto the copier and, unfortunately, into the side of my finger.

Ouch! I flinched and stuck my bleeding finger in my mouth. My mind filled with self-pity. *Can my luck get any worse?* I pulled my finger out to take a look. It was really bleeding. I winced and put it back in my mouth, reaching down with my other hand to flip over and align the paper on the copier. That's when I saw it—the drop of blood covering the S in Stuart. I'd soiled the original signature page! Frantically, I scanned the copy room for a paper towel, a tissue, anything to wipe off the blood and minimize the stain, but there was nothing. Why wouldn't a room that carries ten different colors of "sign here" tabs have one freaking roll of paper towels? I grabbed a plain piece of paper, crumpled it up, and began rubbing. Images of Lady Macbeth washing her hands of Duncan's blood flooded my mind. *Out, damn'd spot! Out, I say!* After a few frantic strokes I lifted the wad of paper to assess the damage.

The blood was now covering all of Stuart and part of the H. I stuffed the blood-stained page inside the file folder and darted down the hall, my hands shaking.

"Mackenzie!" I heard a voice belt out behind me.

I whirled around, panic pulsing through my body.

"What are you doing here?" Ben asked incredulously. "You need to get the signature page over to Highlander's lawyers. Is that it?" He gestured to the file I was clutching.

There was a dim ringing in my ears and my mouth went bone dry. *Remain calm.*

I gulped for air. "Yes, I was just making a copy of it before delivering the original," I finally answered, my voice trembling.

"Well, get it the fuck over there. Everyone is waiting."

I nodded briskly and continued down the hall to Rita's cubicle.

"Rita," I whispered anxiously, gesturing for her to come into my office and shut the door.

"Geez, hon, you look like ya've seen a ghost or something," she said. "What's the matt-ah?"

"Rita, I fucked up." My voice shook as I slid the soiled signature page out of the folder and placed it on my desk. The stain looked browner than it did in the copy room, causing a fresh wave of anguish to wash over me. I squeezed my eyes shut as a sharp pain shot through my chest. It was as if my lungs could only reach twenty percent capacity, and for a brief moment I wondered if I was having a heart attack.

"Hm. Hm. Hm." I heard Rita pick up the paper and examine it. Swiftly, she moved behind my desk and slipped into my chair. "What's ya password, hon?"

"Cupcake2013," I answered obediently. I was so vulnerable at that point she could have asked me for my social security and credit card numbers and I would've given them to her, no questions asked.

"Cupcake?" Her mouth twitched with humor as she pecked at the keys. "I'm not even gonna ask."

I felt a twinge of embarrassment, knowing that most people choose something dear to them for their password. Rita probably thought it was a pet name, but in reality, when I was prompted for a password, it was what came to mind.

A minute later my printer was whirring, spitting out a single page, which Rita pulled out and placed in front of her. "Gimme." She gestured to the soiled page.

In a trance-like state, I slid it across the desk.

Rita studied it before scrolling swiftly but purposefully across the freshly printed page. She handed it to me with a triumphant expression. "Problem solved." She crossed her arms over her chest and a wide grin spread across her face.

"But how did you . . . " I stared in awe at the exact replica of Stuart's signature, minus the blood.

"Ya can't grow up in Long Island without learnin' to forge a signature, hon."

My mind raced through my options for how to handle this. I could come clean, delaying the signing, possibly killing the deal, and most certainly killing my career or . . .

My phone blared, the caller ID flashing BEN GIRARDI.

Rita looked at me expectantly, pressing the speakerphone on.

Ben's anxious voice filled the room. "Mackenzie, I have Highlander's lawyers here in my office. Do you have Stuart's signature with you?"

There were a few beats of heavy silence as both Ben and Rita waited on my answer.

"Yes," I finally croaked, holding the paper up with trembling hands. "I have it right here."

———

"Mackenzie, our fearless leader, here's to you—the only female lawyer I can bear to be around!" Patrick boomed, holding his Stella high in the air. We were on our second round and the toasts were heading downhill.

"I don't think I *should*, but I'll take that as a compliment." I clinked his glass. The Highlander purchase agreement was officially signed and a huge weight removed from my chest. I was one step closer to StarCorp. Gavin and Patrick had pressed me on my time at Bearhurst Lodge. *What does Stuart look like? How big is his house? Is his wife hot? Is he as weird as they say?* I'd answered the questions about his wealth, but was purposely vague about his personality. For some reason the short time I spent with Stuart felt . . . private. His peculiar behavior made him seem so vulnerable to me. As if by sitting in the same room with you and exposing his odd behavior, he was confiding in you. Sharing his secret. And, even with everything he had, all the possessions he'd accumulated and the power he'd amassed, I actually felt sorry for him. I didn't want to add to the rumors.

Ben was positively gleeful that the deal hadn't fallen apart. "Great work with Stuart," he'd praised when he tracked me down in my office following the signature page exchange. "Take the juniors out to celebrate—firm treat." I knew the hard work was far from over—a closing date had been set for May 15, so there were closing documents to draft and regulatory approvals to gain, but I was trying to push that out of my mind. Tonight was about celebrating.

"It *is* a compliment!" Patrick gave me a hearty pat on the back. "That's as good as it gets, Mac Lucky."

I laughed, feeling pleasantly buzzed. I actually had an embarrassment of riches tonight. Sadir had updated me on "the latest" just before I left the office, which included the delightful nugget of information that Sarah had been staffed on a large IPO with Maxwell, which would essentially amount to her being exiled to the printers for an indeterminate amount of time. Not only did it mean that I wouldn't have to see her smug face around the office, but it also meant she wasn't working for Ben now. Out of sight, out of mind.

"Mac Lucky?" Kim looked at me inquisitively. Despite the last minute invite, Kim agreed to join us. "Well, I'd planned on watching a marathon of Girls, but I suppose that can wait for another day," was her response when I gave the 5 P.M. call. "But do we really have to hang out with a bunch of boring lawyers?" I gently explained to her that I couldn't ditch my comrades tonight, so the evening would have to involve lawyers and possibly boring law talk. But it would also involve free drinks. "Well, twist my semi-alcoholic arm," she'd joked.

The Biglaw survival technique I was employing tonight: streamlining your social life. Free time is a limited resource in Biglaw, so when you get it you need to use it efficiently. Which means if you're ever given time away from the office, you invite everyone in your contact list to join you. Sure, it can make for some strange co-mingling of worlds. Like maybe you're doing shots with your cousin and your hairdresser, but at least you avoid the "it's been six months since I've heard from you—are you still alive?" email.

"Has Mackenzie not filled you in on her gambling nickname?" Gavin put his hand on my shoulder, giving a light squeeze. "You gotta take this one to Vegas. She's got a knack!"

"Is that so?" Kim said disinterestedly, clearly unhappy about being the odd man out of the inside joke.

"Here's the story," I started, hoping I could bring her in on the humor. "There's this senior associate, Russ."

"He's a dick!" Gavin piped in.

"And he's super cheap," I continued. "So he's always scrounging for food in the conference rooms. Every day at four o'clock he'd come by the war room."

"War room?"

"Sorry, I mean the conference room. We call it 'the war room' because . . . " Why *did* we call it that anyway? "Whatever, it's not important." I waved my hand dismissively. "Anyway, we started to notice his pattern. He'd come into the conference room and imme-diately hit the tray of desserts left over from lunch. He'd pop all the leftover brownies in his mouth, one after the other."

Patrick acted out Russ stuffing food into his mouth, as Gavin burst out laughing.

"We were bored one day, so we decided to make a game of it. We took bets to see how many brownies Russ would stuff into his mouth in one sitting. And the winner was yours truly." I took a mini bow.

"How many did he eat?" Kim looked horrified rather than amused.

"Eight!"

"Ew, gross."

222

"Oh, but the funniest part was, right before Russ came in we called Sheldon, another associate on the deal, to ask him if he wanted in on the bet. He says . . . " I paused, snickering, as Kim looked at me expectantly. "'No, but I'd like to come *watch*.'"

Patrick, Gavin, and I dissolved into laughter, as Kim turned her gaze to the TV behind the bar, ignoring us.

Maybe I mistakenly left out some of the funny bits because Kim was failing to see the humor in the story. What was with her tonight?

"Hey, have you guys seen the new *X-Men*?" Kim asked, changing topics. "A-maze-ing. I mean, I don't usually like the whole superhero thing, but in 3D . . . " She trailed off awkwardly, reading our blank faces.

"We've kind of been living in a conference room." I explained. "We haven't had any time to see movies, but it *looks* really good."

Streamlining my social life was clearly not working tonight. Bringing Kim here reminded me of the time when Mom made me invite the French exchange student to my sleepover in the fifth grade.

It was a disaster—she had no idea who the Backstreet Boys were and the best question she could come up with for Truth or Dare was "do you like your teachers?" Granted, it was probably the only English she knew, but still. Kim might as well have just asked us if we liked our teachers.

"Another round?" Patrick offered, but Kim politely declined, grabbing her coat and mumbling something about needing to get up early.

"I promise, when this deal is over we'll go out for a girls' night," I said, giving her a quick hug goodbye.

"Sounds good. Lemme know when it's done."

I nodded enthusiastically.

"Don't be a stranger," she called out over her shoulder, but I had already turned my attention back to the group.

24

I PULLED THE LATEST copy of the closing checklist off the printer and flipped through the pages, feeling light. I'd been working around the clock for the past eight weeks to meet the implausible timetable for closing, and finally the end was here. The regulatory approvals were in hand, all transaction documents were signed, and, through the magic of wire transfers, Pegasus Partners would become the proud owner of Highlander Hotels today.

Alex poked his head into my office. "Big day! Has it closed yet?"

I shook my head. "The funds are set to move at noon."

"Congrats. I'm sure you'll be happy to put this monster deal behind you." He came in and closed the door. "Have you heard anything about the secondment yet?"

"Nope. But Sadir regaled me with 'the latest' this morning and supposedly Ben makes the announcement after Memorial Day weekend every year. So, I should know in a few weeks."

I didn't mention that after Sadir had passed on that tidbit of information, I'd high-tailed to the bathroom to practice my best surprised face in the mirror. *You're choosing ME for the secondment? The one that assures me I'm on partnership track?* Palms to the face, like Macaulay Culkin in Home Alone — too theatrical. Hand covering mouth, Miss America style—too dramatic. Tiny grin, Mona Lisa style—too aloof. I'd settled on charmingly surprised à la Jennifer Lawrence at the Oscars.

"Well, there's no better authority than Sadir." Alex snickered. He picked up a book from my shelf and began flipping through it absentmindedly, before his facial expression changed. "And no word on the other . . . " He trailed off without looking up.

"No word." I shook my head.

It was the first time either of us had brought up the insider trading investigation since that night at the bar. Even now, Alex was choosing his words carefully enough to avoid being implicated. I'd think he was overly paranoid, if I hadn't already torn my office apart to ensure it wasn't bugged. Clearly, we'd both seen Homeland too many times.

"Well, no news is good news." He returned the book to the shelf, like he no longer needed the shield. "Want to grab a drink after the closing dinner tonight?" His jovial tone had returned. "I've got some work to do for Russ, but it shouldn't keep me here past nine. We can celebrate the end of the Highlander deal and your impending good news."

"Don't say that!" I scolded. "You'll jinx it. Ben could give the secondment to *anyone*."

"Oh, come on, Mac. The biggest deal in the firm right now is about to close and you're the reason. You've got to be feeling pretty confident."

He was right. I was.

———

Ding, ding, ding—Vincent clinked on his wineglass, pushed back his chair, and stood up.

A team of white-shirt clad wait staff descended upon our table, placing massive porterhouse steaks in front of each of us. What I really craved was a fresh salad packed with all the vitamins and minerals I was certain my body was crying out for, but lawyers always celebrate accomplishments with red meat. Like it will somehow make everyone feel like a successful hunter instead of some robotic paper pusher.

Glancing around the table, I subconsciously took inventory—nineteen men, one woman. The mixture of pride and discomfort was a feeling I'd grown familiar with, but never got used to. I tugged at the hem of my skirt, wishing I'd worn pants instead.

"I just want to welcome everyone and tell you how impressed I am with all of your hard work on this transaction." Vincent paused for applause. "A deal of this magnitude takes a lot of ground soldiers on the battlefields. Each one of you is responsible for getting the ball across the finish line." I fought the urge to laugh. He'd managed to check off lawyers' two favorite metaphors—war and sports.

"For that I am eternally grateful." Another pause to look around at each of us, hoping individual eye contact properly conveyed his sincerity. "This transaction will probably be known as the 'deal of the decade.' It was the most complex deal I've worked on in my career."

Hyperbole—check!

"You should all consider yourselves very lucky—you will be better lawyers for having been on it."

There was the "giving up the last six months of your life to fill the firm's coffers was really for YOUR benefit." Check!

He cleared his throat. "And, while I hope this isn't the most high-profile deal you work on in your careers, I suspect it will be."

Ah, good old fashioned arrogance. The Biglaw congratulatory toast checklist was complete. Hear, hear.

"Let's just drink the fucking wine, for Christ's sake!" Anton Waldorf bellowed from the other side of the table, tossing a dinner roll at Vincent. "At the rate you're going with this toast we'll all finish this night fucking sober."

"You've never been sober a day in your life, Waldo!"

"And fuck if I want to start tonight!"

With that, hearty guffaws were exchanged around the table as everyone raised their glass and the evening descended into a buzz of ego, testosterone, and meat eating.

The next two hours continued in this vein, as we made our way through four courses and countless bottles of wine, with the conversations headed downward as rapidly as the wine.

"Vinny and I started our careers at a firm called Nixon Weiss," Anton slurred, holding the attention of the entire table. "I was a third year associate and Vinny was just a fresh first year associate. We had some good times. Good times," he repeated, looking reflective. "But definitely the thing that sticks out most in my mind has to be the morning that my secretary arrived at work and announced, 'I fucked Vincent Krieder last night.'" Everyone at the table roared with laughter and hoots. I shifted uncomfortably in my chair and grabbed my wineglass, wanting to disappear into it. My God, these guys were so vile. Did they even notice I was here? Worse, did they think I found it *funny*? I half expected them to shout "yee haw" and lasso a calf or whatever it is that good ol' boys do.

"Don't crucify me for that one!" Vincent exclaimed, pointing his finger at Anton. "I was BETWEEN wives at the time. Besides, your secretary was hot!" More guffaws. "Not like your secretary NOW."

"Well, YOUR secretary has fucked so many lawyers on that floor that they should name it after her," Anton retorted. Now poor Rita was being dragged into this drunken debacle.

"Yeah, first name TRAILER last name TRASH," Vincent quipped. There was a burst of laughter and everyone swilled back more wine. I'm sure Vincent would be surprised to know that Rita expressed pity for him, rather than admiration. Even more surprised to know that his inabilities in the bedroom with his ex-wife were a source of comedy for her (and most likely the countless people she's confided in). If this was the direction of the conversation, maybe I should just bring up the whole no orgasm thing. It would serve him right.

While I contemplated the idea, Ben piped up from the other side of the table. "Did you hear Fox Paper is finally going to file tomorrow?" He'd been silent most of the evening. Given the woman he's married to, he must be used to taking a backseat to the drunk and disorderly. My ears perked up for the first time all night. Fox Paper was the IPO that Sarah was working on with Maxwell, the one responsible for her being banished to the printer for the past eight weeks. If it was going to file tomorrow that meant Sarah's ugly mug would be back haunting the halls of F&D.

"We've racked up so many fucking hours on that—it's going to make Maxwell's fucking year," Vincent bellowed. "Well, hall-a-fuck-ing-lu-jah, it's finally going to file. Hear, hear." Glasses clinked all around, as I plotted how best to avoid the Ice Queen. With Ben's

StarCorp announcement around the corner, I didn't want anything getting in the way.

Walking into the Pig 'n' Whistle minutes after I'd ducked out unnoticed from the drunken closing dinner, I felt my shoulders start to relax. A drink with Alex was just what I needed to unwind after that shameless display of swagger. I gave my name to the hostess and attempted to stand off to the side, avoiding the jostling from all sides by eager patrons.

"Excuse me." I felt a tap on my shoulder. "Have you put your name in yet?"

"Uh huh," I answered, my eyes fixed on my BlackBerry as I scrolled down an email from Alex saying he was going to be late due to Russ's need to be kept company at the office, rather than any actual work that needed to be done. "Jackass," I muttered out loud to no one in particular.

"Hey, it was just an innocent question! It doesn't make me a jackass!"

"No, it's my friend—I mean, not my friend, a guy he's working for ..." I looked up from my BlackBerry and the most gorgeous brown eyes were smiling back at me.

Staring at me, actually. "You don't remember me, do you?" He chuckled, looking sheepish.

"Umm ... refresh my memory," I hedged.

"From the plane?"

The plane? My mind started to race like a slot machine until it landed on ... oh ... my ... God. The guy from the flight to Dallas. The guy I fell asleep on.

"Oh ... uh ..." My face reddened. "It's ... you ... I mean, we uhh ... right ... we met on the plane." I suppose "met" was a bit of a stretch, but saying, "Oh, you're the guy I drooled on and ranted to about not showering" seemed somehow inappropriate. Standing up, this guy was even cuter than I remembered. He had the body of a swimmer—tall, muscular without being obnoxiously big, wide shoulders, and a chiseled stomach. "Sorry, I ... uh ... never got your name."

"It's Lawrence," he chuckled, "but you can just call me jackass." He smiled and I noticed the adorable dimple he had on one cheek.

"Oh, sorry about that." Flustered, I waved towards my BlackBerry and started to explain. "My friend was supposed to meet me . . . "

"Mackenzie for two," the hostess called out, thankfully interrupting my stumbling attempt at an explanation.

"That's me." I stepped forward.

"Is your whole party here?" she bellowed. I hate that question in a restaurant. New York seems to be the only place in the world where they refuse to seat you unless everyone is present and accounted for. Do they think you're lying to them in a sordid attempt to get a table for four when you're only a party of two? You just want the extra space?

"Oh, he'll be . . . "

"Right here!" Lawrence stepped forward. "Just go with it," he whispered, giving me a quick wink.

Walking over to our table I was suddenly aware of how dowdy my black Theory suit looked in a bar. I felt like Hillary Clinton at a frat party. I wriggled out of my blazer and hung it over the back of the chair, thankful that I had a silk camisole on underneath rather than a boxy blouse.

"What can I get for you?"

"Heineken for me and . . . " He gestured to me.

"Same," I nodded, looking around the bar, trying to hide the fact that I was replaying our previous encounter and cringing inside at the things I'd revealed. Maybe he'd forgot.

"Soooo, last we spoke you were miserable and unshowered," he said, a half smile playing at his mouth.

"I was kinda hoping you forgot about all that." I grimaced and blushed at the same time. "Let's just say that wasn't exactly my finest hour. I was working really long hours, for a crazy person . . . and well, yeah . . ." I trailed off, deciding I'd better just cut the explanation short at that for fear of descending into the TMI abyss again.

"Hey, I'm just hoping things have improved. It looks like you're clean at least." He flashed another smile and looked me over teasingly.

"Yes, yes, I have showered today." I held my hands up in mock triumph.

"And have things improved?"

Good question. Would catching your boyfriend cheating on you with the person you dislike the most in this world be considered an improvement? But, then again, sitting here chatting with a cute guy, with the weight of the Highlander deal off my back and the secondment ahead of me, I felt like things *had* improved. Maybe it wasn't just the Highlander deal that had caused the crushing stress, maybe trying to hold together a stagnant relationship had something to do with it too. "Well, I guess that depends on your definition of 'improved,'" I answered, smiling mysteriously.

He raised a quizzical eyebrow and cocked his head. *Ohhhh . . . he can do the sexy one eyebrow lift.* I've always been a sucker for the sexy one eyebrow lift.

I shook my head and laughed. "You don't wanna know—trust me. And I'd have to be a lot drunker to get into it anyway."

"Waiter!" He raised his hand. "We're going to need a round of shots here," he called out. I laughed and felt my tension melting away.

"So, what led you to working at a big law firm?" He took a long first gulp of beer.

"Well, my uncle is a lawyer and I've always looked up to him. He's just—" I paused, realizing I hadn't made a trip out to see Uncle Nigel since his retirement party, over five months ago. I vaguely remembered that he'd emailed a few times, but I couldn't recollect if I'd ever responded. Uncle Nigel had always been there for me, helping guide me towards my goals. And he'd given me the incredible memento from the World Trade Center. Now he was retired and could probably use the company. I silently hoped I'd at least shown him the courtesy of a response. "He's just someone I really look up to." I swallowed hard. "But why a big firm in particular?" I shrugged, staring into my glass. "Maybe it's just the whole overachiever thing gone awry. And, of course, once you look at your loan repayment schedule, your options start to narrow significantly. The hours are long, but, well . . . you just get used to it, I guess."

"Right," he nodded, looking amused. "Kinda like how someone just gets used to constant physical pain."

"Something like that." I smiled and took another swig of my drink, trying to think of something to say to change the topic, but I couldn't think of anything. It's not like I had any free time to engage in any other activities or even read a newspaper. The result was that I'd become an incredibly boring person with nothing to talk about except my job, which not even I wanted to hear any more about. "Sorry, I haven't always been this boring." I gave a nervous laugh. "There was a time when I read books for pleasure, kept up to date on politics and current events, listened to music . . . " I had to stop myself from recollecting everything I had relinquished for this job. I really was developing serious disclosure issues. *Shut up, Mackenzie!* I urged myself. *You're going to bore this poor guy to tears with your gloominess. And you're descending into TMI territory again. Next thing, you'll be telling him how Tandoori chicken from Bombay Palace gives you the runs. Just stop speaking!* "But enough about that." I waved my hand dismissively. "It's like exhaustion and uncontrollable over-sharing go hand in hand with me. Your turn—anything totally unbecoming or overly personal you want to share with me?" I joked, hoping to keep the mood light.

"Personal? Let's see . . ." He shifted in his seat. "Well, does the fact that I shower daily count?"

"No, no, that's getting off waaay too easy. You need to say something cringe-worthy. Here, I'll start you off—I told you about my job, so what is it that YOU do?" I was relieved to be moving the conversation away from myself.

He leaned back in his chair. "I have an idea. Let's not talk about our current jobs. I'll tell you about the BEST job I've ever had." He gave me a wry look and paused for effect. "Dogwalker."

I laughed in surprise, nearly spitting out the gulp of beer I had just taken.

"Seriously! It was the perfect job. I was in college and new to the city and it combined two things I love. Dogs," he said, planting his elbow on the table and lifting his index finger, "and exploring the city." He lifted a second finger and I noticed his fingernails looked perfectly manicured. Or what is it they call it? Handshake maintenance? His fingernails were perfectly . . . maintained. "I'd take a different route every day," he continued, "and I got to know streets I would never have thought to walk down. I learned so much about the city doing that." He paused, looking reflective. "Did you know that the only wooden townhouses left in the entire city are on 92nd Street in the Upper East Side?"

"I did not know that," I answered.

"It's true, just a few blocks away from where the Marx brothers lived. Their house is still there too. Just a little bit of trivia for you." He gave a confident, charming smile. "And I've got many, many more pieces of useless New York City trivia too. Thanks to my favorite job. Okay, now you." He leaned in. "Let's hear about your favorite job."

"Hmmm . . . " I paused. I was considering how much I wanted to reveal to someone I'd really just met. For some reason it felt easier to talk about F&D than other things in my life—like my job wasn't personal; it wasn't really *me. But, then again, this guy has already witnessed me drooling in my sleep*, I reasoned. In for a penny, in for a pound.

"Okay," I said. "Like you, it was my job in college—I worked at a bakery close to campus called 'Sweet Muffin.'" I leaned back in my seat, getting comfortable. "I loved it from the start—the smell of freshly baked cookies when you opened the door, the cupcakes frosted in pastel pink, the happy customers coming in for their morning indulgence. The atmosphere was always festive. It's just impossible to be unhappy in a bakery, you know?" I couldn't help smiling at the memory. My mind flashed to sitting on a couch with Kim during our Bachelor nights, listening to her rave about my latest creation and insisting I add it to the menu at Sweet Muffin. She was always my biggest cheerleader, even when all there was to cheer about was my homemade Heath Bar crunch cookies. "That association always stayed with me. When I was stressed in law school, the process of baking just soothed me. You take ordinary ingredients—eggs, flour, sugar, milk, and voilà—something delicious. The satisfaction of pulling a pan out of the oven and knowing if you put the right ingredients in, it comes out delicious every time. There's something in the science of it, I guess . . . " I trailed off, remembering how good it used to feel arriving at Sweet Muffin for my shift. "Okay, here's one for you—did you know the busiest day of the year at a bakery is Christmas Eve?"

He gave an appreciative full-wattage grin. "I did not know that," he exclaimed in mock amazement.

"Just a little bit of bakery trivia for you."

The next hour flew by as we flowed from one topic to the next. We talked about everything *but* our careers. I learned he was the youngest of three children, raised by a single mother, and the most difficult part about not having a father in his life was not having someone to show him how to put on his equipment in his first year of football.

I talked about my parents and how I used to be embarrassed when they would hold hands in public, how I realize now how lucky I am to come from such love, and how I enjoy living in New York but miss my family every day. We talked about favorite places we'd traveled to, books we loved, and TV shows we recorded. The conversation was just . . . effortless.

234

Lawrence was one of those rare people who listened with his full attention, making me feel like everything I said was interesting. And he was absolutely hilarious—he made me laugh in a way I hadn't for a long time. The type of laughter that makes you grip your stomach and leaves your cheeks actually hurting. I felt buzzed in a way that I knew had nothing to do with the alcohol. I let the world of abusive partners, inhumane hours, and bitchy mentors slip away. For the first time in years, my mind was remarkably, delightfully void of any thoughts of F&D and it felt fantastic.

Lawrence's cell phone rang just as he was starting in on a story about the time his two older sisters used him as a makeup model. His face turned serious as he peered down at the caller ID. "Sorry, I have to take this," he said, standing.

"Oh . . . yeah . . . you probably should get to whatever it was you were supposed to be doing tonight." I tried to mask the disappointment in my voice. I'd been having such a good time I'd forgotten that we didn't actually plan this—I'd basically hijacked his evening. "And I should probably get going, too," I added, not wanting to sound like I had nothing else to do tonight. Which I didn't, now that I was apparently being ditched by Alex.

"This," he pointed at the table, "is what I want to be doing tonight." He smiled and held my eyes long enough to make it clear that something was happening in this bar. "Why don't you order us another round and I'll be back in a minute."

"Okay, sure." I nodded, feeling a surge of happiness.

"Hello?" I heard him bellow into his cell phone as he made his way through the crowd.

I reached into my purse to fish out my BlackBerry. I couldn't believe that I'd forgotten about it this long. I saw the red light blinking and felt a wave of relief that it was just an email from Alex. He said he needed to take a rain check—Russ's one hour "project" was going to take him most of the night. I smiled and returned my Black-Berry to my purse. For once, I was thankful for Russ's random, needless projects.

Lawrence and I were on our third round when I finally told him about the Sarah and Jason saga. I hadn't planned on it, but there was something about Lawrence that just made me relax and open up. I felt unedited with him. Two months ago I wouldn't have been able to tell the story without my eyes welling up. Tonight, I felt like I was telling a story from years ago that I'd long since put behind me.

"Wow—that's just messed up. I mean, sex in the office? On the *desk*?"

I nodded, realizing just how ridiculous the situation had been. "Total cliché, isn't it?"

"Does that even *happen* in real life? I mean it's so . . . Mad Men."

"Except instead of a voluptuous redhead with a cigarette, it's a neurotic, semi-anorexic woman with OCD."

We laughed, and how I felt in this moment was easily the happiest I'd felt in a long time. Lost in conversation, we ended up closing down the bar.

Lawrence suggested hitting a nearby diner for a late dessert, but my exhaustion was starting to catch up with me. I didn't want the night to end, but I was feeling like if I put my head down on the table, there was a good chance I wouldn't wake up for days. And falling into a sleep coma was probably not a good thing to do considering I'd already fallen asleep on this guy once. As much as I wanted to keep the night going and get to know him better, I knew I had to take a rain check.

"Understandable—rain check it is."

He insisted on at least putting me in a cab, which I gladly accepted. After years of leaving work at odd hours, I was no longer anxious being alone on the sidewalks at late hours, but it was chivalry I appreciated. He put his hand on the small of my back as we exited the bar into the chilly night air. We stood on the corner outside of the Pig 'n' Whistle, each waiting for the other to speak. He broke the silence first.

"I really would like to see you again. Any chance you'll be sprung from prison Friday night?"

My insides did a giddy happy dance. *Be cool, Mackenzie.* "Friday *should* work . . . " I answered, wondering what lay ahead of me now that the Highlander deal had closed. "Work dependent, of course," I added lamely.

I longed to be type of girl that could just say, "Sure, Friday works for me," and not worry that some thoughtless partner was going to screw it up. Would Lawrence understand the unpredictable hours that I had to work?

"Wait a sec," I said, realizing I didn't know what kind of hours *he* worked. "You never did tell me what you do."

"Guess you're just going to have to go out with me again to find out." He grinned, reaching out his hand. "Now let me see that ball and chain of yours for a minute." I reached into my purse, pulled out my BlackBerry, and handed it to him. He punched at the keys with his thumbs. "I'm emailing myself so I'll have your email."

A cab with a lit-up medallion number came barreling down Third Avenue and Lawrence stuck out his hand to hail it. "Your chariot," he said, turning back towards me. Confidently, he pulled me towards him and, looking straight in my eyes, leaned in for a kiss. A delicious jolt of pleasure coursed through me and I felt like my body might actually levitate. His kiss was soft and sweet with the perfect amount of passion. Amazing. The best kiss I'd ever had.

He opened the taxi door for me and gallantly gestured for me to slide in. He handed me back my BlackBerry. "I'll email you, since I know you have that thing attached to your hip." He grinned and closed the door.

I gave a quick wave from my seat as he stood on the corner. "Ninety-first and Third, please," I instructed the driver. I couldn't wipe the smile off my face. Had that night really just happened? I looked down at my blinking BlackBerry and giggled when I opened the email: *Stop checking your BlackBerry and get some sleep! Lawrence*

Still smiling, I leaned back in the seat and gazed out the window. Despite the late hour, the city looked alive.

———

I was beaming as I stood in the salad line at Toasties on Tuesday afternoon, pecking out an email to Lawrence. We'd been emailing each other all morning and I was dying to see him again. My whole body felt light, airy, and for the first time in months, well rested. Last night after I'd met Lawrence, I went home and fell into the kind of sleep that is so revitalizing you're sure you've added years to your life, erasing the bags under my eyes and giving me the kind of energy that made me feel like I could sprint around the Central Park Reservoir. I hit send on my flirty email before firing off a quick email to Kim.

To: Kim Bawolska
From: Mackenzie Corbett

You won't believe my night last night! Are you free Saturday night? Dying to fill you in! xo

I think I was actually humming as I replayed my evening with Lawrence. I'd never clicked with someone so fast. And the kiss. It was such an incredible kiss . . .

"Ma'am? What kinda lettuce you want, ma'am?" An impatient voice interrupted my thoughts.

"Oh." I snapped back to reality. "Mixed greens, please." I moved down the line as the server tossed a handful of lettuce into the large bowl. "Chicken, carrots, croutons, onions."

I scanned the crowded deli for an empty seat. Nothing. I grabbed a plastic-wrapped sour dough roll from a basket at the register and the clerk threw it in the paper bag along with the salad and a fork.

"$10.42," he grumbled and pushed the bag across the counter. The ten dollar salad—only in New York. I paid for the over-priced veggies, did one last check for an open seat and, seeing none, headed out the door.

The sun was shining as I made my way back towards the office. I briefly considered having lunch outside, but the Death Star was smack dab in the middle of an outdoor space dead zone, and my Derek Lam A-line skirt made perching difficult, so I quickly dismissed the idea. I pulled my BlackBerry out of my pocket as I entered the revolving doors, anxious to see if Lawrence had replied. But what I saw in my inbox was the exact opposite of an email from Lawrence.

To: Sarah Clarke, Mackenzie Corbett
From: Saul Siever

PLEASE COME TO CONFERENCE ROOM 27C ASAP.

My breath caught in my throat. I did a full 360 in the revolving door and was deposited back outside the building. For a moment I just stood there, frozen. The memory of working with Saul and Sarah was still burned into my head the way a POW recalls his captivity. I thrust my BlackBerry into my purse and, without knowing where I was going, staggered away from the office. It was a primal fight-or-flight reaction and my body had chosen flight.

Dazed, I crossed the street despite the orange "Don't Walk" blinking hypnotically. I kept going past the man peddling fake Gucci purses spread out on a white sheet, nearly tripping over a large LV patterned suitcase. People blurred past me and the sounds of the city—horns honking, a jackhammer pounding, the loud conversations of the passersby—all blended into a buzz in my head. The air smelled of meat frying from a nearby food truck.

Another deal with Saul and Sarah—this can't be happening. I walked faster as Alex's voice rang in my head. *He can't be bargained with, he can't be reasoned with, he doesn't feel pity, or remorse, or fear. And he absolutely will not stop, ever, until you are dead.* Alex was right. That line from Terminator 2 was a surprisingly accurate description of Saul. Suddenly Arnold Schwarzenegger's voice burst through my thoughts in one clipped line: "Your foster parents are dead." I stopped in my tracks, my pulse quickening, as my mind replayed the scene from Terminator 2 like a movie reel.

The Terminator has just told John Connor that the T1000 has been sent to kill him. In an attempt to warn them, John calls his foster mother from a pay phone. "Something is wrong. She's never this nice," he tells the Terminator. Knowing that this diversion from ordinary behavior means John is now in danger, the Terminator takes the phone, unceremoniously hangs it up, looks John square in the eye, and says, "Your foster parents are dead."

With shaking hands I pulled my BlackBerry out of my pocket. There, in all caps, shouting at me, was the word "PLEASE." Saul had never used that word before. I could hear myself gulp. That's when I knew this had nothing to do with being put on a new deal.

239

25

I PUSHED MY WAY past the large group of summer associates lingering in the elevator bank and made my way to conference room 27C, as Rita had instructed, ready to hear my fate. Questions zipped through my mind. *Did they find out about the forged signature page for Stuart? Am I about to be fired?*

"Mackenzie," Sarah hissed from the other side of the corridor. Her precise and perfect demeanor was harried and disheveled, making me wonder who had finally pulled the bobby pin out causing her to completely unravel. "Everyone is waiting!" She angrily gestured towards the conference room before disappearing back inside.

You can do this.

But when I stepped through the door, I froze. Standing up to introduce himself was a man whose head was as bald as a cue ball, and just as shiny. His enormous arms bulged through his grey suit jacket. Dangling from his left earlobe was a gold hoop earring. My heart began thundering in my chest. He bore a striking resemblance to Mr. Clean, just as Rita had described.

"Miss Corbett, I'm Tucker Sullivan with the Securities and Exchange Enforcement division." He stuck out a paw-like hand, squeezing my hand in a hardy shake. "I have a few questions for you regarding some unusual trading activity we've discovered. Why don't we all take a seat?" He strode briskly behind me and pushed the conference room door shut.

I pulled out a leather rolling chair, sneaking a surreptitious glance at Saul. I noticed he'd perspired through his dress shirt.

"Let me start with some background for you, Miss Corbett."

"Mackenzie," I croaked, my sweaty hands clasped tightly in front of me.

"Mackenzie." He nodded, scratching something down on his pad of paper. "In the past year we've become aware of an unusual amount of trading in the shares of five different takeover targets days before bids were announced. This type of activity is a red flag for us that there is insider trading going on. What we look for in these situations is a common thread among the bids and when we find the common thread, we pull it." He mimed pulling an imaginary thread from his suit jacket. "And what we unravel is *always* securities fraud. The common thread here, in all five bids that were the subject of the suspicious trades, was the law firm negotiating the deal. F&D negotiated all five." He raised his eyebrows ominously. "So let's start tugging at that thread, shall we?" He pulled a piece of paper out of a redweld and slid it across the table with a satisfied look on his face.

"Did you have access to confidential information regarding any of these companies?"

"Yes," I answered, scanning the list. "I worked on transactions involving these five companies." I tried to keep my voice even, worried that a shaky voice would make it seem like I had something to hide.

"And did you work with Mr. Siever and Miss Clarke on the failed bid of Falcon Mobility Inc.?"

Sarah and Saul stiffened. In my nervous haze I'd forgotten they were sitting there. Saul wasn't normally someone who faded into the background, but clearly he had no interest in being front and center at this meeting.

I nodded. "And a number of specialists as well."

He scratched something on his notepad. I noticed he'd already filled a few pages, presumably with answers from Saul and Sarah.

"Let's talk about that deal because that's the one that opened up Pandora's box for us. We uncovered an abnormal amount of shorting activity before Falcon's announcement that the deal fell through. Do you know what that means?"

"I know if you're short selling stock you're betting the stock is going to decline." I could feel the confidence returning to my voice now that I was given the opportunity to utter more than a one word answer.

"And I'm assuming you know how short selling works, then?"

"Yes."

Without looking up from his notepad, he rolled his hand, gesturing for me to go on.

"You borrow shares of stock and then sell them in the open market without ever owning the shares. When the stock drops, you buy back shares at a later date at the cheaper price to return to the owner." I wiped my wet palms on my pants.

"So the goal of short selling is to purchase the shares for less cost in the future and net a profit." His tone sounded more like a question than a statement, so I nodded assent.

He slid another piece of paper out of his redweld, peered down, and pushed it over to me. "Here is a list of individuals or corporations that shorted Falcon Mobility stock. Do you recognize any name on that list?"

243

The room was silent as I peered down at the list. "No." I shook my head.

Out of the corner of my eye I noticed Sarah and Saul exchange a brief, pointed glance.

"So you never knowingly or inadvertently passed confidential information to any person or entity on that list?"

"Of course not!" My tone was flustered. "Are you accusing me . . . Do . . . do I need a lawyer?" My eyes darted to Sarah and Saul, who sat expressionless, averting their eyes from my stare.

"You are the only person that had access to confidential information on all five of these deals. So, here's what I think, Mackenzie." The look on Mr. Clean's face was like he was about to devour a delicious dessert. "I think someone knew that the media reports of your client bidding on Falcon inflated the Falcon stock. That person was also privy to the information that the negotiations ended when Falcon informed your client that they were seeking a loan instead of a sale. Knowing that this meant the stock was ripe for a sharp decline, that person then fed the information to someone on this list, who shorted the stock before the failed bid was publicly announced."

The room was spinning like a carnival ride that I couldn't get off. Nauseous, faces were whirling in front of me—Saul, Sarah, Mr. Clean.

"Yes, Miss Corbett," he continued. "You may want to get a lawyer because this train is pulling out and it looks like you're on the tracks."

26

HE WAS GRINNING WHEN he opened the door, but his smile quickly faded as he took in my sweaty, splotchy, disheveled appearance. Out of breath from running the entire way from the train station, I could barely manage to get the words out. "Uncle Nigel," I puffed. "I need your help."

His hand felt solid and comforting on my shoulder as he guided me inside, reassuring me I'd come to the right place. He had the same look on his face that Mom had when Margaret had called her to tell her she had suffered an injury that would jeopardize her scholarship — unwaveringly calm and pragmatic. For the first time since I left the office, I could feel my rapid heart rate start to decrease a little bit.

"Let's talk in here, Mac." He gestured towards the study.

I sat down heavily on the couch and rubbed my eyes with my palms. I hadn't formulated a script in my mind for how best to explain what was happening to me. It was too dreadful and humiliating to comprehend, let alone explain it.

"Listen," Uncle Nigel started gently. "The economy still isn't great and this happens to the best of lawyers. Law firms just over-hire and then let good quality people go. It's the only way they can maintain their pyramid structure. It is nothing to be ashamed of."

I shook my head. "I didn't get fired, Uncle Nigel." I raised my eyes, meeting his. "It's worse." And then the words came tumbling out of me in a hurried, uncontrollable crush. I told him about when I first heard about the SEC investigation from Rita and when Alex saw the list of associates who'd worked on the five deals. I described the horrible meeting with Mr. Clean, Sarah, and Saul and how I'd been told I may need to get a lawyer. "So." I exhaled a shuddery breath. "Here I am."

Uncle Nigel was rubbing his chin and nodding. He had a quiet, thoughtful look on his face, but it was impossible to read. "What is the firm's position? Have they put you on leave?"

"No, not officially. Mr. Clean said he needed to meet with us again on Thursday. The SEC is still gathering information internally and will have more questions for us then. So, HR told me and Sarah that it would be best if we didn't come back to the office until that meeting." All the times I would have embraced what amounted to a two day break from the office and now here it was. Be careful what you wish for.

He was looking carefully at me now. "Is there any way you passed on confidential information to anyone inadvertently? Maybe carried a file without a codename or talked about a transaction in a public place?"

"No." I shook my head adamantly. "I'm so cautious with stuff like that that people actually make fun of me about it."

"Does anyone have access to your network password?"

"My secretary, but I trust her." I shrugged. "I don't know. Maybe the IT guy?" The room was quiet as my brain whirred. The memory of Sarah in my office standing behind my desk when I arrived one morning suddenly filled my mind. "Maybe Sarah," I whispered.

He furrowed his brow. "Did you give her your password?"

"No, but she was in my office one morning before I arrived. And there's been a lot of weird stuff that I've just pushed out of my mind because I've been too tired to deal with anything but work." I chewed on the side of my fingernail. "But none of it really adds up either." Sarah was crazy, but was she a methodical white-collar criminal? The only thing I knew for certain right now is that I wasn't.

"Is my situation right now as bad as I think it is?" I asked Uncle Nigel in a voice so small I didn't even recognize it as my own.

"Well, you're not going to go to jail." He blew out a long breath. "They certainly don't have enough evidence to turn this into a criminal matter."

I put my hand to my chest in relief.

"But it isn't as easy as that." He paused, and I could tell he was trying to bring himself to say something difficult. "I need to be straight with you, Mac. In situations like this, if you aren't able to prove your innocence there's a good chance you'll be fired. And you know how small the legal community is. No other firm will hire you. There's a possibility you could even be disbarred."

I felt like the wind had been knocked out of me. Everything I'd worked so hard for was crumbling and there was nothing I could do to stop it. This couldn't be the way it all ended. It was too horrible to stomach.

"But how could I ever do that? Prove my innocence?"

His expression was grave. "Unfortunately, the only way to clear your name in this situation is to prove that someone else did it."

———

I left Uncle Nigel's house a little shaken, but with a firm resolve. I hadn't let anything break me before and I wasn't going to start now.

I punched the familiar numbers into my phone. I may have been told not to come back to the office until Thursday, but nobody said anything about calling. She answered on the first ring.

"Rita, it's Mackenzie."

"Oh my Gawd! I'm so glad you cawwwled. Are you okay?"

"I'm okay," I answered, with more certainty than I felt.

"I wasn't sure if Mr. Clean had locked you away somewhere."

"Listen, Rita, I really need your help. I need you to get a paralegal to run the standard corporate searches on the following companies. Everything you can get—bankruptcy, court house, corporate register. Everything." If there was one thing I knew about after nearly three years with F&D it was how to perform due diligence on a company. Luckily for me, the names of the companies on the list that Mr. Clean had shown me that had short sold Falcon stock had been burned into my memory.

"That's going to take a long time, Mackenzie. When would ya' need this?"

"Tomorrow. And listen, no one can know about this. You have to keep it under the radar." I squeezed my eyes shut, praying this would work. There was a beat of silence before Rita answered.

"Meet me at the Starbucks on 59th tomorrow at noon. I'll have it for ya' then."

———

"How are you going to get through all that before the meeting with Mr. Clean tomorrow?" Kim pointed to the banker's box brimming with documents that I'd schlepped on the subway from Starbucks to my apartment an hour ago. Rita had been sporting large, dark sunglasses when she'd entered Starbucks, looking every bit the part of an informant. Spotting me in the corner, she'd set the box down, mouthed "good luck," and turned towards the door. I was so moved by her gutsy act of loyalty that it took me a minute to compose myself enough to walk across the coffee shop to retrieve the box.

I didn't realize how badly I needed to see a friendly face until I saw Kim waiting for me in the lobby of my apartment building when I returned home, my muscles burning from supporting the weight of the box. "I called you at your office to chat about that email you sent me about a great night you wanted to fill me in on, but the receptionist told me you were taking the day off. I knew something had to be wrong," she'd explained. Without any questions, she relieved me of my heavy load and helped me up to my apartment, where I filled her in on the terrible turn of events.

"I've become an expert in reviewing documents in a short time frame. Especially when my ass is on the line," I replied now, lifting the top off the box and pulling out the first manila folder. "And it's not like I have a choice." I collapsed on the couch and began flipping through a company profile.

"Well, then, let's get down to it." She raised my window blinds, letting in the afternoon sun. I couldn't remember the last time I'd been in my apartment during the day and I suddenly wished she would close the blinds so I didn't have to think about it. Out of the corner of my eye I saw her run a finger along my coffee table and peer at the dust on her finger. "I'll just clean up our work space a little." She disappeared into the kitchen and came back with a wet paper towel and set to work wiping down the surfaces around me. I'd never known

Kim to be a fastidious person, which made me think my apartment must be in particularly bad shape.

"So," she said gently, "what do you hope you'll find in these documents?"

"Honestly? I hope I'll find any morsel of evidence that clears my name and implicates Sarah," I replied, without looking up.

I could feel her standing over me, scanning my apartment before fixing her eyes on me.

"When was the last time you've been in this apartment, Mac?"

"Well, I sleep here every night," I snorted.

"Really?" She eyed me doubtingly.

"Most of the time," I mumbled.

"I'm worried about you. You look like you haven't slept in days. Or showered for that matter."

"Does dry shampoo count?"

She sat down beside me and took a slow, cleansing breath, reminding me that I hadn't been to a yoga class in months. "I know you're under a lot of pressure, Mac." She was speaking slowly, her kind eyes full of concern. "But maybe this is all some kind of sign. Maybe what you need is to be heading in a different direction."

249

"No." I shook my head, too drained to talk about anything other than the task at hand. "It's not a sign, it's a set-up, Kim. I know I sound like a crazy person right now, but I was this close to everything I've ever wanted and if I don't fix this then . . . " Unexpected tears prickled the back of my eyes. "I can't even go there in my head."

"Okay." She was quiet for a moment. "Okay," she repeated more resolutely. "Then let's prove the Ice Queen did it. But first we need to deal with the food issue because you're starting to remind me of Kate Moss and not in a good way." She stood up. "Do you have anything in your kitchen to eat?"

I shot her a droll look that said *Do you even know me at all?*

"Right." She nodded. "Sushi it is. You get to work, I'll get to dialing."

When the sushi arrived, Kim set it out on my coffee table along with plates, napkins, and two glasses of wine. "Don't say no." She handed me a glass. "You need it. And I'll force feed you that California roll if you don't stop for five minutes and eat."

"Thank you, Dr. Bawolska." I smiled, accepting the glass. "But I've mastered the fine art of reviewing documents while eating." I buried my nose back in the company profiles.

"Suit yourself." She picked up a manila folder from the box, flopped down on the couch, and began flipping through it. "Man, this stuff looks painfully boring. Sometimes do you just want to scratch your eyes out so you won't have to look at it anymore?"

"Sometimes," I answered distractedly, gnawing my pen.

"Company registration number, tax reference number, VAT number . . . " Kim rattled off in a monotone voice. "Nothing interesting in this one." She tossed it on the table and reached for another file. "Hey, there's a yellow sticky on this one."

"Really?" I felt a sudden burst of hope. "Let's see."

She passed me the file, squinting at the note curiously. "It's about Mr. Clean."

My heart rate sped up as I read Rita's scrolled message. *Mackenzie, I copied this stuff from the file Mr. Clean left for Vincent. I don't know if it will be helpful, but if it is, you didn't get it from me.—Rita*

"Rita, I love you," I whispered. "And you too, Kim." I squeezed her hand.

"Does it have what you're looking for?"

"Hopefully." I hunched over the coffee table and examined the folder's contents, scrutinizing lists of associates, spreadsheets of trades, and names of companies until my eyes blurred.

"Anything?" Kim finally asked, peering over my shoulder.

I shook my head, feeling defeated. This was a waste of time. There wasn't going to be a smoking gun with Sarah's fingerprints all over it in this pile of useless documents. I was screwed. After all those nights spent hunched over a computer and weekends spent fielding angry emails, all those movies I'd missed and vacations I didn't take, this was how it was all going to end. I wasn't going to be awarded the StarCorp secondment. I wasn't going to be a partner at F&D. I wouldn't reach the top of the mountain after all. I wouldn't even be employed.

Reading my expression, Kim reached out and put her hand on my shoulder. "Why don't you take a break from this and get some rest?

When you wake up tomorrow maybe you'll see something different with fresh eyes."

"I know she did it, Kim." I buried my face in my hands. "But nobody is going to believe me."

"I do," she replied without hesitation.

I leaned into her. "Thanks, Kim. I can't thank you enough for sticking by me through all of this."

She fluttered her hand. "You'd do the same for me."

We were both quiet for a moment. I couldn't help but wonder if she was right. God, I hoped so.

"I'll clean this up." Kim broke the silence and began gathering the foil containers with the remains of our half-eaten dinner. "The last thing you need is for your apartment to smell like day-old sushi when you wake up."

I tilted my head back against the couch and closed my eyes. A heavy exhaustion radiated down to my bones. My body was crying out for sleep, but my jittery, anxious mind refused to acquiesce, leaving me stuck in some kind of sleep purgatory. All of the peculiar things that had happened in the past year began floating around in my consciousness like tiny particles drifting through the air. Suddenly my mind reached out and held onto one of them. Our anniversary dinner. Our disastrous anniversary dinner. My eyes shot open. "Wait a second," I breathed, frantically flipping through the papers fanned out on the coffee table before I found the spreadsheet with the timing of every trade.

Bingo.

27

I SAT IN THE refuge of my office, clutching the piece of paper still warm from the printer. Outside my door, the familiar morning noises buzzed, but all I could hear was the sound of my own breathing. I'd been awake most of the night, repeatedly running possible scenarios through my mind, ensuring I'd be prepared to introduce my piece of evidence at just the right moment. With adrenaline and caffeine coursing through my veins, I felt like a boxer before a bout. I just needed a trainer to mop my brow with a towel, and toss out a "go get 'em, champ."

"They're ready for ya' in the conference room." Rita's voice blared over my intercom.

"Tell them I'm on my way." I slipped the print-out into a manila folder and stood up. After taking one last deep breath, I walked past Rita's cubicle, mouthed a silent "thank you," and headed down the hall. I reached the marble elevator bank and pushed the down button. It wasn't lost on me that someone had booked conference room 23A for this meeting, the largest in the office. I pressed the button for the twenty-third floor and leaned back against the wall, wondering how many people Mr. Clean had brought with him this time.

"Hold the door," a shrill voice rang out as a red Louboutin pump poked through the gap, stopping the elevator doors in their tracks. Like a scene right out of a horror movie, the doors pulled back, slowly revealing Sarah, looking pressed and manicured. Even when

I was about to bring her down, she still somehow managed to show me up. "I presume we're going to the same place," she said, stepping inside and standing next to me.

"I presume so." I matched her sharp tone.

We stood in silence, watching the numbers decrease as a sudden wave of unease washed over me. I held in my hand the piece of paper that would lead to my tormentor's demise. "Sweet, sweet revenge," Kim had called it. But standing next to her now, I realized I wasn't going to take any joy in watching what was about to happen to her. A tiny part of me even felt sorry for her.

The doors dinged open and Sarah gestured for me to go first. Either she was feeling magnanimous or she wanted to be the first one to direct me towards the guillotine.

I decided to assume it was the former and stepped out.

"Dead man walking," she mumbled. Of course it was the latter.

I whirled around. "Excuse me?"

She stepped off the elevator and burrowed her eyes in mine. "I've just been banned from the office for two days because of you."

"Because of me? You're delusional, Sarah."

She crossed her arms over her chest. "You didn't really think you were going to get away with all this, did you?"

I took a step towards her and felt every ounce of uneasiness drain from my body and anger, red hot fury, take its place. "That's funny, Sarah, because I had the same question for you. But I'll save you the time of considering your answer and let you in on a little secret." I returned her full force eye contact and knew there was no way I was going to be the first to blink this time. "*You're* not going to get away with it. And it's going to be *me*, the person that you screwed over the most, who ensures *you* don't."

Shock and perhaps even fear flashed in her eyes, but her expression quickly reverted to her default look—brittle and smug. "We'll see about that," she spat.

"Yes. We will."

We walked down the rest of the long corridor in silence. The only sound was our shoes pounding on the floor.

I changed my mind. This was going to be fun.

———

Mr. Clean was waiting for us at the door when we reached the conference room. "Ladies." He gestured towards the enormous oak table in the middle of the room where three dark suited men I didn't recognize were sitting next to Saul. "Please have a seat and let's get started."

My palms felt moist as I pulled out my chair. I briefly wished I'd taken Uncle Nigel up on his offer to come along today. If Mr. Clean had three grey suits on his side, I wanted at least one on mine. But having the evidence on my side was even better. I just needed to play this very carefully so I didn't inadvertently expose Rita.

The grey suits muttered something to each other before Mr. Clean said, "Miss Corbett, let's start with you."

I nodded, clasping my hands on top of my manila folder.

He flipped open his legal pad and readied his pen. "The last time we spoke, I showed you a list of persons and entities that had short sold Falcon stock. You said that you didn't know anybody on the list."

I nodded assent.

"And that answer hasn't changed, has it, Miss Corbett?"

"No." I shook my head. Judging by his demeanor, Mr. Clean really did think he was starring in his own blockbuster legal thriller. I half expected him to point his finger at me and shout, "You can't handle the truth!"

"I want to ask you a question about a company called Kerrisdale Inc. Are you familiar with that company?"

I drew a sharp breath in. I knew from the documents that Rita had obtained from the registrar that a company called Kerrisdale Inc. was the sole shareholder of Pemberton Corp., one of the seven companies that had short sold Falcon Stock, but I couldn't find any information about Kerrisdale Inc. on the internet and it had been too late to have Rita get anything more from the registrar.

"Miss Corbett?" Mr. Clean repeated, his voice stern. "Are you familiar with Kerrisdale Inc.?"

255

Everyone in the room stared expectantly in my direction as a tiny bead of sweat trickled down the back of my neck. I cleared my throat. "No, I am not."

Mr. Clean scratched something on his notepad.

"I'm passing you a list of the names of the directors and officers of Kerrisdale Inc." He slid a piece of paper across the mahogany table. "Can you tell me if you recognize any individuals on that list?"

The grey suits mumbled to each other as I peered down at the list. My eyes stopped at a name in the middle of the page. Suddenly everything went quiet except for a dim ringing in my ears. Tapping my finger on the name for a moment, I tried to understand how he could be on this list. I swallowed hard. "I know Eddie Esposito. He's my doorman. Uh, *was* my doorman," I corrected myself, remembering the story that the old lady in 8H had told me. "Apparently one day he just didn't show up to work," she'd whispered to me by the mailboxes. "Never even picked up his last paycheck. I always *knew* he was shady." She'd scrunched up her eyes and studied me carefully, presumably trying to decipher if I fell under the same umbrella.

The grey suits exchanged a pointed glance.

"Well, Miss Corbett, then we have a problem." Mr. Clean whipped off his reading glasses and tossed them on the table. "Actually, YOU have a problem because Eddie Esposito and every other director of Kerrisdale Inc. has skipped the country. Can you tell me about your relationship with Eddie Esposito?"

"I didn't have a relationship with him," I sputtered.

"Okay, then, let me try this again. Did you ever knowingly or inadvertently pass confidential information on to Mr. Esposito?"

"No!" I had the sudden feeling that I was sitting in a witness box of a court room, looking over at the jury who were all shaking their heads solemnly, seemingly certain that I was guilty. This was not one of the scenarios I had prepared for last night. Somehow this meeting had gone terribly, terribly wrong. "Wait a minute," I breathed, my muddled thoughts finally clearing. The evidence. Now was the time for the evidence. "*When* did Pemberton Corp. borrow the Falcon shares and sell them?"

"Friday, November 20th."

"And when did they buy the Falcon shares from the market and return them to the broker?"

"After the public announcement on Monday, November 23rd. Making $273,000 in the process."

"Then it *couldn't* have been me. I didn't know the Falcon deal had died on Friday. I was still working on the deal on Saturday." I was speaking quickly now. "I remember because I had to come into work on my anniversary that Saturday night. And I worked all day Sunday on the deal." I turned to Sarah just as the color drained from her face. "Sarah knows that. She's the one that requested the work on Saturday night." I pulled the print-out from the manila folder that I'd been clutching so hard my knuckles had turned white. "Here is an email from Sarah dated Saturday, November 21st giving me instructions to come into the office and complete some research related to the Falcon deal."

Mr. Clean had the look of a goaltender who'd just been scored on in the final minute of the game. Saul, on the other hand, looked like the bookie who'd just lost a lot of money on the game and was now out for blood. "What is she talking about, Sarah?" His irate voice boomed.

257

"Mackenzie," Sarah sputtered, her eyes darting around the room like a trapped animal. "Don't try to pin this on me. I only asked you to work on Saturday because—" Her voice was faltering as Saul's angry eyes burrowed into her. She waved her hand dismissively. "I don't even remember why. It was such a crazy deal and there was so much going on." She swallowed hard. "And who cares if it was your anniversary? I don't see how that's relevant at all. He didn't want to be there with you anyway. You're . . . you're . . . I see what you're doing here. You're trying to nail me to the wall and I know why, but it's not going to work."

Mr. Clean and the grey suits were staring curiously at Sarah now. She reminded me of a fish that had been dropped on the dock—thrashing about wildly, doing anything to find its way back to the water.

"I don't know what you are trying to prove here, Mackenzie, but I do know I have NO idea who Eddie Esposito is." She crossed her arms over her chest triumphantly.

I looked squarely at her, the truth in sharp focus now. "But Jason does."

28

MY LEGS WERE TREMBLING when I walked out of conference room 23A. I felt like I'd just been dangled over a balcony with my life on the line, only to be snatched back at the moment when I was about to fall. I'd survived. Barely.

"Mac, there's . . . there's someone in there," Rita stammered as I passed by her cubicle, but my dazed mind didn't catch up to what she'd said until I walked into my office and saw him standing there, leaning up against my book shelves like he somehow belonged here.

"What are you doing here?" I faltered.

"Mac," Jason began, a pained expression on his face.

"What are you doing here?" I repeated with more force in my voice, surprising both of us. I always knew that this moment had to come at some point. Since the Sarah incident, I'd somehow managed to avoid being face to face with Jason. It really hadn't required any effort, being that I was practically living in the war room, arriving at the office and leaving at times most people reserved for sleeping. He could've switched jobs sometime in the past three months and I would've had no idea. Unfortunately for me, he hadn't.

"You okay in there, Mac?" Rita peered in.

I nodded. I'd just gone toe to toe with Mr. Clean. I could handle this.

"I need to talk to you," Jason whispered, stepping around me and pushing my office door shut.

I crossed my arms over my chest, glaring at him as the room filled with a thick, tense silence. There was no way he could've known what had just happened in the meeting with Mr. Clean, so I was baffled as to why he was here in my office. A small part of me was actually curious what he was going to say. "So talk," I said flatly.

"Listen, I heard that the SEC is questioning you about insider trading. Specifically about that deal you were working on with Saul. I *know* you didn't do it, Mac. I know this because —" He hesitated, raking his hands through his hair as his expression grew more and more anguished.

I was stupefied. He had the look of a man who'd been carrying around a giant barbell on his back and was ready to finally relieve himself of the burden. Was he going to admit to me right now that it was *him* that the SEC should be questioning?

"Because . . . " I prompted. Despite already putting the pieces together and knowing that he was the one who had conspired with Eddie to trade on insider information, I suddenly needed to hear him admit it to me, face to face.

"Because I know that's not the type of person you are, Mac. This job means everything to you and I just want to help you." He jammed his hands in his pockets and started pacing around my office, avoiding eye contact. "You've worked so hard and I can't let you go down like this." He was rambling quickly now, uttering sentences like "lots of people would have access to this information" and "What about the cleaning lady?" For a moment I had the strangest feeling that I wasn't really there in my office, but was instead watching the whole scene unfold from a seat in a movie theater. I wanted to stand up and throw popcorn at the screen and shout, "Of course it wasn't *her* because it was *you*, you asshole!" I tuned back in to hear him say, "I really want to help you. Could I be some kind of alibi for you or something? I mean, I know you would never insider trade. You're my rule follower."

"I'm not your anything," I snapped, taking a small pleasure in watching him flinch. Too bad I didn't have a bag of popcorn to dump over his head.

He pinched the bottom of his nose a few times, a nervous habit that I used to find endearing, but now realized that it was actually pretty gross. "Look, I know when we were together we had our differences . . . "

I held up my hand to stop him. "Differences?" I choked out a humorless laugh. "If by 'differences' you mean you were screwing someone behind my back, then yes, I guess we had our differences."

He looked at me with tears in his eyes and dropped his voice to a whisper. "I swear on my life I never meant to hurt you."

Fury started to boil up inside me and I had to close my eyes to keep from screaming at him. After a moment, I opened them and looked at Jason, *really* looked at him. For the first time, I realized I'd been in love with someone who never truly existed. I was in love with the person I thought he was. I didn't even know the person standing in front of me now. But I didn't say any of that out loud. The last thing I wanted to do right now was have a discussion about our relationship. It was history. And he was about to get what he deserved. I reached over and opened the door, holding onto the handle so there would be no mistaking that our conversation was over.

261

"Okay. I'll go," he whispered, lowering his head like a dog being reprimanded.

"Jason?" I could hear my voice crack slightly.

He looked up and met my eyes.

I cleared my throat, surprised by the sudden lump. "You're right. I would never insider trade. But when you get back to your office, you might want to give your lawyer a call because apparently *you* would."

A wave of panic swept over his face before receding and being replaced with what looked like resignation. He gave a slight nod, as if agreeing with me, before turning to leave.

As I watched him walk out the door I gave the inside of my cheek a gentle bite. Jason was not going to get one more tear out of me.

———

Sarah was let go from F&D the next day. Staring down the barrel of being accused of insider trading, she confessed that she had confided in Jason that the Falcon deal was going to die before a public announcement was made. Since she was able to establish that she had no involvement in any of the other illegal trades that had occurred, Mr. Clean concluded that she'd inadvertently tipped Jason, meaning she wouldn't face any legal charges. F&D had not been as forgiving, though. Sarah had breached client confidentiality by giving away material information to someone not involved in the deal. They agreed not to turn the matter over to the Bar Association, which would mean that she would most likely lose her license to practice law, if she agreed to sign an agreement relinquishing any claim to severance.

Jason's departure from F&D was not as discreet. "All Directions Point to Jail for Son of GPS Mogul," screamed *The New York Post*. According to media reports, Jason had managed to arrange trades in public companies using important deal information not yet known to the public on at least eight deals during his time at F&D. He'd find out what deals were impending then feed the information to Eddie and the other directors of Kerrisdale Inc. Through Pemberton Corp., Kerrisdale Inc. would then buy the shares with an online brokerage account before an acquisition was announced. Once the shares jumped, another trade was made and the shares were sold at a handsome profit. Kerrisdale Inc. and Jason would split the profits down the middle. Most of the time the consortium of Jason's misfits and acquaintances made money on a stock rising, but in the case of Falcon, they reversed it and made money as the stock sharply decreased on the bad news that no deal was going to happen. The scheme was stunning in its simplicity.

I tried to pinpoint the exact time when Eddie and Jason had formed their partnership. Maybe it was on the day I'd moved in, when Eddie had helped Jason navigate my dresser into the elevator. I pictured Jason slipping him a fifty and saying "there's plenty more where that came from." Or maybe it was Eddie who'd approached Jason, convincing him that there was an easier way for him to make his mark. I decided to stop reading the papers and torturing myself with the details, though. I was on to bigger and better things.

Even a petrifying meeting with the SEC couldn't distract me from my ambition. If anything, the fear of having F&D pulled out from underneath me made me more motivated, more fixated on the final goal. I was back in my office early Friday morning, wanting to prove to myself and the firm that this loyal F&D foot soldier could survive an ambush attack.

It was just before noon on Friday when Rita popped her head into my office. "Glad to have you back, strange-ah. Ben Girardi wants to see you in his aww-fice." She crossed her arms over her chest, smiling knowingly. It was still two weeks until the typical time the StarCorp secondment is announced, but if Rita was smiling she must know something I didn't. Rita was plugged into everything around here.

"Thanks, Rita. Tell him I'll be right there."

"Good thinkin', Mac. Make *him* wait for you after all the shit they pulled." She winked and pulled the door closed behind her.

I smoothed my hair with my hands, pushed my chair back, and began the walk down the carpeted corridor to Ben's office. I'd done this walk so many times, bleary eyed and anxious. Today, it felt like I was striding down the red carpet. Any moment Joan Rivers was going to call out, "Mackenzie Corbett, who are you wearing?" It was time to collect my prize.

Ben's secretary stood up to greet me when I reached his office. "Great to see you again, Mackenzie. Ben's just finishing up a call, but asked me to have you wait."

"No problem." I smiled, my eyes focused on the inspirational calendar pinned next to her computer. A sunset shot of a well-muscled woman standing at the top of a mountain, with her hands on her knees, taking in the panoramic view. *With great sacrifice comes great reward,* it read. All of the times I'd disappointed my family or canceled plans with Kim at the last minute. Every time I'd been humiliated by Saul or been rendered so thick-tongued with exhaustion that I slurred my words. It would all be worth it now. It had to be.

"Looks like he's ready to see you now," Ben's secretary sing-songed, interrupting my thoughts.

I squared my shoulders, took a deep breath, and entered Ben's office.

"Good morning, Mackenzie." He smiled, revealing a charmingly small dimple in his cheek. How is it that I'd never noticed that before?

I had the sudden realization that this was probably the first genuine smile I'd witnessed on Ben's face. "Have a seat," he said, gesturing to the chair in front of his desk.

"Mackenzie," he began, "there is nothing more important to an employer than loyalty. If there is a silver lining to the recent unfortunate events, it's that we were able to trim some fat, leaving us with only the juicy meat."

I nodded uncertainly. Was I the juicy meat in this scenario?

"You've done some excellent work for the firm."

"Thank you," I murmured, pleased that we were moving away from the steak analogy.

"We usually wait until after Memorial Day to make these decisions. But given the circumstances, I wanted to break with tradition and reward your loyalty." Ben looked down at his folded hands.

My heart was pounding. It was like Ben standing on the stage, clad in a tuxedo, taking his time to open the envelope and announce the winner. *And the Oscar goes to . . .*

"Mackenzie, we'd like to award you the StarCorp secondment."

Yes! Yes! Yes! I did my best humble, surprised face. I felt like I was making my way to the stage, giving a few high fives and posing for a selfie with Ellen on my way up.

I didn't need any notes. My speech was memorized. "I'm really grateful for this vote of confidence, Ben. I look forward to expanding my skills at StarCorp. The learning experience will be invaluable and I'll surely be a better lawyer because of it."

He stood up and came around the desk, clapping me on the shoulder. "I know you'll knock their socks off at StarCorp. And when you return, you'll be ready to put your nose back to the grindstone."

I wanted to respond, but my voice wouldn't cooperate. Suddenly it felt like I had the weight of a grand piano on my chest. All the blood was rushing from my head. The room needed to stop spinning or I was going to throw up. I'd only experienced this feeling one time before, but I knew what it was right away. I was having an anxiety attack.

Ben was still smiling at me, completely oblivious to the hurricane swirling inside me.

Somehow I managed a barely audible, "Thank you."

———

With wobbling legs, I walked out of the Death Star. "You headed out for a celebratory lunch, Mac?" Rita had asked when she saw me minutes after my meeting with Ben, purse slung over my shoulder headed to the elevator. I'd nodded, not exactly sure where I was headed. All I knew for sure was that I needed fresh air.

The last time I had an anxiety attack was two years ago, after a Yankee playoff game I attended with Jason. When the Yankees' fate was sealed in the ninth inning, there was a mass exodus to the exits. The subway platform outside Yankee stadium was so packed I had to pull my purse to my front because there was no room on either side of me to keep it swung over my shoulder. I was at the front of the platform when the train pulled up, causing the crowd behind me to surge towards the doors. Suddenly I was swept up by the powerful wave of people, no longer in control of my own movement, being pushed towards a train that wasn't even the one I wanted to get on. Thankfully, Jason ended up on the same train. He spent the ride back to Manhattan calming my scarily racing pulse.

265

This was not supposed to be happening now, just when I reached the goal I'd been working so hard to achieve, was it? I should have been popping into the nearest bar, calling out "drinks are on me," but instead I only felt like a crate of bricks had been placed on my shoulders. *Get a grip, Mackenzie,* I admonished myself. *Everything's going the way you always wanted. The glittering prize is finally yours.*

I kept walking uptown, stepping over the littered coffee cups on the sidewalk, as I tried to quell the questions zipping through my mind—*Is working at F&D ever going to get any better? Can I submit myself to another round of Saul's abuse? Did Ben really think forcing me to prove my own innocence was simply an "unfortunate event"? If I stay at F&D am I destined to end up like Ben or, worse, like Saul?* They were the antithesis of everything I wanted to be.

I thrust my hands through my hair, struggling to calm my thoughts. I'd never felt so uncertain in my life. I'd always been positive about what I wanted and where I was headed. Now, the sounds of a nearby jackhammer seemed to be beating like a tribal drum, the city noises chanting, *Is this what you want out of life? Is this what you want out of life?*

I considered my life in the last few years—the countless hours, the inhumane work schedule, numerous greasy dinners eaten at my desk or in some windowless conference room. What struck me most was how much I'd changed.

Had I really used an air canister to keep another associate awake? Had I really just sat there and let Vincent call Rita trailer trash? Had I let months go by without seeing Kim? Had I even bothered to email Uncle Nigel back? A hot rush of shame flooded my body. I paused for a red light. I had walked ten blocks. Tension grew in my body and my heart pounded until I could barely breathe. Deep down I knew why I hadn't left F&D sooner—because I had bought into it. The firm had managed to convince me that working in Biglaw was the only symbol of success and that anything outside Biglaw's doors was failure. I had drunk the Kool-Aid. The whole damn glass jug with the smiley face on it. Biglaw just does that to you. It wears you down until you see things its way.

I rummaged through my purse with trembling hands, looking for my phone but not yet sure who I was going to call.

"Excuse me," a voice called out. "I think this fell out of your purse." A kind-looking older man walked towards me holding out a plastic card. "You look much too young to have such a worn employee ID card," he observed, smiling.

"Oh, thank you," I said, reaching out to accept the card. "It's uh . . . it's not actually mine." He looked at me, confused. "I mean, it is mine. It's just . . . thank you." I smiled warmly, stopping myself from getting too far into the explanation. He walked away as I stared down at Uncle Nigel's World Trade Center ID, my heart pounding in my chest.

I suddenly knew it with the deepest certainty I'd ever felt. I don't want this. I don't want to spend my life in a war room. I don't want to miss out anymore.

29

ALL OF MY PERSONAL items fit into one banker's box—my diplomas, three framed pictures, and various toiletries. I bagged up the Seamless rations that filled my shelves and donated them to Henderson's Bodega—twenty-four granola bars, eighteen Diet Cokes, eleven bottles of water, nine bags of M&Ms, and three boxes of cereal. Some night soon a weary associate was going to need a caffeine and sugar fix and would get it from my provisions. I silently hoped that the winning lottery ticket would come from the proceeds. Everything else went into a giant recycling bin that seemed to magically appear outside my office minutes after I had walked out of Ben's.

Ben had been surprised when I told him I had to respectfully decline the StarCorp secondment. His surprise turned to irritation when I told him I was also resigning from F&D. There wasn't any dramatic "take this BlackBerry and shove it." I simply thanked him for the opportunity and gave my two weeks' notice.

"You're making an irreparable mistake," Ben snarled. "If you pull out of this race, there's no way to reach the finish line."

I wanted to tell him that the race he was running was unwinnable. Biglaw was like a perpetual marathon, where someone from the sidelines passed you a Dixie cup of water that you swigged, crumpled up, and tossed back. You could be sustained, but you'd never be fulfilled. "I'm okay with that," I replied confidently.

Perhaps thinking that I was going to grab a megaphone and lead a mutiny of Biglaw associates everywhere, Ben had rejected my offer of two weeks' notice and suggested I leave today. "It's for the best that way. Just provide me a list of all of the matters you're working on so we can assign them to another associate," he'd ordered before giving a curt nod of his head.

"Will do," I'd replied. All the work I'd obsessed over like the future of the human race depended on it would be reassigned to some other hungry young associate. The Biglaw beat would go on without me. There would just be one less Storm Trooper in the Death Star.

When I pulled his office door shut behind me, I noticed my hands were shaking. Not with fear, but with relief.

"Mac, I just got your email!" Alex swept into my office now, looking flustered. His eyes grew wide as he took in the state of disarray. "Holy crap, this is all going down *today*?"

I nodded, a little shell-shocked myself. Luckily, I didn't need the money that came along with two more weeks of work. I had saved up enough from expensing my life away to last me about three months. Pawning the earrings Jason gave me would give me another two months. And then ... then I'd have to figure out what I wanted to do with the rest of my life. I was nervous, but felt lighter than I'd ever felt before. I was twenty-eight years old and could do anything I liked. As Kim pointed out to me, I was living in the city *designed* for people reinventing themselves.

"I wanted to tell you before you heard it from Sadir's latest," I said to Alex, as I briefly considered popping my car-shaped deal toy into the banker's box before rejecting the idea and tossing it in the trash.

"I'm surprised he's not here hiding in this recycling bin to get the nitty gritty details."

I snickered. "I wouldn't be surprised."

My BlackBerry suddenly buzzed, causing the Pavlovian response of a tight band of stress around my lungs. Thankfully, this email had nothing to do with work.

To: Mackenzie Corbett
From: Lawrence Brogan

Still on for tonight? Can't wait to see you—Lawrence

Still on. See you at eight, I replied, reveling in how wonderful it felt to make promises I knew I could keep.

"Wow." Alex blew out a long breath, shaking his head in disbelief. "I can't believe you won't be here Monday. Who am I going to grab coffee with?"

"Well, word on the street is you won't be too lonely . . . " I trailed off with a mischievous edge.

A look of confusion crossed Alex's face before it clicked. "Oh, you mean Jane?" His eyes lit up.

"Yes, Jane." I grinned. Sadir had finally managed to include one interesting tidbit in his "latest" before I left. Alex had been quietly dating the same girl for the past month and a half, an unheard-of length of time for him. "I heard she's an ar-tist," I joked, with a hoity tone.

"She is. Can you believe it? Me with a creative type?"

I nodded approvingly. "I can see it."

He paused for a minute, seemingly trying to decide if he should reveal what was on his mind. "Looks like I won't be the only one with a creative type." A tiny grin played at his lips.

Now I was the one who was confused.

He cocked an eyebrow. "The guy you were out with on Monday night at the Pig—Lawrence Brogan. He's the author of all those vampire books that turned into movies. Didn't you know that?"

I shook my head. Lawrence was a writer? A famous one? I hadn't even Googled him.

"I thought you knew, but I guess you haven't had a lot of time for reading lately. See how much you've been missing out on?"

I smiled, considering this. "I can't really remember the last time I read for pleasure. I can actually read a book now."

"Maybe you'll even discover some hidden talent, like they do in the movies. Hey, you could always write a book about this crazy world." Alex gestured grandly towards the bustling office outside my door. "There's a mountain of outrageous material just dying to be exposed. I've always thought I sensed creativity in you that was just being stymied by this place. Maybe dating a creative type will bring it out."

"You never know." I shrugged, blushing slightly.

"Just make sure you don't lump me in with these idiots. Make sure I'm a good guy."

"If I ever did write a book, I can assure you, you would be the one anomaly." I smiled, realizing I would've never made it through the past six months without him. "Wait a sec. How did you know that I was out with Lawrence the other night?" Not even Sadir would have been able to collect that information this quickly. Slowly, my mind pieced it together. "You . . . you came by the Pig that night?"

He nodded, looking the slightest bit guilty.

"But why didn't you . . . " I squeaked, my voice shaking.

"I know how much you've been through lately. And when I saw you, you looked happier than I've seen you in a long time. I figured I shouldn't interrupt." He shrugged.

I looked into his eyes and there was a brief charged moment that felt like if the timing had been different with us, things might have gone the other way. Then the moment was gone.

"Thank you," my voice croaked. "For everything."

"Anytime, Mac." He opened his arms for a hug. Without hesitation, I stepped into them.

Before I left the offices at 919 Third Avenue for the final time, I took one last nostalgic look at my office, which had at times filled me with dread and other times been the place where I sought refuge. The desk was clear, the shelves empty, except for a lone air canister. I smiled and threw the canister in the trash. Hide the evidence and remove the temptation for a future diligence drone to torture junior associates. My old office was now ready for its next inhabitant. I took a deep breath and closed the door.

ACKNOWLEDGMENTS

I AM DEEPLY GRATEFUL to my agent, Allison Hunter, who believed in *BigLaw* from the very beginning. Allison, you have been an outstanding advocate, therapist, and friend. This book would not have flourished without your tireless efforts.

A big thank you to my talented editor, Jon Malysiak, for your keen insight and making the publishing process virtually painless. Working with you has been a delight and a privilege. Thank you to Sonali Oberg for your contributions with marketing and to the many others at Ankerwyke for helping this all come together. Much appreciation to my publicist Crystal Patriarche and the BookSparks team. Thank you to Kaitlyn Bitner for your creative and eye-catching cover design and to Shari Smiley at Gotham Group for taking this book under your wing.

I've been so fortunate to have the support of friends and family during my time working in biglaw and writing *BigLaw*. And though the list is endless, many thanks to the following people: Kimberley Hall, Gosia Bawolska, Rick Royale, Paige Moss, Sonja Cameron, Bert Cameron, Lauren Waters, Amber Bagnulo, Michele Murphy, Erik Magraken, James Magraken, Owen Magraken, Chi-Yon Lamprecht, Nigel Lamprecht, Mike and Lis Steinberg, the Bohaker Family, and the Akerly Family.

I owe a special debt to Ellen Montizambert. If you had not gotten on a plane and worked with me to shape this book it would still be collecting dust on a shelf. You're also the reason I made it through my first year of law school. Is there nothing you can't do?

Thank you to the friends and colleagues that crouched with me in the trenches of biglaw. I would list you each individually, but then I would miss someone and that's how rumors get started. You know who you are. Know that your humor and kindness made the all-nighters much more bearable.

My heartfelt thanks to Serena Palumbo for helping me keep the faith and for pointing me in the direction of my lovely literary agent. You always have my back and I'm so grateful.

Thank you to my parents for being an endless source of love and encouragement. Dad, on September 11 you walked down 103 flights of stairs and kept going. With your unwavering strength, you taught me the true meaning of pressing on. Mom, you have always been in my corner and are as fierce and loyal as they come. And I know that right at this moment you and Dad are sitting in a restaurant telling the waitress that your daughter wrote a book. Thank you for championing the cause.

Thank you to my sister, Catherine Magraken, who has been a faithful cheerleader throughout. You are the one who convinced me I should be a writer based solely on the Easter bunny story I wrote in the second grade. And to my brother, Michael Lamprecht, who will always indulge me in a good debate about hockey. Gretzky is better than Lemieux. There—last word. Another problem solved.

Very special shout out to everyone who has ever enjoyed a good Happy Hour on the deck at Reef Road. You are my people. Now pass the Fritos.

Last but not least, thank you to the loves of my life. Gord, you always manage to make me laugh in any situation, even when we're traveling cross-country with children and that's no small feat. Ethan and Elise, I see all that is good in this world in your smiling faces. You are everything.